The Yale Critics: Deconstruction in America

Jonathan Arac, Wlad Godzich,
Wallace Martin
Editors

Theory and History of Literature, Volume 6

University of Minnesota Press, Minneapolis

The University of Minnesota Press
gratefully acknowledges assistance provided
by the Andrew W. Mellon Foundation
for publication of this book.

Published by the University of Minnesota Press,
2037 University Avenue Southeast, Minneapolis, MN 55414
Printed in the United States of America
Second printing, 1984

Library of Congress Cataloging in Publication Data
Main entry under title:

The Yale critics.

(Theory and history of literature; v. 6)
Bibliography: p. 203
Includes index
1. Deconstruction—Addresses, essays, lectures.
2. Criticism—United States—Addresses, essays, lectures. I. Arac, Jonathan, 1945-
II. Godzich, Wlad. III. Martin, Wallace. IV. Series.
PN98.D43Y34 1983   801.95'0973   83-1127
ISBN 0-8166-1201-3
ISBN 0-8166-1206-4 (pbk.)

The University of Minnesota
is an equal-opportunity
educator and employer.

The Yale Critics: Deconstruction in America

Theory and History of Literature

Edited by Wlad Godzich and Jochen Schulte-Sasse

Contents

Key to Brief Titles

The following abbreviations are used for citations; publication information appears in the bibliography. When authors or full titles are cited in parentheses—e.g., "(Norris, p. 70)" or "(Bassett, 'Tristes Critiques')"—the references can be found in the bibliography.

ABW   Miller, "Ariachne's Broken Woof"
AI   Bloom, *The Anxiety of Influence*
AR   de Man, *Allegories of Reading*
BF   Hartman, *Beyond Formalism*
BI   de Man, *Blindness and Insight*
BT   Hartman, "Blessing the Torrent"
BV   Bloom, *The Breaking of the Vessels*
CCC   de Man, "The Crisis of Contemporary Criticism"
CW   Hartman, *Criticism in the Wilderness*
DC   *Deconstruction and Criticism*
DDW   Hartman, "Diction and Defense in Wordsworth"
DG   Miller, *The Disappearance of God*
EHH   de Man, "Les Exégèses de Hölderlin par Martin Heidegger"
EM   Derrida, "The Ends of Man"
FCI   Bloom, *Figures of Capable Imagination*
FR   Hartman, *The Fate of Reading*
G   Derrida, *Of Grammatology*

Preface

The "Yale Critics"—Harold Bloom, Geoffrey Hartman, Paul de Man, and J. Hillis Miller—are often represented as a group that one should defend or oppose rather than as individuals whose ideas deserve critical scrutiny. Our intention in this volume has been to stimulate serious, careful assessment of their writings in relation to recent American criticism and to the critical tradition. Thus W. K. Wimsatt, Cleanth Brooks, and M. H. Abrams form one context of reference for our contributors, while Longinus on the sublime, Schiller on the aesthetic, and Wordsworth on the poet's relation to the public all come into play at other points. To achieve this initial location, we have had to refrain from pursuing other important current concerns, such as feminism, semiotics, and ethnic and regional studies.

The largest context that continually concerns us is that of the gap between Anglo-American and Continental criticism, resulting from a difference in social experience. This gap has made significant dialogue between the two extremely difficult, and to the extent that the Yale Critics are important voices in that dialogue it has made them hard for American readers to understand. By selecting contributors who, in different ways, find themselves between these two traditions, we hope that we have made our volume interesting and accessible to the American reader. The introduction offers a brief history of the Yale Critics and deconstruction. It is followed by two essays on the relations of deconstruction to the characteristically Anglo-American enterprises of speech-act philosophy and new criticism. Essays giving individual attention to Hartman, Miller, de Man, and Bloom come next. Two essays then return to modern Continental philosophy and are followed by an afterword that discusses the volume as a whole and tries to see "beyond" the Yale Critics.

If the space of this book is particularly that of the "gap" between Anglo-American and Continental criticism and philosophy, then the problem it continually addresses is that of "translation," not only literal matters of turning one language into another, but also the larger matter of cultural transference in general. In this sense we rejoin the centuries-old topic of the *translatio studii*, related always to the *translatio imperii* ("Westward the course of empire . . ."). Beyond these large political and cultural dimensions, critically elucidated by Frank Kermode in *The Classic, translatio* is also the term in Latin rhetorical treatises for what we call in English, adapting from the Greek, "metaphor." In all these senses, "translation" raises problems of distance from an origin, of possible inauthenticity, unreality, or duplicity. It is tempting, but perhaps also necessary, to raise this question about the Yale Critics' work of translation, even as we recognize that one of the major projects of deconstruction in philosophy has been to challenge severely the privilege of an "original" place or language that remains superior to what has been borne away (*translata*) from it.

Nonetheless, there has long seemed something puzzling, even disturbing, in the relation of American culture to European culture. When not closed into willful provincial isolation, the United States has appeared over-receptive. If the "greatest" and most "difficult" European writers have often had, even before in their homelands, their "first vogue" in America; if we have "patronized Nietzsche, found something entertaining in every kind of revolutionist, and welcomed the strangest philosophies," could it be, worried Van Wyck Brooks in 1918, because our "culture of industrialism" could find "nothing real to us" in iconoclasms that threatened no idols which were actually ours? As we now in 1982 contemplate the impact of advanced European philosophy on American critical thought and practice, when we reflect on how Americans respond to the curious blend of Hegel, Marx, and Heidegger that has had some five decades to brew in France—through the Action Française and Popular Front, the Occupation and Vichy government, wars of decolonization in Indo-China and Algeria, May '68—Brooks's words still carry a disquieting relevance: "Those very European writers who might . . . have done the most to shake us out of our complacency have only served the more to confirm us in it. Our immediate sphere of action being sealed against them, their influence has been deflected into 'mere literature,' where it has not been actually inverted" (*America's Coming-of-Age*, New York, Doubleday, 1958, pp. 109-10). We too think that literary criticism may play a significant part in national life, all the more a criticism that raises to explicit attention the problems that so worried Brooks of "influence" and its, perhaps necessary, deflections.

This volume, then, inquires into the current state of literary study in the United States by focusing on four critics who since the early 1970s have shared an institution and many intellectual concerns. They are different enough from each other so that a considerable sense of variety emerges from our essays on them, yet their shared ground allows us also to address a more particular subordinate question: how does their work relate to "deconstruction in America," the controversial impact of the philosophical problems and practices associated with Jacques Derrida? After the postwar decades of new criticism and the confused search for relevance in the later 1960s, the last dozen years have seen an extraordinary set of debates shake American critical culture. One epicenter for this shaking has been what Richard Poirier in 1975 designated the "community enterprise" at Yale. We do not find that community achieving the coherence of a "school," and so we focus on four "critics." Although Derrida is a regular visitor to Yale and lectures there, we do not devote an essay to him alone but allow his effect to be diffused throughout our discussion.

"Deconstruction in America" goes on in many places besides Yale, and there is much more that goes on in New Haven than deconstruction. Frank Lentricchia has gone so far as to insist that it is "self-deluded" to identify Harold Bloom "with what is called deconstruction" (*BV*, p. xii). Nonetheless, in the very book Lentricchia is introducing, when Bloom relates Whitman to Stevens, he begins by asserting that between the two poets "there came Nietzsche's deconstruction of the self" (*BV*, p. 9). Even where they disagree with each other, and in their recent work they have often done so, the Yale Critics speak in terms that distinguish them from most of their agemates in the academy but that they share with many younger critics. The contributors to this volume are almost all members of a younger generation committed to engagement with the terms, and issues, that the Yale Critics have set working. Neither their students nor their disciples, we find that our future leads through their problems. This generational question touches upon another of our self-limitations in this book. For there are not just four "critics" at Yale. Shoshana Felman, for example, works brilliantly within the problem areas that Americans associate with de Man, Hartman, Miller, and Bloom. Her work, however, we have judged part of another story. Written in French, it has helped make the "Ecole de Yale" known in Paris, but it is only beginning to be known here, as translations of her major books appear.

If it is a delicate matter of judgment to decide where to draw the circle, to give a workable subject that is reasonably comprehensive yet still coherent enough to yield essays that make sense side by side even if they do not perfectly intermesh, it is no less difficult to know how most accurately to gauge the effects of the Yale Critics. Are they merely an elite coterie, whose prestigious institutional affiliations (Harvard, Johns Hopkins, and Cornell before Yale) have won them attention that their accomplishments have not merited? Since they have come together, no one of them has won the James Russell Lowell Prize of the Modern Language Association of America (MLA) or the Christian Gauss award of Phi Beta Kappa. If these very names suggest a discredited belletrism, the open market has been no more receptive. De Man's *Blindness and Insight*, the work most cited in this collection and by any judgment the beginning work of "deconstruction in America," reached no paperback edition for over a decade. In remaking the *Introduction to Scholarship in the Modern Languages and Literatures* (1962, 1981), the MLA has followed the lead of the Yale Critics by replacing a single chapter on "Literary Criticism" (by Northrop Frye) with two, on "Literary Criticism" and "Literary Theory." But neither is by a Yale Critic. On the other hand, critics doing the new work most respected by a professionally authoritative screening group have drawn heavily from the Yale Critics. In 35 essays that recently reached the Editorial Committee of *PMLA*, the American critics most cited were Miller (in 6 essays), de Man (5), Bloom and Hartman (4 each), while Derrida (10) led foreign sources (reported by Joel Connaroe in *PMLA* 95, 1980, p. 3).

Consider yet another measure of impact, spreading from elite private institutions to public institutions with broader student bodies. The contributors to this volume include some with doctoral degrees from Yale, Cornell, Harvard, but their doctoral and current institutions embrace much more of the United States: Binghamton (SUNY), Buffalo (SUNY), Illinois at Chicago, Iowa, Minnesota, Oregon State, Pittsburgh, Temple, and Toledo, as well as the traditionally elite Chicago, Columbia, Dartmouth, and Princeton. And one would immediately name Texas (Austin) and the California campuses at Los Angeles and Irvine as places where the issues associated with the Yale Critics and deconstruction are vigorously pursued.

Finally, we would draw attention to two related aspects of this book. First, we hope that the essays here will not only shed light on the Yale Critics but will also help to indicate critical possibilities—tempered by engagement with the Yale Critics as the Yale Critics were by their engagement with New Criticism—that may give a sense of new directions in American criticism. Second, we hope that our collaborative undertaking itself indicates a new direction, through the flexibility it achieves as the work of "critics," neither of a "school" nor of a single individual.

May, 1982
Jonathan Arac
Wlad Godzich
Wallace Martin

Introduction
Wallace Martin

The purpose of this volume is to disentangle the themes and theories of four critics who are often treated as a group because of their association at Yale, and to assess the implications of their writings for the future of literary study.

If they had not intimated that they have something in common, J. Hillis Miller, Harold Bloom, Geoffrey Hartman, and Paul de Man might never have been grouped as a critical school. Among the theoretical strands running through their writings, there is not one that would serve to unite them or distinguish them clearly from other contemporary critics. When presenting themselves as a group, they scrupulously point out their differences. However, for their opponents, among whom are numbered many of the most distinguished critics in the country, the Yale critics can be lumped together because regardless of how they differ, they represent what we (as critics, scholars, humanists, teachers, and perhaps citizens) should be against.

The reaction against the Yale critics and deconstruction has followed a pattern evident in the early years of the new criticism: innovative critics who have little in common evoke the collective opposition of critics and scholars who have even less in common. The same kind of reaction occurred against structuralism in France during the 1960s and against Russian Formalism in the 1920s. The history of criticism is in large part a history of polemics, with only one party to the dispute surviving in anthologies. Reversing a distinction made by Thomas Kuhn, one might say that revolution or revisionism is the norm of noteworthy criticism, and that "normal" criticism (judgment according to sanctioned standards, or codification of shared principles) is for the most part forgotten. Thus one test of a critic's importance is his ability to touch the soft spots or trigger the anxieties in the critical practice of his time—by which test the significance of the Yale critics is beyond dispute.

The Yale critics have already evoked more commentary than those interested in their work are likely to read. Testy allusions to their ideas began to appear in the early 1970s; 1976 marked the beginning of the staged debates on deconstruction that have been annual features of many conferences and professional meetings since then. Papers presented on such occasions have appeared in print, adding to the flood of articles that explain, in a few pages, precisely what each Yale critic says, and (often) why he is very wrong about it. In view of this mass of secondary materials, some of which are listed in the bibliography, our reasons for adding to it require comment.

To say the worst that can be said of both parties to the dispute (for the Yale critics have also picked quarrels with potential opponents): their analyses of each other have seldom been probing, and the choices offered to presumably disinterested readers involve not the complexities of criticism, but simplifications of philosophy, ideology, and sociology (all -isms vs. skepticism, meaning vs. free-play, cultural relevance vs. academic elitism, rational inquiry vs. pointless paradox; or, positivistic reduction vs. philosophic subtlety, Locke vs. Nietzsche, reassuring unities vs. labyrinthine uncertainties, blind propagators of Apollonian pieties vs. the blinding insight of Dionysian vision). Most of the abilities evident when a critic writes well about literature seem to leave him when he enters this dispute and writes about criticism: his tact, attentiveness to nuance, and imaginative insight are subordinated to a partisan rhetoric on its way to a predestined conclusion. In its simplest forms the debate seems to concern the Lewis Carroll-Hegelian question of who shall be the masters of modern American criticism.

There are, of course, reasons for the reductiveness of these polemics. Criticism about criticism has never been held in high esteem. Many complain that there is too much of it, and even the few journals devoted to critical theory emphasize what should properly be called the theory of literature. Since this battle of the critics has in large part been conducted in nonspecialist journals, opponents of the Yale critics often feel compelled to provide capsule summaries of their thought. Perhaps this is a form of flattery (on the assumption that the audience has the good sense not to pay much attention to newfangled theories) or a discreet form of pedagogy (explaining intricacies that might understandably befuddle the mythical common reader). In any case, criticism of criticism is not a genre on which writer or reader wants to spend much time, and the only alternative to summary seems to be apodictic assertion.

The contributors to this volume assume that literary criticism deserves detailed discussion, especially when the issues at stake are fundamental ones, as they are in this case. We also assume that readers of such a volume are already acquainted with some writings of the Yale critics and, therefore, we have not attempted to provide a vade mecum of their works. The first group of essays concerns backgrounds—their reception, or refraction, of Continental thought and the ways in which our critical tradition has reasserted itself in their attempts to depart from it. Essays on individual critics follow in the second section; the third reverses the perspective established in the first by remarking distinctions between Continental thought and its American proponents. The contributors do not always agree in their interpretations of the Yale critics. If there is any theme that could unify so heterogeneous a volume (the afterword reflects on this question), it is that criticism is in the process of enlarging its scope beyond the precincts of pedagogical and national compartmentalization, and that the certainties within which its debates have traditionally been contained have broken down, throwing everything, once again, into question. While critics remain free to commit themselves to one or another sort of "normal" criticism—even deconstruction has been institutionalized and now produces predictable rereadings of literary masterpieces—genuine engagement with the issues raised in recent debates will be necessary if literary study is not to descend into intractable dogmatisms and hostilities.

To say that everything is in question in the quarrel of the critics may seem hyperbolic. The implication is that they disagree not just about issues and interpretations, but about the assumptions on the basis of which disagreements are usually defined and discussed. Straightforward description of the positions involved can be misleading if it seeks to reduce disparate modes of thought to a common vocabulary. The hope that there might be a metalanguage into which all critical languages could be translated has long since proved delusive, in practice as well as in theory. Rather than attempting to knit up the loose ends in received accounts of the Yale critics, the remainder of this introduction will unravel parts of them in order to question the idea that it is appropriate to conceive criticism in America as divided into camps and then to choose between them. In doing so, we may be able to open the conceptual space within which the essays that follow will be intelligible.

I

A genetic account of the Yale critics and deconstruction would trace both through the conflicts and complications of the 1960s to their problematic convergence in 1970, when Hartman and de Man published books collecting their earlier writings, and Bloom and Miller set out in new directions. In 1975-76 Miller brought about the crisis in this critical plot by identifying its protagonists as ''a new group of critics gathered at Yale'' and listing their distinguishing characteristics. The antagonists Miller identified accepted their assigned roles in the debates of 1975-80, and the dénouement remains in doubt. However, this historical plot, constructed in retrospect, is not one that any critic could have imagined before 1975. The years in question were marked by continuous change and shifting allegiances in criticism, with at least half a dozen identifiable trends competing for attention. To recover the points of reference that marked critical differences before they had been turned into antitheses, it may be helpful to review the relationship between the Yale critics and their contemporaries.

The selection of a starting-point for a history of contemporary criticism is inevitably arbitrary, but the year 1966 has much to recommend it. For those who were then interested in critical theory, that was the year in which Barthes's *Critique et Vérité*, Foucault's *Les Mots et les choses*, Lacan's *Écrits*, Dubrovsky's *Pourquoi la nouvelle critique?*, Todorov's *Littérature et signification*, the English translation of Lévi-Strauss's *La Pensée Sauvage*, the ''Structuralism'' issue of *Yale French Studies*, and the issue of *Communications* devoted to structuralist analysis of narrative were published. It was also the year in which Robert Martin Adams's *Nil* and Richard Poirier's *A World Elsewhere* appeared—books that, however memorable, offered no new theoretical prospects.

Publications in the humanities are usually a year or two behind the state of discourse; for an accurate index of historical moments, one must turn to conferences and colloquia. The conference at Cérisy in France that year was directed by Georges Poulet, and the proceedings subsequently published with the title *Les chemins actuels de la critique*. In the prefatory essay to that volume, Poulet proposed a definition of contemporary criticism (''la critique nouvelle''): It is, he said, ''above all, a criticism of participation—better yet, of identification. There is no authentic criticism without the coincidence of two consciousnesses'' (p. 7). One month after the conference at Cérisy, Poulet attended a symposium at Johns Hopkins which gave a very different picture of the central concerns of contemporary French criticism. Its subject (according to the preface of the published proceedings) was "the impact of contemporary 'structuralist' thought on critical methods in humanistic and social studies," and its speakers included Barthes, Todorov, Lacan, and Derrida. In 1966 theoretical criticism was largely French, and the antagonists in critical agons were structuralism and the criticism of consciousness. The Johns Hopkins symposium attempted to domesticate the former; translations of Poulet's books and J. Hillis Miller had already introduced the latter to the American audience.

In 1970 the proceedings of the 1966 symposium at Johns Hopkins were published under the title *The Languages of Criticism and the Sciences of Man*. The latter half of the title calls attention to the awkwardness of attempts to translate *Geisteswissenschaften* or *sciences humaines* into English, and serves as one index of the inescapable difficulties in interactions between Continental and Anglo-American thought. But as the discussions recorded in that volume show, disagreement, and even incomprehension, can exist within a single national tradition. A few examples:

I should simply like to ask Derrida . . . for some explanation . . . of the concept of the center of structure, or what a center might mean. . . . Is this what you wanted to say, or were you getting at something else? (Jean Hyppolite, pp. 265-66.)

I would like to express the very great pleasure I felt in listening to Roland Barthes and also a certain feeling of melancholy, for there seems to exist between us a sort of misunderstanding. (Georges Poulet, p. 145.)

It is not "One" who speaks, but "I". And even if you reduce the I, you are obliged to come across once again the concept of intentionality. (Serge Doubrovsky commenting on Derrida's paper, p. 271.)

When I hear you refer to facts of literary history, you say things that are false within a typically French myth. I find in your work a false conception of classicism and romanticism. . . . You distort history *because* you need a historical myth of progress to justify a method which is not yet able to justify itself by its results. (Paul de Man commenting on Barthes' paper, p. 150.)

I would like to say that I find that Derrida, with whose conclusions I do not agree, has a catalytic function in French cultural life. (Lucien Goldmann, p. 269.)

It is only in retrospect that these statements about Derrida, and by Paul de Man, seem noteworthy; they were among the least-known participants, and at the time there was no reason to think that their opinions constituted a serious challenge to the goal of the conference (which was intended to introduce structuralist thought to the American audience). But the changes in theoretical criticism, and attendant changes in our method of understanding the past, were revealingly registered when the proceedings of the 1966 symposium, published in 1970, were republished in 1972. In the latter volume, title and subtitle changed places: What had once been *The Languages of Criticism and the Sciences of Man* became *The Structuralist Controversy*. In retrospect, the editors questioned "the very existence of structuralism as a meaningful concept," and found in the same volume "evidence . . . of the ensuing moment of theoretical deconstruction."

To put these later developments in perspective, it is necessary to return briefly to American criticism. Some critics in this country were following developments in French structuralism, and essays in English, such as Geoffrey Hartman's "Structuralism: The Anglo-American Adventure" (1966), were introducing it to a wider audience. In the absence of the critical debates that had characterized the 1950s, American literary study in the following decade produced works that are likely to prove of permanent interest. Rosalie Colie's *Paradoxia Epidemica*, Robertson's *Preface to Chaucer*, Lipking's *The Ordering of the Arts in Eighteenth-Century England*, Bate's *Keats*, and Levin's *The Gates of Horn* exemplify what that decade contributed to scholarship and intellectual history. It was a time when the close reading popularized by the new critics was being combined with a greater awareness of historical contexts to the profit of both. The exegetical skills of the new critics had been turned against their complacent historical assumptions in Kermode's *Romantic Image* and Langbaum's *The Poetry of Experience* (both published in 1957); thereafter, Romanticism began to regain its rightful place in English literary history. If one were to select critics exemplary of the best that American criticism had to offer during the 1960s, Geoffrey Hartman, J. Hillis Miller, and Harold Bloom would certainly be on the list.

Valuable integrations of careful reading and historical awareness appeared in Hartman's *Beyond Formalism: Literary Essays 1958-1970*. The title essay in that volume showed how intrinsic and extrinsic criticism, attention to formal and thematic-existential features of literary texts, could be combined. While expressing reservations about "Anglo-Saxon formalism," Hartman argued that the Continental neglect of formal aspects of literature, as exemplified in the works of Poulet, led to another dilemma: Poulet's conception of literary history appeared to be an afterthought, an external framework discarded because of his single-minded concentration on consciousness, but then subsequently re-imposed, in an awkward fashion, on the minds that he analyzed. In *The Disappearance of God* and *Poets of Reality*, J. Hillis Miller attempted to solve this very problem. Using Poulet's method of intrinsic analysis, he produced an evolutionary account of literary consciousness since the Romantic period. In Miller's sacramental history, the Reformation marked the second Fall:

"Instead of being a sharing in the immediate presence of Christ, the communion service becomes the expression of an absence" (*DG*, 6). Harold Bloom had a different conception of literary history after Descartes and the Reformation. In his view, theology and "existing conceptions of the world" were both undesirable limitations on imaginative vision. The virtue of Protestantism was that it provided a sanction for heterodoxy, thereby authorizing the independence of the poetic imagination (*The Visionary Company*, 1961).

Despite their differences, Hartman, Miller, and Bloom shared a number of convictions during the 1960s. For all three, the defining characteristic of literature was its interiority, as consciousness or vision. The conception of literature as artifact was factitious, in their view; the mind needs a garb of words to transport its interiority to others, but (as Hartman showed in *The Unmediated Vision*), post-Enlightenment poets strive to transcend mediation. "Literature is a form of consciousness. . . . Though literature is made of words, these words embody states of mind and make them available to others" (Miller, Preface to *DG*). "An emphasis on words is discriminatory as well as discriminating unless it guides us to larger structures of the imagination" (Hartman, Preface to *BF*). "The plea for literary history merges here with that for phenomenology, or consciousness studied in its effort to 'appear' " (Hartman, *BF*, 368). Bloom did not indulge in programmatic statements about criticism before 1970 (in the preface to *The Visionary Company*, he said that "in matters of critical theory, I have been guided by Frye's *Anatomy of Criticism* and by Abrams's *The Mirror and the Lamp*"). But it was evident that he was more strongly committed to a conception of poetry as vision that was either Hartman or Miller. For all three, the imaginative consciousness underlying the words of literature was connected with the sacred—with those impulses and experiences that, before the second Fall, had given rise to religion and theology.

Before 1970 Miller, Bloom, and Hartman were practical critics: the value of their interpretive criticism was not dependent on their occasional statements about theoretical matters. They opposed emphasis on linguistic and structural aspects of literature not simply because it drew attention away from consciousness, but because in the hands of earlier critics, it had been used to denigrate Romanticism. The new criticism, said Hartman, "concentrated all its attention on teaching a methodical suspicion of the word, on demanding even of poetry an ironic or tensional structure, and on establishing by that criterion a new and exclusive line of modern classics." Its imitators had become "formalists, hunting structures by means of what they believe to be value-free techniques and confusing art with ideas of order" (*BF*, xii-xiii).

Paul de Man was also opposed to "formalists" who assumed that the language of a literary work embodies the author's consciousness without remainder and that the critic can, therefore, reconstruct its meaning through verbal or stylistic analysis. (Corngold discusses this "mistake" in his essay on de Man.) To attribute this view to the new critics on the basis of passages taken from I. A. Richards and Stephen Ullman is to oversimplify (ICF; *BI*, 22-23). However, de Man did not equate new criticism with formalism: he pointed out that the new critical emphasis on ambiguity and irony called into question any "purely empirical notion of the integrity of poetic form" (*BI*, 32). Unlike Miller and Hartman, he looked less to the criticism of consciousness and French phenomenology than to their German antecedents for a poetics that would correct the positivistic excesses of formalism. From his point of view, all types of criticism that either subsumed consciousness in verbal surfaces, or attempted to dissolve language in a totalization of reflection or sensation, were equally attempts to "fill the abyss that rends Being," the abyss between sign and referent, or consciousness and matter (ICF, 500).

The intermediary (if not mediating) position of de Man between Continental and American criticism has not been sufficiently appreciated, and this is one reason for the attention accorded him in the essays that follow. On several crucial issues, de Man agreed with the new critics, in opposition to Hartman, Bloom, and M. H. Abrams, who were then resuscitating a quasi-spiritual conception of Romanticism. In *Literary Criticism: A Short History*, Brooks and Wimsatt defended allegory against the charges leveled against it by Coleridge and German critics; and they defended fancy, which they associated with wit, against the imagination as it was conceived by defenders of Romanticism (pp. 400-03). De Man would probably be sympathetic to their attitude on both of these matters. In his contribution to this collection, Paul Bové identifies several important areas of agreement between de Man and the new critics. Abrams complained that they had distorted Coleridge's ideas by displacing them in the direction of Friedrich Schlegel—whose conception of irony de Man later used (in RT) to criticize Anglo-American conceptions of Romanticism. Just as the new critics had used Metaphysical poetry and wit as a means of covertly criticizing the Romantics, so de Man used Empson, Andrew Marvell (ICF), and Benjamin's conception of allegory in Baroque literature to question the criticism of consciousness and the poetics of Romanticism and Symbolism. However, despite these affinities, de Man's criticism cannot be adequately characterized through reference to Anglo-American criticism, French criticism, or some judicious combination of the two. The conceptual structure underlying this convenient but misleading dichotomy can be understood only if one sees "*through* French culture to German lines of thought" (Hartman, *CW*, 44)—to Hegel and Heidegger (who also surface in Blanchot and Derrida), Gadamer, and perhaps even Jauss.

If structuralism had simply been another formalism, it might have been added to the array of analytic methods employed in criticism without altering the balance of forces between formalists and their opponents. But de Man and Hartman evinced an uneasy awareness that structuralism posed new problems. In "Structuralism: The Anglo-American Adventure," Hartman attempted to assimilate the movement by representing it as the latest development in the tradition of the Cambridge anthropologists and the myth and archetype criticism they inspired. However, he did not gloss over the fact that it challenged the commonly accepted distinction between literary and nonliterary language (*BF*, 20-21).

In an essay written before the Johns Hopkins symposium of 1966, de Man said that a critique of structuralism would involve "the same set of problems" that he had addressed in discussing formalism, but noted that "the theoretical assumptions that underlie the methods of structuralism are a great deal more powerful and consistent" than those of the new critics (*BI* 33; slightly altered from NC, 35). His view of structuralism was soon to change. "The great contribution of the New Criticism," in de Man's view, "had been to retrieve the autonomy of the literary work and to preserve the delicate equilibrium of its structure from the onslaughts of crudely deterministic systems" ("Spacecritics," 643). In a paper read at the University of Texas three months after the symposium, de Man showed that this conception of autonomy was threatened by structuralism. The central section of the paper draws on the one that Derrida had presented at Johns Hopkins: de Man refers to the symposium, mentions Derrida, and discusses a passage from Lévi-Strauss that Derrida had quoted. He describes the fundamental tendency of structuralist criticism as follows:

If the radical position suggested by Lévi-Strauss is to stand, if the question of structure can only be asked from a point of view that is not that of a privileged subject, then it becomes imperative to show that literature constitutes no exception, that its language is in no sense privileged in terms of unity and truth over everyday forms of language. The task of structuralist literary critics then becomes quite clear: in order to eliminate the constitutive subject, they have to show that the discrepancy between sign and meaning (*signifiant* and *signifié*) prevails in literature in the same manner as in everyday language. . . . The so-called "idealism" of literature is then shown to be an idolatry. (CC, 48-49; *BI*, 12).

The Johns Hopkins symposium of 1966 served as evidence that all forms of criticism attributing a privileged position to literary language were under attack. On that occasion, Derrida made explicit the critique of structuralism that had been implicit in his earlier writings, thereby enabling American critics such as de Man and Miller to identify the reasons for their wariness of the movement. Thus the symposium could be interpreted in two ways. On the one hand, it showed that problems of literary form, language, consciousness, and intentionality, as traditionally conceived, lost their specificity when redistributed among the linguistic and cultural categories of structuralism (the papers by Todorov, Barthes, and Goldmann were exemplary in this respect). On the other hand, Derrida showed that the structuralist method of effecting this redistribution could in its turn be dismantled; but to endorse Derrida's deconstruction as an alternative to structuralism might in the end prove more threatening to literature than the threat it warded off. The development of theoretical criticism during the following decade could be interpreted as an attempt to resolve the dilemmas created by these alternatives.

If Lacan and Derrida had traveled together to attend the symposium, one might appropriately have said to the other (as Freud is reputed to have said to Jung when they arrived in this country to attend a conference at Clark University in 1909), "They do not know that we come bringing the plague."

II

In describing Continental criticism as it was perceived by English and American critics, we have misrepresented it; but from this distorted perspective, it is possible to record with some degree of accuracy the seismic tremors and aftershocks of deconstruction in this country, at a considerable distance from its epicenter in Paris. Derrida's thought is like the purloined letter in Poe's story, as analyzed by Lacan: "As it passes from hand to hand, and moves from point to point within a complex web of intersubjective perception . . . it attracts different meanings to itself, mediates different kinds of power relationship and determines subjects in what they do and are" (Bowie, in *Structuralism and Since*, ed. John Sturrock, p. 141).

Rather than choosing sides in any of the controversies then current in France, Derrida scrupulously retraced the implications of other positions (Hegelian, phenomenological, Marxist, structuralist, psychoanalytic, anthropological, linguistic, literary), acknowledging the necessity of their assumptions and the inevitability of their conclusions. Then he pushed those conclusions further toward their logical limits, to a point at which they were linked to the consequences of all modes of thought, in a vast web of complicity that had neither inside nor outside, no identifiable temporal or conceptual limits. The strategy he attributed to Lévi-Strauss— that of exploiting traditional concepts in such a way that "the language of the human sciences criticizes *itself* "—is similar to his own strategy of "repeating what is implicit in the founding concepts and in original problematics, by using against the ediface the instruments or stones available in the house" (*SC*, 254; EM, 56). His unique achievement was to expose the complicity of positivism and idealism, showing how reductive empiricisms and formalisms exist in a symbiotic relationship with immanent and transcendent supplements. His immediate references were Continental, but his analysis ultimately applied to most varieties of Anglo-American criticism. Those who read him properly could not be "influenced" by his thought; they could only be infected with it.

A discussion of Derrida cannot be undertaken in this context. As he has said, his ideas are best understood in relation to the tradition of Husserl and Heidegger (*Positions*, p. 15); for those who grew up with the tradition of Hume, logical positivism, Wittgenstein, and linguistic analysis, there are aspects of his thought that will remain puzzling until they learn to think about philosophical problems in a different way. Because they were conversant with Continental philosophy, Hartman, de Man, and Miller experienced the impact of Derrida's thought more immediately and deeply than many American critics. One of the following essays discusses de Man's response to Derrida. A complete account of his relationship to the Yale critics (which would include discussion of Miller's "Preface" to *Thomas Hardy* and his *Daedalus* essay of 1970; Bloom's *clinamen* and *tessera* against Derrida as precursor; and Hartman's ambivalent response in his writings up to and including *Saving the Text*) would exceed the limits of an essay. It would also accord Derrida an exaggerated prominence in relation to their own critical theories. They have viewed him not as a lodestar or harbor light, but as a channel-marker near which they might founder.

Consider the position of Miller. In his history of the world, there was a time when "God, man, nature, and language participated in each other" and "the words of the poem incarnated the things they named." But then there was a "splitting apart" (cf. Freud's *Spaltung*; Derrida's *brisure*; the bar between Saussure's signifier and signified) of "the cultural unity of man, God, nature, and language." What brought about this failure of medieval symbolism and consequent fragmentation? Despite all the plausible explanations that have been suggested, its cause "remains mysterious" (*DG*, 3). Derrida would agree: this historical script has been rewritten so many times, in different terminologies and disciplines, that it might be called the story of history itself. And Derrida would also agree that most explanations of this Fall are inadequate. With this splitting of word and thing, signifier and signified, subject and object, comes the Pandora's box of subjectivism, nihilism, humanism, historical relativism, and perspectivism. Again Derrida would agree: the primal split is like a demonic logic machine that generates these consequences.

Can the wound be healed? Miller's solution involved setting aside the question of language as such: literature is in essence a form of consciousness, and words are only its outside, a necessary but contingent supplement used to resolve the primal dichotomy of consciousness and reality. If there is a tertium quid in his scheme, it is the ghostly, immanent "presence of things present" (*PR*, 10). In the works of modern poets who have moved beyond dualism, words "coincide in closest intimacy" with mind and thing, contributing nothing of their own to the blissful liaison. Admitting that he has made certain choices in constructing this account, Miller's deployment of concepts is in itself logical and is sanctioned by the philosophical tradition.

Derrida not only understood this; he described the systematic disposition of concepts in this tradition with such precision at the Johns Hopkins symposium that Miller might well have felt Derrida's analysis was directed specifically at him. (Some critics still cite the paper that he delivered on that occasion—"Structure, Sign, and Play in the Discourse of the Human Sciences"—as if it were a canonical account of deconstruction.) When Derrida said that the center of a structure is "the point at which the substitution of contents, elements, or terms is no longer possible," but which at the same time authorizes "the free-play of elements around it," he was describing the "being" that dwells in all objects and that fleetingly reveals itself as a "fugitive presence" that "flows everywhere" in *Poets of Reality* (p. 10). As Derrida pointed out, this tradition had been called into question by Nietzsche, by Freud's critique of self-presence, and by "the Heideggerian destruction of metaphysics, of onto-theology, of the determination of being as presence." In contemporary thought, "the metaphysics of presence is attacked with the help of the *sign*" (*SC*, 247-50). Thus Derrida's analysis bridged the gap between the two philosophic traditions that in contemporary criticism were exemplified by the criticism of consciousness and structuralism—displaying not only the logic of each, but also the larger system of distinctions that served to authorize both. Given Miller's intelligence and integrity, there was no way he could evade this subversion of his thought. Derrida was not a polemicist who could be challenged; he was a *pharmakon*, a medicine or poison one must swallow, even if the cure achieved turned out to be a cure of the ground.

De Man was less vulnerable to Derrida's deconstruction because he had long been critical of any "redemptive poetics," such as those of Miller and Poulet, that aspired to reunite subject and object (ICF, 496-500). Until 1966, he seemed to be laying the groundwork for an "ontology of the poetic" inspired by Heidegger but avoiding Heidegger's errors; traces of this project survive in *Blindness and Insight* (1971). The conceptual pairs employed in that volume (empirical vs. ontological self, intention vs. verbal expression, immediacy vs. pastness, desire vs. reality, self vs. language) have suffered more from the passage of time than the interpretations produced through their use. When philosophical terms are appropriated by critical theorists, they become part of the rhetoric of criticism. During the past fifteen years, phenomenology and existentialism (once important to the Yale critics) and the idealistic aesthetics of the Kantian tradition (important to the new critics) have lost their rhetorical force. When a critic finds it necessary to forgo his philosophical terminology, he must remake his rhetoric. This had never proved an easy task; it is tantamount to remaking his theory.

Because he acknowledged the importance of the traditions on which the criticism of de Man and Miller was based, Derrida could reveal to them why they needed to rethink, systematically, the place of language in relation to ontology. Because he understood and was able to employ the methodologies of the structuralists, he was able to show them why they needed to reconsider the relationship of metaphysics and ontology to theories of language. By 1970 Barthes and Todorov (to name only two) had shifted away from the scientism of their publications a few years earlier, and while this shift can be explained through reference to the logic of structuralism itself, Derrida was responsible for hastening it toward its conclusions. Like the structuralists and semioticians, Derrida was interested in the *sciences humaines*—in linguistic theory, psychoanalysis, history, Marxism, anthropology, as well as philosophy and literature. Anti-formalists such as Hartman, de Man, Miller, and Bloom have traditionally discussed the relationship of literary study to other disciplines with only one purpose in mind: They want to show why the methodologies employed in the sciences are not of any relevance to literature—after which they can return to their own methods of hermeneutic meditation. Quite apart form the rights and wrongs of the arguments involved (and the anti-formalists may be right), the effect of their position is to insulate, if not isolate, literary study from other spheres of contemporary knowledge.

Even if we were to contend that structuralism in the 1960s was both too formalistic to be relevant to literary study and not nearly formal enough to justify its scientific pretensions (since it used linguistics as a source of analogies rather than as a model of how to satisfy the constraints imposed on theory formation in the exact sciences), we would still have to concede that its effects on literary study were beneficial. Structuralism recreated the bond between literary and linguistic studies; it reawakened interest in the relationships between "high" literature and folklore, popular literature, and (via anthropology) non-Western literatures; it provided methods of "reading" cultural phenomena and thereby relating literature to its social and historical contexts; and as a movement that proved intelligible throughout the Western world, it renewed a sense of community in humanistic and literary studies that had long since disappeared, each nation having sunk into its own forms of criticism and pedagogy.

Considering their achievements and commitments, there was good reason for Miller, de Man, Bloom, and Hartman simply to turn their backs on these developments and to continue producing the valuable interpretations for which they were known in the 1960s. That they were willing to undertake the difficult and unusual task of changing their minds has led them to occupy a place in contemporary criticism that they would not otherwise have. Miller's change was the most dramatic; de Man's was the least apparent and most arduous, as he painstakingly readjusted his critical terminology in the series of essays that were collected in *Allegories of Reading* (1979). What Hazlitt said of Shakespeare might be said of Hartman: he is a true mirror of criticism, reflecting all; he has only "to (read) anything in order to become that thing." But a troubled tone has surfaced in his essays, and his thought has been extended to acknowledge challenges to his earlier self. Bloom, on the other hand, is Hazlitt's Milton—all subjective intensity, revealing his own mind no matter what he talks about; "his imagination melts down and renders malleable, as in a furnace, the most contradictory materials." The structuralist concept of intertextuality, French readings of Nietzsche and Freud, and the shards of occult traditions emerge from the foundry of his mind in forms that are almost entirely his own. What Bloom said of Yeats is true of himself: we can best understand him by studying not his "doctrines in themselves but the experience of their psychological meanings" (*Yeats*, p. 212).

Although many American critics thought that the theoretical revisionism of Miller, de Man, and Bloom in the early 1970s resulted from their acceptance of ideas current in Continental criticism, others interpreted it as an essentially defensive maneuver, intended to ward off the threat of a more radical critique of literature (Riddel, "A Miller's Tale"). From one point of view, de Man's and Miller's argument that literature demystifies or deconstructs all attempts to accord it a special status can be seen as an attack on the Anglo-American critical tradition and on literature itself. From another point of view, this argument may be intended to save literature from irremediable deconstruction: it acknowledges the validity of anti-idealistic theories and claims that literature has already anticipated them. Thus it is possible to forestall the death of literature by a Hegelian negation that preserves what it cancels.

Depending upon which perspective is selected, we can view the Yale critics as iconoclasts or as wily conservatives. It is even possible to view them as the last stage of a decadent tradition inaugurated by Modernism, or Romanticism, or Descartes. The Yale critics would reject these generalizations and, in all probability, the very attempt to characterize them collectively. Those who have attended to their comments on each other know that their mutual esteem has been qualified by flashes of trenchant criticism, and that their differences have become more overt with each passing year. In planning their first joint appearance in *Deconstruction & Criticism* (1979), they apparently agreed to write on Shelley (p. ix), but even this minimal accord proved impossible to sustain. De Man's essay in that volume deconstructs Bloom's earlier interpretations of *The Triumph of Life*. Bloom's essay mentions Shelley only to insist that he can be read in various ways; several pages are devoted to criticism of de Man. Swerving from Bloom and de Man, Hartman wrote on Wordsworth; subsequently, in *Criticism in the Wilderness*, he recorded his ambivalent response to de Man's reading of Shelley (pp. 106-10; 261-62).

Hartman and Bloom have often disagreed (Michael Sprinker discusses their differences in his contribution to this volume), but they stand together in their opposition to the forms of deconstruction practiced by de Man and Miller. As Hartman points out, we should not be misled by Bloom's bluster: "He *accuses* poetry in order to save it" (*CW*, 60-61). Hartman's own method of incorporating deconstruction in order to overcome it differs from Bloom's only tactically. Both have been driven to defend literature by claiming that it is a *necessary* fiction. "Poetry works to *remind* us of what we may never have known," says Bloom, "yet need to believe we have known" (*KC*, 86; cf. Hartman, *ST*, 109-11, and his discussion of "forgetfulness of the sacred," *CW*, 42-45). Their position approximates that of Vaihinger's philosophy of "as if," or the conventional reading of the later Wallace Stevens.

In the writings of all four, language has come to occupy a place that all but de Man had denied it in their earlier theories. Developments in criticism as a whole, as well as Derrida, suggested that such a change had to take place if they were to remain relevant to the current state of critical discourse. They have helped each other make this transition: de Man, for example, showed Bloom how to translate his polyglot terminology into terms taken from rhetoric (Godzich, "Harold Bloom as Rhetorician"). Aside from de Man's use of speech-act theory, they remain content to discuss language as if Saussure and Jakobson's essay on metaphor and metonymy were the only significant developments in the field since the codification of the trivium. Those who think of language in terms of the distinctions used in modern linguistics and logical theories may find it difficult to translate the "grammar," "rhetoric," and "logic" of the Yale critics into their modern equivalents, or to determine what has been demonstrated by arguments based on these terms. (For example, de Man and Miller seem to think that the law of identity is in some way crucial to language and thought, despite what twentieth-century philosophers and logicians have said on the subject; any standard reference work, such as the *Encyclopedia of Philosophy*, provides an adequate critique of their views.) But their writings have helped restore rhetoric to its rightful place in literary study, and an interest in the philosophy of language is one that they share with critics of other schools. In keeping with another contemporary trend, the Yale critics have turned from a defense of literature, beset on all sides by positivistic methodologies, to an offensive reconquest of the disciplinary and cultural territories that humanists have been losing since the Renaissance.

III

By 1975 Bloom, de Man, Miller, and Hartman had each established a distinctive presence in American criticism; but in view of their declared differences, no one acquainted with their writings could think of them as a group. Miller might understandably have sympathized with the attitude toward such eminence expressed in the preface to Hartman's *The Fate of Reading* (published that year): "The critic today is as necessary and ineffectual as ever. His text is simply another text added to the heap. . . . A critic should be scrupulous in dealing with particular texts and tonalities, yet how magnanimous a scrupling is this? Are we trapped in minute criticism, end-stopping it, as it were, making it a value in itself rather than a procedural means to some greater end?" (viii).

At the time, there were several paths available to connect intrinsic analysis of literature with other concerns. It was then possible to renew the relationship between literary studies and other disciplines—the path of structuralists and semioticians. Alternatively, it was possible to expand the concept of literary study itself—to show that the discipline had legitimate claims to an importance not hitherto recognized. Or, disregarding disciplinary mediation, these critics could have entered the arena traditionally occupied by the man of letters. They had access to the weeklies and quarterlies in which the first generation of new critics—and their opponents—had bridged the gap between traditional and contemporary literature, on the one hand, and that between academic and cultural criticism, on the other. The second of these possibilities, in some way the most ambitious, deserves further comment.

Since attempts to enlarge the province of "literature" involve either expansion of that term to include more kinds of writing, or (more radically) a questioning of the disciplinary divisions on which our civilization's conception of knowledge is based, the obvious starting-point for any such endeavor is in philosophy. It was, after all, philosophers who established the distinctions that place figuration, pretence, play, and fiction outside the pale of truth. The crossing from philosophy to literature often becomes a chiasmus in the writings of those who would explain the difference between the two: the "referential-nonreferential" and "fictional-nonfictional" oppositions get shuffled, and the territory of literature, where certain questions about truth-value can properly and crucially arise, is either not accurately mapped or simply set off limits for philosophic purposes. Meanwhile, philosophy and the sciences tranquilly pursue their course, relying on analogies, metaphors, structural models, hypothetical examples, paradigms—all of which are, by definition, "fictions"—to discover the truth. If this system of distinctions were to be subverted, literature would be liberated from its traditionally subordinate position. Derrida's arguments on this issue are relatively well known. Here, then, is an apparent fissure in the defenses of the *epistēmē*. To breach it (in which case literature would be everywhere) would require an immense amount of knowledge. Furthermore, it would require a type of philosophical sophistication that is not common in literary critics.

Despite Hartman's impatience with "minute criticism," he had no inclination to redirect it toward "some greater end" by following any of these three paths. He pointed out the dangers of two of them in explaining that his own goal was to produce "a genuinely reflective history writing," which, he said, "protects the very concept of art from the twin dangers of ideological appropriation and formalistic devaluation. The demand for contemporaneity on the one hand, and endlessly competing formal systems, on the other, pressure the reader as much as the artist" (*FR*, xiii). "Formalistic devaluation," the preface to *The Fate of Reading* makes clear, is the threat posed by structuralist and semiotic methods of renewing relationships with other disciplines. "Ideological appropriation" and "contemporaneity" result from crude attempts to relate literature to life. He has recently argued that literary study can prove itself relevant to other disciplines and professions, but his commitment to the autonomy of literature (which in his view includes criticism and literary theory) remains unchanged (*CW*, 284-300).

For Bloom, who in the mid-1970s was recording and at the same time reordering his insights into interpretation and literary history, there was no time or occasion to reflect on strategic choices. When he had anything to say about the contemporary world, he simply said it, reviving the critical tradition of which Ruskin is part; when he needed materials from other disciplines, he plundered; and he had already violated literature's prudish autonomy by arguing that it was in the end a direct expression of the self's struggle with life. Hartman and de Man had expressed their uneasiness with this conclusion in their reviews of *The Anxiety of Influence*; de Man called it "a relapse into psychological naturalism." Like Bloom, de Man was then engaged in reordering his own theory. As he later noted, he had found it necessary to forsake his intention to write a historical study and to investigate instead the problems of reading. As he did so, the distinctions between the empirical and the ontological, consciousness and reality, pastness and presence in his earlier work were assimilated to linguistic categories (tropes, the rhetoric of persuasion, grammar, reference, constative and performative speech acts, logic)—purging his vocabulary of its existential attachments and of the psychological naturalism toward which Bloom had swerved. De Man's strategic choice, then, had been the second: he challenged traditional distinctions between literature and philosophy, arguing that literary language incorporates an awareness of its rhetorical status that is lacking in the language of philosophy.

In the course of dismantling the demarcation between "fictional" and "true" discourse, de Man has found it necessary to reinterpret a number of philosophic distinctions—including those traditionally used to interrelate words, concepts, and referents. His arguments on this issue lend themselves to misunderstanding. If they are construed as implying that there is something fundamentally wrong with our references to the real (to objects, literature, the self, language) we will probably conclude that the theory being advanced is some form of idealism, skepticism, or negative theology (cf. Gasché, "Deconstruction as Criticism"). De Man is aware of this danger, increasingly vigilant in attempting to avoid it, and presumably resigned in advance to being misunderstood, since his theory is intended to explain why such misunderstandings are inevitable.

In view of the differences between them, the Yale critics were scarcely in a position to undertake an offensive reconquest of any disciplinary territory. There was no agreement about what that territory would be, and they were entirely at odds on questions of strategy. J. Hillis Miller was able to solve both of these problems. Following the example of the Geneva school, Miller created a fictional critical school through resort to metonymy: they became the "Yale Critics." This trope in itself defined the antithetical territory to be retaken: that possessed by the rest of American critics. Since there could be no strategy, preliminary probes were purely tactical: idealism, structuralism, traditional historicism, new criticism, rationalism, naiveté and/or ignorance of Continental thought were among the units first engaged. In one sense, the original conception of the campaign proved to be a success, in that it led these parties and others (Marxists, reactionaries, highbrow journalists, creative writers, Aristotelians, Wittgensteinians, quarterlies left and right) to set aside their traditional differences and to decide that they were in fact American critics who had something in common—even if it was only that they were against the Yale critics.

The resultant polemics, an account of which might occupy the center of a history of the Yale critics, will not be discussed here—not because they have not been important, but because they have simplified and confused the issues that this volume is intended to clarify. From a theoretical point of view, the antagonists misrepresented the issues involved for rhetorical purposes. The controversy was not one that pitted Continental against Anglo-American criticism (as Wellek has repeatedly pointed out, chapters in *Theory of Literature* often cited as archetypal of new criticism had been published abroad before he arrived in this country; most West and East European critics have more in common with American critics than with the Yale critics and Derrida; structuralism itself is in important ways an offshoot of Anglo-American empiricism and philosophy of science . . . etc.). It was not a controversy that involved any intelligible disposition of philosophic positions; the participants could not be classified on the basis of their ideas about the relationship between theory and practice. It was not a dispute about whether or not one should read poems aloud, to be decided by the ways in which the philosophic tradition refers to speech and voice.

With those who wished to turn it into a dispute about academic elitism, the social responsibilities of professors, the nature of post-industrial capitalism, the cultural status of academic institutions, and the economic interests of critics, one may or may not take issue. What de Man said of French criticism in 1966 is true of American criticism today: "Actual institutional and economic interests are involved. There is more at stake than a mere turnover of generations" (CCC, 40). But to judge criticism on the basis of some pedagogical, economic, or social goal is as crude as to claim that literature and criticism have nothing to do with those realms. Criticism, economics, the sociology of knowledge, and political science are different fields of study involving different practices. An understanding of how they interact is different from a decision that the theories of one should be dictated by the theories or goals of another. Paul Bové, Donald Pease, and Michael Sprinker discuss these issues in the essays that follow.

In one sense, then, the debate never took place, and the gains and losses involved were not those that the participants envisaged. If some of them hoped to forestall the dissemination of Continental theorizing in journals and universities, they were already too late. J. Hillis Miller could never have thought that a controversy so staged would win his beleaguered party much sympathy or understanding, but it is doubtful that he envisaged the hardening of attitudes that ensued. What was really lost as a result was any possibility of defining the issues that have been most important in recent critical theory and of making them more widely understood.

IV

The preceding account of the genesis and development of the Yale critics might serve as an introduction to a collection of essays that would sort out and adjudicate the issues raised in their writings, thereby enabling criticism to progress beyond the impasse of current polemics. Given the thesis and antithesis of traditional criticism and deconstruction, the lure of synthesis is almost irresistable, if not historically necessary. But the Yale critics have taught us to be suspicious of this conception of "history as a temporal hierarchy that resembles a parental structure in which the past is like an ancestor begetting, in a moment of unmediated presence, a future capable of repeating in its turn the same generative process" (BI, 164).

The influence of the Yale critics on the contributors to this volume is evident from the ways in which the latter dismantle the complacent chronology of the preceding pages. Where I have attempted to identify critical schools and issues, they see tissues and textures, overlapping strands of thought. My account of how Derrida "influenced" Miller and de Man, presupposing the transmission of self-identical ideas from one mind to another, becomes, in their interpretation, a story of displacement and appropriation. For my conceptual topography, they substitute economic models of intellectual exchange. And where I see a logic lurking in chronology—an orderly development of thought—they see repetition and difference.

Thus Derrida becomes, in the essays by Wlad Godzich and Rodolphe Gasché, not an influence on de Man and Miller, but a radical philosopher whom they have domesticated and whose conception of the text they have reworked for their own purposes. (Gasché's "Deconstruction as Criticism" and his contribution to this collection are among the best accounts available of the philosophical issues involved in deconstruction.) Likewise, in Donald Marshall's view, Blanchot proves to be an ambivalent tool in the hands of critics: we see not a sublation of his thought in the Yale critics, but an attempt to lift from him ideas that might well be used to question the conclusions they are employed to authorize. The essays on Miller, Hartman, de Man, and Bloom cast doubt on the adequacy of any chronological account of their work. Where many would see an evolution proceeding by stages from phenomenology and the criticism of consciousness to deconstruction and analysis of language, the writers of these essays identify a recuperation of the idealism from which these critics began, based in part on a negative theology.

Rather than placing the Yale critics at a distance appropriate for disinterested scrutiny, the writers of these essays (in my prejudiced view) tend to merge with their subjects and find themselves entangled by the very ideas they are discussing. What one sees, as a result, is how the problems of close reading disrupt traditional certainties about literary history and critical theory—and thus how the influence of the Yale critics subverts any attempt to describe them. The polemics that have engaged other writers on the Yale critics recur here, with a difference: disputes emerge within the field of thought loosely circumscribed by these critics, rather than being imposed on them from the outside.

The task of summarizing this volume (interpreting the interpreters) is left to the afterword; for present purposes, it is sufficient to note that the contributors can be viewed as symptoms, as well as analysts, of the current situation in criticism. In both capacities, we bear witness to the fact that the extremes of traditional criticism and deconstruction do not offer viable alternatives for the future of literary study. The reading of critical history that would pit them against each other is too transparently a literary plot; if our critical fathers insist on playing it out, they will do so on a stage somewhat removed form the middle ground where their epheboi attempt to make sense of the historical and theoretical problems they have raised but not resolved.

We are left with a critical situation in which the traditional compartmentalization of disciplines and the clearly defined conceptual structures within literary study (national literatures, historical periods, genres, and attendant divisions of labor) can no longer be maintained. Having emulated the specialization that is characteristic of the natural sciences, on the assumption that theories and methods of literary study were sufficiently defined for the accumulation of positive, progressive knowledge, the profession of literary study acquired a secure place in the academy, able to satisfy institutional demands for scholarly "productivity," on the one hand, and to discharge the duties of pedagogy, on the other. Those who fear that the breakdown of this system of specialization will lead to superficiality should remind themselves that it is a fairly recent innovation and that the production of Ph.D. students who specialize in one or two centuries of a national literature and cannot really read a foreign language has not noticeably enhanced the quality of scholarship. The burden on the critic who does not confine himself to literary specialization and polite learning is immense; he must emulate the scholars who took the Western tradition as their province. Edward Said has suggested Curtius and Auerbach as models. Such examples must make us feel that in our belated times, only the foolish and the heroic would attempt to be strong critics.

The critics now teaching at Yale did not bring about this change, but they experienced and have contributed to it. American critics who resent the flood of foreign terminology that has engulfed their discourse have only themselves to blame. In every discipline except psychoanalysis, they have access to theories as interesting, powerful, and relevant to literary study as those that recent French critics have employed. It is ironic that after several decades of deconstruction in Anglo-American philosophy (cf. Richard Rorty's *Philosophy and the Mirror of Nature*), American critics should be startled by Derrida. Because we have not made use of native resources, American criticism has not until recently been as interesting as that produced on the Continent.

What place might the Yale critics occupy in the future of literary study? To begin with the most limited of expectations: Hartman's insistence that we must rethink literary history is salutary, and his colleagues should take upon themselves the responsibility of fulfilling the expectations they have raised on this subject. Wellek can be said to have initiated the redefinition of Romanticism in our time with his essay "The Concept of Romanticism in Literary History" (1949). In "Romanticism Reexamined" (1963), he called attention to the contributions of Bloom, Hartman, and de Man to this ongoing project. Since then, their paths have diverged: Hartman and de Man have reservations about Bloom's conception of Romanticism, but they have not undertaken the sustained exposition of alternative views that one was led to anticipate on the basis of their writings in the 1960s. De Man's recent comment that "the question of history and of ethics can be seen to reemerge" from discussions of Romanticism making use of his methods (I, 499) may indicate that he will once again undertake reflection on literary history.

De Man's reference to ethics and Miller's recent statement that he is trying to "think through" the ethical and epistemological responsibilities of teachers (TP, 613) imply that they are preparing to address subjects that their critics have accused them of neglecting. Hartman's point that the role of the contemporary critic seems trivial, when compared to that of the humanists of the past, is well taken. He has recently written that "the tradition of practical criticism, so narrow at present, has limited our awareness of the relation of literature to the practical life, which includes law, religion, economics, and the process of institutionalization itself" (CW, 300). The justice of his stricture is confirmed by the fact that every major critic has also been something more than a literary critic. We may disagree with the social and political attitudes of Pope, Shelley, Arnold, Ruskin, Eliot, or Sartre. But the perennial interest that attaches to their criticism appears to be directly related to the fact that it is rooted in something other than the verbal complexities of fictional artifacts.

I would add one other burden to this imponderable list of expectations that we might have of our best critics—a burden suggested by Goethe, the Schlegels, Emerson, Arnold, Richards, and Eliot. The awareness of Near and Far Eastern literatures that characterized the nineteenth and early twentieth centuries has been lost, at a time when it is even more important to understand them. Scholarly integrity may dictate that we should not dabble with literatures we cannot read in their original languages. If so, the alternative is learning those languages. The critic might argue that we are in no position to understand other cultures until we can understand our own. But as Edward Said has shown (in *Orientalism*), we have for too long defined our culture through an imaginary antithesis to our "other"—those peoples who occasionally impinge on Western Civilization courses and whose caricatures inhabit the press. While social scientists and governments are amassing facts and creating policies to deal with our recalcitrant others, distinguished critics might show that literature can play a crucial role in encouraging a humility and humanity more appropriate to self-understanding. Our theories have been based on too limited a canon; we should expose them to the world's literature.

Part I

Variations on Authority:
Some Deconstructive Transformations
of the New Criticism
Paul A. Bové

There have been recently many attempts to describe, rebut, "go beyond," and account for deconstructive criticism. They have come from Marxist, phenomenological, humanistic, and political quarters. Occasionally, there have been sympathetic accounts, sometimes bordering on the apologetic, from a younger generation of scholars nurtured in the excitement of the Derridean era.[1]

John Brenkman and Michael Sprinker, for example, both remark on the power of deconstructive discourse within the academy and account for this fact by seeing deconstruction as the mirror image of contemporary society. Sprinker specifically identifies the source of deconstruction's power in the "technicality of [its] procedure." For this reason, Sprinker concludes, "Deconstruction . . . mirrors the effacement of ideology under the mantle of technical rationality which is the principal feature of ideology under late capitalism. . . . Deconstruction is the specular image of the society of the spectacle."[2]

Far from the rigor of such a critique, Gerald Graff, in *Literature Against Itself*, asserts that deconstruction is the heir of earlier Modernist formalisms which deny reason, common sense, and referentiality.[3] Unfortunately, Graff's characterization is too broad and fails to account for its own position, thereby devaluing his genealogical insight. His polemic attempts too naive a recuperation of conservative humanism to fulfill the scholarly demands for historical precision required by this topic.[4]

In a closer focus, Jonathan Arac identifies the New Critical and deconstructive fascination with Coleridge, rather than Shelley, as a mark of their common genealogy. For as Arac suggests, "Even the rhetorical subtlety of Paul de Man . . . may remain as partial a tool . . . as Northrop Frye, or . . . the New Critics, in its restriction to discourse, in its attempt to deny the possibility of any other realm than that of the text."[5] In thus suggesting the continuity of deconstruction and New Criticism—indicated by the conservative reappearance of Coleridge and the persistence of textual priority—Arac identifies a persistent trend in Modern American criticism. For the similarities in technique between New Criticism and deconstruction produce a critical impasse not easily broken. Since neither New Criticism nor deconstruction bothers to account for its own function and position historically in society—precisely because they are both radically anti-historicist—even the most sophisticated employment of the latest reading techniques merely repeats and extends a power formation already in place. I will return to this idea in the body of my essay.

In a remarkable series of essays, Daniel O'Hara has recently outlined a history of the romance structure of interpretation in Modern criticism. Taking the case of Walter Pater as paradigmatic, O'Hara has specified that in Eliot, Valéry, Bloom, Frye, Ricoeur, Said, Graff, Lentricchia, Hartman, and Derrida a certain ironic repetition encircles all these and others in a pattern of (self-) parody. O'Hara finds: "The oppositional critics of our culture would simultaneously critique the last vestiges of the ascetic ideal [which Arac identifies with Coleridge, O'Hara with Kant] as it makes its appearance in the work of art of our culture and the latest models of the revisionary ideal by mating with their own self-created phantasmagoria in the voids of past texts. Their aim is to reproduce themselves as the divine child of yet another potentially liberating vision that deserves to be parodical."[6] O'Hara's devastatingly all-inclusive critique denies the critical intelligence any easy hope to make a new beginning or to avoid the ancestor's romance pattern. For his reading is not led by the witty inventiveness of deconstructive play to forget its place in an ironic tradition or to accept deconstruction's goal of hearing "unheard of thoughts."

Invoking Heidegger's phenomenological destruction, W. V. Spanos finds terms to analyze not only humanistic and New Critical procedures but also deconstruction, discovering the persistence in our recent criticism of the critical impulse to spatialize time. Spanos has produced a cumulative indictment of the New Critical-structuralist-poststructuralist hegemony which cannot be ignored. Focusing his attention relentlessly on the areas of nondifferential identity between humanism, formalism, and deconstruction—Babbitt, the New Critics, Derrida—while bracketing their reducible differences, Spanos has now named the deconstructors the true heirs of the Modernist critical aesthetes. Spanos's opinion on this matter is seminal and needs quotation:

In thus reducing the signifiers emerging from and addressing *different* historical/cultural situations to a timeless intertextual (ironic) text, deconstructive criticism ironically betrays its affiliation with the disinterested—and indifferent "inclusive" formalism of the New Criticism . . . which it is one of its avowed purposes to repudiate. The deconstructive reader, like the New Critic . . . , becomes a distanced observer of the "scene of textuality" or, in Kierkegaard's term, an aesthete who perceives the text from the infinitely negative distance of the ironic mode. With his levelling gaze, he, too, like his adversaries, refines all writing, in Derrida's own phrase, into "free-floating" texts. All texts thus become the *same* text.[7]

One cannot allow the deconstructive response to such charges too much authority. Such a response might, for example, fasten on terms like "time" and "aesthetic" and on "oppositions" like "interested" and "disinterested" to mark their metaphysical entrapment and perhaps "totalitarian" implications. Of course, conceding authority and persuasion to such a response is, in advance, to concede the argument. The temptation to do so testifies to the power of deconstruction. But it also testifies obliquely to the truth of Spanos's claim; for the ubiquity of the dissent to his position from critics of all camps reveals the very relationship he is trying to name.

Perhaps the argument needs to be developed in a complementary direction. The authority and dissemination of deconstruction can be accounted for by seeing it as a transformation of the critical variation called "New Criticism." But one must not insist upon the repetitive or recuperative nature of deconstruction too exclusively. One must not attempt to "reduce" it to a preexistent "tradition" or "institution" which, for various reasons, it cannot escape. Yet one can recognize that deconstruction is a redeployment of the forces which sustained academic literary study in its univocal, pluralistic, and New Critical modes, that is to say, in critics as seemingly different as W. K. Wimsatt, E. D. Hirsch, and Wayne Booth.

Literary study is an institution with certain persistent as well as varying characteristics. Like all institutions, academic criticism repeatedly "reforms" itself, transforming its appearance while elaborating and conserving its institutional power and thus ensuring its survival—or delaying its demise. Persistent "right-wing" critics of deconstruction argue that it is a threat to the civilization, a threat to the profession, and furthers the separation of academia from the public.[8] But is it not possible that the decade of deconstruction encompassed by Paul de Man's brilliant performances in *Blindness and Insight* and *Allegories of Reading* has helped preserve the academy during economic and methodological changes, and epistemological and evaluative doubts, so grave as to mark a "crisis"? Is deconstruction not the perfect institutional response to this crisis (rather than its cause)? Is it not a strategy for taking up the crisis into the academy in a self-preserving act which, as Donald Pease has suggested, fuels the institution with its own impotence?

For there can be no denying that the representation of "crisis" in criticism in the late 1960s is the work of deconstruction and those it influenced. Nor can it be denied that the polemical conflicts which resulted both from this declaration of crisis—to which deconstruction is the rigorously appropriate response—and the rising prominence of deconstructive techniques sustained the seeming vitality of the institution through the 1970s and into the 1980s. Careers have been made, books published, journals begun, programs, schools, and institutes founded, courses offered, reviews written, and conferences held. The point is simple: no matter which "side" one takes in the battle, the fact is that deconstruction effectively displaced other intellectual programs in the minds and much of the work of the literary avant-garde—a group of which M. H. Abrams is as much a member as J. Hillis Miller.

In fact, if one concedes that repetition is a sign of institutional persistence and identity, then two parallel gatherings at Columbia University must be remarked. On February 23, 1978, in a Lionel Trilling Seminar, before several hundred people including Stanley Fish, Abrams delivered "How to Do Things With Texts," a critique of Derrida, Harold Bloom, and Fish. Edward Said and A. Walton Litz responded. On February 19, 1981, Frank Kermode presented, again to a Trilling Seminar, "To Keep the Road Open: Reflection on a Theme of Lionel Trilling." His respondents were Abrams and de Man. Kermode, too, chose to address the issue of the burgeoning of theory, of the threat this poses, "from above," to the identity and survival of the institution—illiteracy is the threat "from below"—and of the difficulty for critic/teachers to carry out their "pastoral" role of producing what Kermode calls, borrowing rather ironically, I think, from Fish, an "interpretive community." One is, of course, tempted to open an ideological critique of Kermode and Fish, to remark that the old and new criticisms are linked by this common traditionalist goal to reproduce, so to speak, the means of production. This is especially true when Kermode—in a passage the sentiments and figures of which are traceable back, at least, to Irving Babbitt and I. A. Richards—points out the dangers to the institution and the society it serves in the tendency to authorize various and competing canons.[9] "Yet it must be obvious," says Kermode, "that the formation of rival canons, however transient, is very dangerous; that in allowing it to happen we risk the death of the institution. Its continuance depends wholly upon our ability to maintain the canon and replace ourselves, to induce sufficient numbers of younger people to think as we do.''

One must suspend the tendency to demystify, or to defend, this position long enough both to mark its genealogy throughout the history of critical study and to understand that this position is a necessary and repeated element in a debate so central to the ''pastoral'' mission of literary study that it may be said to be a constituent element of its discourse and its institutional survival. Indeed, the tendency to demystify this position is one of the relays of power sustaining and implementing the institution by pressuring the dominant discourse—here represented by Kermode—to reshape and defend itself. The institution is not then simply represented by Kermode's variation on Richards. But this variation is itself supported and identified by the various antagonists attacking, ''defeating,'' and sustaining it. The institution is the terms of the debate. It is historical variation without rupture, crisis, or new beginning.

We may conclude that deconstructive criticism and its interpretive, humanistic opposition function as specular images within an institutional and discursive system akin to Lacan's idea of the Imaginary. This specularity is clearest in charges which, on the one hand, accuse deconstructors of chaotically threatening civilization and, on the other hand, denounce humanists as totalitarians. Even J. Hillis Miller's outrageously inventive play on the host-guest paradigm points to this ''unity'' of antagonists on the practical, semantic level of critical performance (*DC*, 217-53).

To accept Spanos's perhaps too unqualified certification of the identity of New Critic and deconstructor is impossible for the academy so long as it sustains its own power structure by waging these endless battles between civilization and chaos, or, in the latest version, between man and language. It must be stressed that the critiques of Arac, O'Hara, and Spanos which I have mentioned do not simply cry, ''a curse on both your houses.'' On the contrary, these analyses draw detailed attention to the ways in which the institution of academic letters sustains itself in service to our society.[10] They point out how the institution has managed, within variable limits, continually to redeploy itself around a central, functional structure whose rules for producing ''knowledge'' about literature, texts, reading, and writing we are only now beginning to understand.

A description of some of the various deconstructive transformations of the New Criticism would be useful in understanding the nature of academic institutions. For it would provide an opportunity to test methods for evaluating the various tactics and strategies adopted by such institutions in relation to and as a reflection of their larger socioeconomic contexts. A preliminary sketching of these transformations would reveal how deconstruction has redeployed the discursive power of the New Criticism's representations of irony, author, the ideogram, propositional language, etc. A complete list will have to await the production of a full institutional history of criticism.

What is beyond doubt, however, is deconstruction's attempt to represent itself as "different" enough from its American predecessor as to be "distinct." The *locus classicus* of this representation is de Man's "Form and Intent in the American New Criticism." In this essay, de Man argues that the New Criticism is essentially contradictory. For the poem, as Wimsatt and the others saw it, must be "hypostatized" to be an object of critical concern. Yet, as such, the fundamental structures of the poem appear to be irony and ambiguity. De Man charges that the New Criticism does not fully understand the nature of the hermeneutic circle as an ongoing, open process of interpretation occurring *in time*. Since Wimsatt's and Beardsley's "intentional fallacy" demarcated the limits of critical activity and investigation, it prevented the formation of "a truly coherent theory of literary form." The New Critics rested their readings on an incorrect boundary of poetic closure even while correctly affirming "the necessary presence of a totalizing principle" to any critical project (*BI*, 32). The New Critics conceived and treated of the poem as a natural or an organic object rather than as an act or intentionally produced "object." For de Man, this ontological error results in the New Critic's belief that complete understanding of the organic form of a poem is, in fact, *possible*. Upon this idea, de Man's essay brings to bear Heidegger's notion of the hermeneutic circle to point out that the "dialogue between work and interpreter is endless. . . . Understanding can be called complete only when it becomes aware of its own temporal predicament and realizes that the horizon within which the totalization can take place is time itself. The act of understanding is a temporal act that has its own history, but this history forever eludes totalization. Whenever the circle seems to close, one has merely ascended or descended one more step on Mallarmé's "spirale vertigineuse conséquent" (*BI*, 32).

De Man effectively subverts the New Criticism's already declining authority by this epistemological assault. He has indicted the Americans for theoretical naiveté while acquiring for himself the authority of their practice. They had, after all, in their reading succeeded in correctly revealing the unstable and indeterminate nature of ironic texts, but had been woefully blind to the insight of their own practice. So de Man is successful in his struggle with a dying enemy and carries off as spoils the riches of their accomplishment: "It is true that American textual interpretation and 'close reading' have perfected techniques that allow for considerable refinement in catching the details and nuances of literary expression. . . . The ambivalence of American formalism is such that it was bound to lead to a state of paralysis. The problem remains how to formulate the model of totalization that applies to literary language and that allows for a description of its distinctive aspects" (*BI*, 27, 32). De Man's deconstructive project can be described as the attempt to solve this problem, but certainly his rigorous mode of disciplined and self-reflexive ironic reading acquires power in the very scene of communion with and cremation of the dying fathers of American formalism. In a way which we have long since come to think of as de Manian, his precise, studied ambivalence in this scene effectively disarms his subject by remarking the inevitable and previously unnoticed *aporia* while equally effectively conserving those elements constituent of his own procedure and project.

Despite the erudition, intelligence, and persuasion of "Form and Intent in the American New Criticism," its most remarkable feature is its intentional forgetting of New Critical moments of de Manian insight. It is precisely such forgetting in such a formidable scholar and critic as de Man which indicates that a transformational struggle for authority is going on.

In "The Heresy of Paraphrase," Cleanth Brooks, the most redoubtable of critical totalizers, at a strategically important moment hesitantly acknowledges the impossibility of producing critical closure. Brooks is arguing the impossibility and yet the simultaneous necessity of paraphrasing a poem in propositional language. Suddenly he suggests that the allegory of closure cannot be sustained, for the critical text is itself metaphorized and destabilized as it tries to be more "adequate" to the poem, that is, as it tries to close off its metaphorical play:

As [the critic's] proposition approaches adequacy, he will find, not only that it has increased greatly in length, but that it has begun to fill itself up with reservations and qualifications—and most significant of all—the formulator will find that he has himself begun to fall back upon metaphors of his own in his attempt to indicate what the poem "says." In sum, his proposition, as it approaches adequacy, ceases to be a proposition.[11]

In other words, the critic's language becomes more similar *in kind* to the language of the poet the closer he comes to "adequately" representing the "meaning" of the poem. This may mean that the New Critical text aspires to be a stable simulacrum of the poetic text, an imagistic or ironic totalization of the infinite possibilities of the poem; but it might better be seen differently. For this passage testifies above all to Brooks's sense that the attempt to close the poem in the discursive language of heretical but inescapable critical paraphrase throws the critic into the dialogue of understanding de Man describes. Paradoxically, the attempt to find "adequacy" in a critical reading merely destabilizes critical discourse to the point—not of silence or reduplicating the poem—but of producing a text itself the record and process of the discovery of critical discursive inadequacy. Put simply: the ubiquitous ironic structure the New Critics, like de Man, attribute to all poetry, reflexively destabilizes the attempt to duplicate it in closure. Closure gives way to *aporia*, if you will, as the critical text indecisively oscillates between its own tendency to allegorical closure and its own ever increasing awareness of its metaphorical status.

The most amazing thing about this passage is that it self-consciously announces the instability of the New Critical project in one of the most dogmatic essays of that school. Moreover it is a climax of sorts in the essay, marking the final turn in Brooks's argument on the alienation of poetry from proposition. And while the essay sadly marks the inescapability of propositional contamination of poetic discourse in the critical attempt at closing the text, it extravagantly remarks the equally inevitable "transcendence" of that contamination into metaphor as the result, and, therefore, as the root, of the New Critical project.

De Man's essay is not "in error." It joins the analysis of the limits of the New Criticism in the work of Northrop Frye, Murray Krieger, and R. S. Crane.[12] De Man's particular contribution is to accuse the New Critics of failing to transfer the practico-semantic knowledge produced by their techniques and readings to the theoretical or syntactic level. Without this oscillating self-reflexivity, the New Criticism, de Man charges, is paralyzed and doomed. It is typical of de Man's ahistoricism not to describe the beginning, survival, and persistence of this paralytic. For the very possibility of New Criticism is defined by its separation of syntactic and semantic, or theoretical and practical levels. The supreme and ubiquitous reflexivity de Man finds missing is an ecological mode of safe (nonparalyzing) relations between levels of discourse which are not epistemologically or syntactically homogeneous. Brook's essay indicates that the New Critics are not ignorant of the "arrangements" they have made in their practice to ensure the continuation of their project and its authority. Transporting the practico-semantic discovery of irony to the technico-theoretical realm of stylistic reflexivity would, in fact, have paralyzed the New Critical project of presenting, in poetry, a form of nonlinear cognition and signification as an alternative to "positivism," "journalism," and the social sciences. De Man's critique displaces the goals of this project while preserving both the theoretical and practical insights—totalization and irony—of the New Critics. The effects of this acquisition, the preservation of irony as the trope of tropes, the production of an authentic "totalization," mark deconstruction's remaking of its predecessor's program.

The continuities of this remaking appear both in the deconstructive revision of New Critical touchstones and in the way the practice of certain deconstructive essays echoes the formalist paradigm. The Derridean critique of the "author" in *Of Grammatology* is an example of the poststructuralist extension of that very New Critical assault on "intentionality" which de Man studies. So, too, influential pieces like J. Hillis Miller's reading of Shakespeare's *Troilus and Cressida*, "Ariachne's Broken Woof," illustrate the reformation of the New Critics' practice and the form and shape of their essays.

Miller's essay is important not for its speculative contributions to deconstruction, but for its success in putting deconstruction into play as a literary critical practice which can be schematized, abstracted, copied, and disseminated. While Miller argues for the radical and destabilizing effects of deconstruction on the critical establishment authorized by and sustaining metaphysics, the uniqueness of his achievement consists in his simultaneously providing brilliant examples of how deconstructive reading "is done." Miller's antagonists frequently concede him his destabilizing goals and accuse him, too, of being a threat to civilization. Others suggest that like de Man and Derrida, the other "boa-deconstructors," as Geoffrey Hartman calls them, Miller is a "negative theologian," an ironic metaphysician. While the first charge must be acknowledged by those who feel threatened by Miller's antihumanistic project to destabilize the univocal or privileged "reading," it is obviously unfairly leveled against a critic of such erudition, sophistication, and wit. As to the second charge that deconstruction is itself metaphysics—this is something the deconstructors have themselves first made us aware of. For as Miller tells us himself, the irony of deconstruction is that its texts "contain both logocentric metaphysics and its subversion" (ABW, 59). It is this "double-bind" which marks all deconstructive projects and which seems to escape many of its critics. "Deconstruction," Miller concludes, "attempts . . . a consequent vibratory displacement of the whole system of Western metaphysics. That this attempt always fails, so that it has to be performed again and again, interminably, is indicated by the way my terms . . . imperturbably reaffirm the system that I am using them to challenge" (ABW, 60). Deconstruction is not naive, and the power of its self-reflexivity which redeploys the power relayed by the figures of failure always already preempts those criticisms which impotently name it metaphysics.

Yet the interest of Miller's concession of failure and the need for repetition of the deconstructive move is not so easily exhausted. Abrams charges that deconstruction is parasitical upon "the obvious or univocal reading." Miller's response in "The Critic as Host" subverts the set of oppositions that lie unquestioned in Abrams's discourse.[13] Miller effectively demonstrates that such notions as "priority" and "secondary" are metaphorical, unstable, and constantly oscillating in crosscurrents of figural exchange. So Miller disarms Abrams et al. and further extends the deconstructive weaponry in the academy by demonstrating and enacting the repetitive nature of his critical project and its extensive subversive implications for critical shibboleths.

But would Abrams's charge have more force if it included Miller with himself, Wimsatt, Trilling, Bloom, etc. as paragons of the profession empowered by the conservative transformation of the system he believes he is challenging? I take it that Miller's text confesses to this complicity when he remarks that "my terms . . . imperturbably reaffirm the system that I am using them to challenge." Quite rightly, in the context of Derrida and de Man and of Miller's own questioning of logocentrism in this essay, the passage must be read as a sign of the closure of metaphysics, of the ongoing cover-up of the trace, and of the power of the system of presence. Yet, more specifically, the "system" Miller challenges is that of the critical machinery which produces univocal, obvious readings or determinate sense. In acknowledging the limits of deconstruction's ability to "go beyond" metaphysics, i.e., in marking the closure of metaphysics as the horizon of our reading, Miller defends the authority of his text against the charge that there is no distinction in being a deconstructor. But this self-justifying apology also confesses that it can do no more than continually transform the New Critical project or system in the very process of challenging it.

Yet Miller the etymologist must know that to challenge an opponent is not only to call an opponent into question by demanding its identity, but is also to attack an opponent with false accusations. A challenge is calumny. Having put "truth" out of the question, Miller's deconstruction aspires to power by means of a false accusation which ironically reaffirms the identity of the slandered opponent. Miller shows that the univocal or New Critical reading is mystified and more unstable than it suspects, so much so that it depends upon the self-reflexively destabilized deconstruction for its own determinate identity. So Miller reverses priority and secondarity. Yet none of this is true, since calumny is the "nature" of all challenge. So Miller's devastating critique of univocality, of the logocentric monology of narrative, not only reaffirms the authority of the system it accuses, but reduplicates its own oscillating status, its own crisscrossing claims to power and truth.

Simply and specifically, "Ariachne's Broken Woof" appears as the mirror image of such texts as Wimsatt's "Concrete Universal."[14] Miller's ability to represent *Troilus and Cressida* and, by implication, all narrative in the figure of anacoluthon simultaneously shifts and reaffirms Wimsatt's desire to represent the organic form of harmonious totalities by the metaphor figured in Hegelian terms. Miller has shown that editors and critics comically attempt to erase the absurd "i" in "Ariachne." He has also dismissed I. A. Richards's solution of the problem by demonstrating that "Ariachne" is not a portmanteau since the two stories—Arachne and Ariadne—are contradictory. So like Rousseau's *supplément* (as Derrida explicates it), Shakespeare's "i" is both too much and too little, differing and deferring the pursuit of presence in a transparent sign. Miller's figure for this recognizable deconstructive trope is "anacoluthon."

Most interesting is the way this term expands in its "reference" from the interpretive "i," to Troilus' mind, to Ulysses' speech on order, to the entire Western metaphysical tradition. Miller could not have done us a better service than so clearly to illustrate his deconstruction's conservation of New Criticism's universalizing tendencies. "Anacoluthon," Miller writes:

describes a syntactical pattern in which there is a shift in tense, number, or person in the midst of a sentence so that the words do not hang together grammatically. An anacoluthon is not governed by a single *logos*, in the sense of a unified meaning.

If the word "Ariachne" is an anacoluthon in miniature, a similar structure is repeated in the syntactical and figurative incoherence of Troilus' speech [which critics try] to reduce. . . . The grammatical analocuthon parallels, in the other direction, the anacoluthon of Troilus' divided mind, the narrative discontinuity of the entire play, and so on up to the immense analocuthon of Western literature, philosophy, and history as a "whole." (ABW, 56)

The point here is not that Miller has made a "negative metaphysical" category of anacoluthon nor that he has seen "ontology" as "rhetoric." More important, in his subversion of the Hegelian project of monology, Miller mirrors—albeit with some disfiguring intent—the New Critical play of extending rhetorical tropes like "paradox" and "metaphor" into versions of the Idea figured as verbal icons and well-wrought urns. Miller's transformation of the critical process is a substitutive, inverted mirroring of the New Criticism. More: it is a reversed replication of the New Critical structure de Man calls paralysis and I call survival. For with the partial exception of his etymological games, Miller's theoretical insight seems not always to transport itself onto the practico-semantic level of style or technique; for his prose preserves the same complex tension of clarity and irony as does Brooks's and his method the same contextual, global attention to detailed iconic reading as Wimsatt's. Miller's inversion of the New Critical project appears in his reiterated demonstration of a text's *instability* while offering *stable* representations of textuality in the figure of anacoluthon. Is this not analogous to Brooks's repeated claims for a text's *stability* while offering *stable* representations of closed form in the various versions of the well-wrought urn? And do not both Miller and Brooks inscribe in their texts tropes calling their projects into question and display these tropes at the center of their bids for authority?

While Miller may not so effectively transform his insight into the ironic play of style which marks Derrida and de Man at their best, it is also true that their stylistic play, crucial as it is to their success in unsettling academic criticism, must not obscure the variations in their works on New Critical tropes. Of course, these variations ''define'' themselves precisely in their play. Especially in the case of Derrida, ''style'' is the only space for his project. To reduce or minimize the nature and complexity of his prose is to neglect his achievement, to prejudice the case hopelessly beyond recall, and to announce one's own blindness to the entire deconstructive project. If deconstruction can legitimately claim any distinction in the academy, it is less on the level of technical reading power than on the level of style.[15] Even so, the frequency with which some readers and critics ignore the precision of Derrida's stylistic deployment of key nonconcepts, such as *supplément* or *différance*, suggests that the utility of these ''terms'' for the institution should be momentarily considered apart from the style of their representation.

The point is not just that, as Edward Said suggests,[16] certain of Derrida's neologisms taken together form a deployed system of reading—despite his intentions; but that, in some cases at least, this happens because Derrida *appears to be offering* only more vigorous and severe forms of common critical tropes. This is perhaps more true of the early Derrida, especially in *Of Grammatology*. It is certainly more obviously true of some ''nonconcepts'' like ''supplément'' or ''trace'' than of others like ''hinge'' or ''*différance*.'' Perhaps the clearest example of how Derridean deconstruction is, as it were, already written into American academic criticism involves not a neologism at all, but Derrida's critique of ''author,'' ''intentionality,'' and ''proper name.''

Wimsatt and Beardsley had, in ''The Intentional Fallacy,'' effectively made the ''author'' a function of the text: ''It is only because an artifact works that we infer the intention of an artificer'' (*The Verbal Icon*, p. 4). Explaining the paradox that ''internal evidence'' of a poem's working is also ''public,'' they go on to write of it: ''It is discovered through the semantics and syntax of a poem, through our habitual knowledge of the language, through grammars, dictionaries, and all the literature which is the source of dictionaries, in general through all that makes a language and culture" (p. 10). While this rhetoric can be easily deconstructed by examining the figural priority of "literature" to "dictionaries" and the sense of causal opposition which masks the "leakage" of each figure into the other, it is worth seeing how this *presages* Derrida's demonstration of the textuality of the author, even of the autobiographical "*je.*" In fact, Wimsatt and Beardsley, like Derrida, point out how the text is a record of the struggle to master tropes rather than be mastered by them. For them, this insight is couched in the psychologistic language of contextualism and in the aesthetic rhetoric of the pure art object. But there can be no ignoring how for them the battle to control or efface "context" and "life" to produce a text is a conflict between self and language waged for control of tropes: "There is a gross body of life, of sensory and mental experience, which lies behind and in some sense causes every poem, but can never be and need not be known in the verbal and hence intellectual composition which is the poem. For all the objects of our manifold experience, for every unity, there is an action of the mind which cuts off the roots, melts away context—or indeed we should never have objects or ideas or anything to talk about" (p. 12).

In the "Introduction to the 'Age of Rousseau'," Derrida, with *pointilliste* precision, thematizes exactly what is going on in Wimsatt and Beardsley. This should not be surprising since at the "center" of Derrida's project is the recognition that this epoch announces itself as the "end of metaphysics" precisely in the way in which it seemingly everywhere calls into question the fundamental tropes and functions of logocentrism only to reestablish them. Derrida's writing on the "author" brings out and supersedes Wimsatt's and Beardsley's assault on authorial intention as a designation of writing's once again remarking on itself and its previous obscurity.

Derrida, of course, unlike Wimsatt and Beardsley, realizes that the mere substitution of terms—"internal" for "external," "public" for "private"—does not allow one to think the problem of poetic or any other discourse outside the realm of metaphysics. So Derrida can write: "The names of authors . . . have here no substantial value. . . . The indicative value that I attribute to them is first the name of a problem" (*G*, 99). Derrida moves *to open* the text by reinscribing the "author," whereas the New Critics try *to close*, *to totalize* the text in the same movement. The New Critical move, we can see with Derrida's help, exemplifies the inevitable entrapments of a restricted economy. Derrida refuses to consider discourse in terms of the "author" since it is one of the primary signs of metaphysical closure; but, unlike the New Critics, he also refuses to attempt such a consideration by a mere substitution of "poem" for "author": "I think that *all concepts hitherto proposed in order to think the articulation of a discourse and of an historical totality are caught within the metaphysical closure that I question*" (*G*, 96). The "autotelic text" becomes, in Derrida, a metaphor for exploring the theory of writing. Derrida examines texts, free of the traditional authorial illusion, to discover and question their internal structures, not for formal closure and meaning, but as symptoms of the problematic of the closure of metaphysics. Inscribing texts into this problematic further extends the "dehumanization" of writing which is itself enabled by the detachment of text from consciousness. This leads Derrida to a statement remarkably similar to that of Wimsatt and Beardsley on the way the mind de-contextualizes itself to produce a poem. Since for Derrida the "proper name has never been . . . anything but the original myth of a transparent legibility present under the obliteration" (*G*, 109), the "author" cannot function as cause, origin, or source of texts. In a passage which recalls Wimsatt and Beardsley, Derrida articulates the deconstructive desire to speak an unheard-of thought on the matter of a text's production:

If in a rather conventional way I call by the name of *discourse* the present, living, conscious *representation* of a *text* within the experience of the person who writes or reads it, and if the text constantly goes beyond this representation by the entire system of its resources and its own laws, then the question of genealogy exceeds by far the possibilities that are at present given for its elaboration. We know that the metaphor that would describe the genealogy of a text correctly is still *forbidden*. In its syntax and its lexicon, in its spacing, by its punctuation, its lacunae, its margins, the historical appurtenance of a text is never a straight line. (*G*, 101)

Although most often the New Critic allegorizes these lacunae in a myth of totalization, the deconstructor duplicates the traces of the genealogy in the text with a rigor exceeding that of the "writer." If anything defines in common the best work of Derrida and de Man, it is this duplication. "We should begin," Derrida writes, "by taking rigorous account of this *being held within* [prise] or this surprise: the writer writes *in* a language and *in* a logic whose proper system, laws, and life his discourse by definition cannot dominate absolutely. . . . And the reading must always aim at a certain relationship, unperceived by the writer, between what he commands and what he does not command of the patterns of language that he uses. This relationship is . . . a signifying structure that critical reading should *produce*" (*G*, 158). This statement, of course, summarizes the deconstructive reversal of the New Critical project. It authorizes the redeployment of critical energies into a new alignment of forces which preserves the integrity of the institution while providing original and praeter-naturally subtle insight into both the operations of textuality and the primordiality of writing "as the disappearance of natural presence" (*G*, 159). Ironically, the very critical movement which *produces* the abysmal (*en abyme*) relationship between authorial control and linguistic excess in fact sustains the institution of literary study. While Kermode and others might see deconstruction and literary theorizing in general as a threat to literature and criticism, precisely because of its abysmal concerns, because of its subtle perceptions into the theory of writing, it seems that deconstruction is, despite its "radical" impulses and procedures, truly conservative. "Contrary to received opinion," de Man remarks, "deconstructive discourses are suspiciously text-productive" (*AR*, 200).

Deconstructive reading is a writing. It is a necessary doubling commentary which must be transgressed *to open* a text and a reading. For de Man, the perpetuity of text-production is a function of error: "There can be no writing without reading, but all readings are in error because they assume their own readability" (*AR*, 202). Deconstruction appears to name and seemingly dispel this error. But such error is ubiquitous, a function of the sign itself: "The problem is . . . that a totally enlightened language, regardless of whether it conceives of itself as a consciousness or not, is unable to control the recurrence, in its readers as well as in itself, of the errors it exposes" (*AR*, 219, n. 36). De Man's "reading" of *Julie* leads him to offer an emblem of all error in a textual image of demystification: "The paradigm for all texts consists of a figure (or a system of figures) and its deconstruction. But since this model cannot be closed off by a final reading, it engenders, in its turn, a supplementary figural superposition which narrates the unreadability of the prior narration" (*AR*, 205). So reading/writing produces allegory. One cannot say of these remarks with Gerald Graff that they are referentially self-contradictory. Such a comment is unappreciative of de Man's ironic play with the levels of discourse in such a statement. Nor can one argue that this is *merely* pessimism or impotence. The difficulty consists in realizing how these seemingly despairing remarks *produce* texts and representations of writing/reading and criticism which have power.[17] It is the quintessence of deconstruction that it responds to the decline of academic literary criticism by inscribing within the academy a project for preservation. The repetitiveness of deconstruction is an institutional necessity fortunately fulfilled by the vigorous texts of subtle critics.

In a sense, Edward Said's objection that deconstruction becomes by repetition merely a "new" system, a "new" method of reading is unutterably true and moot. Deconstruction can be nothing else. It is always already the case that the ubiquity of error in the sign determines deconstruction as an institutional practice, as a succession of more or less interesting misreadings. "Deconstructions of figural texts" (and what other kind are there?), de Man writes, "engender lucid narratives which produce, in their turn and as it were within their own texture, a darkness more redoubtable than the error they dispel" (*AR*, 217). One could speculate upon or play with the figure of darkness de Man so trenchantly probes. One might even offer a "counter" idea of darkness or condemn de Man for moral or political reasons for making darkness such a key element in his representation of literature and criticism. But doing so would, of course, testify to the ecological success of the figure as it emerges in de Man, with a complex genealogy—a success in sustaining the institution ironically marked by its power to provoke so many *challenges*.

No legitimate argument can be made denying the importance of ethical, political, epistemological, or pedagogical critiques of de Man, Derrida, and the other deconstructors. But political critiques of deconstruction must take into account the subversive effects it has had on an academy still largely unwilling either to accept the rigor of its analyses and the intelligence of its speculations or to employ its students. Similarly, a complete genealogical analysis, of which I have presented here only the barest outline, would have to describe deconstruction's specific turns upon the shape of the academy in order to avoid merging deconstruction back into the relief of institutional criticism out of which it has raised itself. A criticism which sees no differences between deconstruction and its predecessors is naive and does a disservice to our self-understanding. Yet such an understanding requires an awareness that deconstruction, in a seemingly paradigmatic way, redeployed critical power and sustained much of the institution. The curious can only ask if the increasing number of intelligent and distorting attacks on deconstruction, from both right and left, as well as a sense in some quarters that it is "finished," mark the beginning of another local variation in the forms of the institution. Has the energy of deconstruction begun to flag, and is all the current critical dance around it a ritual feast of renewal? Has it been co-opted or will it persist and flourish? Is a new transformation of the New Critical-deconstructionist "line" to appear? If so, then we might ask, what dark shape marches forward threatening to be born?

NOTES

1. See, e.g., Barbara Johnson, "Nothing Fails Like Success."
2. Brenkman, "Deconstruction and the Social Text," *Social Text*, 1 (1979), 186-88; Sprinker, "The Ideology of Deconstruction: Totalization in the Work of Paul de Man," paper delivered at MLA Convention (1980) Special Session, "Deconstruction as/of Politics," p. 13.

3. (Chicago: University of Chicago Press, 1979). See also my review of Graff, *Criticism*, 22 (1980), 77-81; Michael Sprinker, "Criticism as Reaction," *Diacritics*, 10 (1980), 2-14; Joseph Riddel, "What is Deconstruction, and Why Are They Writing All Those Graff-ic Things About It?" *SCE Reports*, no. 8 (Fall, 1980), 17-29; and William V. Spanos, "Deconstruction and the Question of Postmodern Literature: Towards a Definition," *Par Report*, 2 (1979), 107-22.

4. See George Levine's review in *College English*, 43 (1981), 146-60. I want to thank Jonathan Arac for pointing this out to me.

5. "Repetition and Exclusion: Coleridge and New Criticism Reconsidered," *boundary 2*, 8:1 (1979), 261-74.

6. "The Genius of Irony: Nietzsche in Bloom," see below, p. 109-75.

7. "Retrieving Heidegger's De-Struction," *SCE Reports*, no. 8 (Fall, 1980), 30-53. On the spatialization of time, see especially "Modern Literary Criticism and the Spatialization of Time," *JAAC*, 29 (1970), 87-104.

8. See, e.g., M. H. Abrams, "The Deconstructive Angel."

9. See Paul Bové, "The End of Humanism: Michel Foucault and the Power of Disciplines," *On Foucault, Humanities in Society*, 3 (1980), 23-40.

10. See also Joseph A. Buttigieg, "The Struggle Against Meta (Phantasma)-physics," *boundary 2*, 9:3 and 10:1 (1981), 187-208.

11. *The Well Wrought Urn* (New York: Harcourt, Brace, and World, Inc., 1947), p. 198.

12. See Frye, *Anatomy of Criticism* (Princeton: Princeton Univ. Press, 1957); Krieger *The New Apologists for Poetry* (Bloomington: Indiana Univ. Press, 1963); Crane, "The Critical Monism of Cleanth Brooks," *Critics and Criticism* (Chicago: University of Chicago Press, 1952), pp. 83-107.

13. See "The Deconstructive Angel," 457-58 and "The Critic as Host," 217-26.

14. *The Verbal Icon* (Lexington: The Univ. of Kentucky Press, 1954), pp. 69-83.

15. See Daniel O'Hara, "The Genius of Irony," and Rudolphe Gasché, "Deconstruction as Criticism."

16. "The Problem of Textuality: Two Exemplary Positions."

17. See Geoffrey Hartman, preface to *DC*.

The Domestication of Derrida

Wlad Godzich

On July 17, 1976, H. M. Queen Elizabeth II. rose from her seat, approached the microphone, and, staring into the Canadian Broadcasting Company camera's eye which re-transmitted the event simultaneously to over a hundred countries around the world, said, in heavily accented French: "Je déclare ouverts les dix-huitième Jeux Olympiques de l'ère moderne, que nous célébrons dans la ville de Montréal."[1] For the speech act theorist, even more than for the sports enthusiast, the moment was particularly savory: *The* most competent agent one could summon in all of one's examples, the Queen herself, speaking as the Sovereign of Canada from the specially constructed podium in the Olympic Stadium at the appointed time and with full knowledge of her responsibilities, had just uttered the perfect illocutionary sentence, to be followed imminently by the release of balloons and doves and the start of the parade of the national teams, thereby confirming the perlocutionary force of the utterance. The event was indeed a classic illustration of J. L. Austin's theories.[2] But, before anything happened, indeed even before the throng assembled under the unfinished dome of the stadium had begun to roar, the Queen was speaking again, this time in her own English: "I declare open the Olympic Games of 1976, celebrating the 21st Olympiad of the modern era."[3] This time the crowd did roar and the released pigeons and balloons rose toward the gap in the roof of the stadium and the parade started. But for the speech theorist, there was only shock: How could she do it? how could the games be "opened" twice?

Here was a conundrum for the theory. Surely, it must be the case that the sentence in French "opened" the Games and the English was merely a translation of it; yet all about the declaration in English, from its formal characteristics to its conditions of utterance, qualified it for the same sort of description as illocutionary act as the French, even more so perhaps since *it* was followed by activity actually characteristic of an "opening." But, if that were the case, then what was the status of the utterance in French? It too had qualified; nothing in its initial evaluation had been wrong. But between it and the realization of its (?) perlocutionary force stood the second utterance. And the two sentences were not symmetrical translations of each other: One spoke of the Games of the 21st Olympiad, accurately placing the event within the four-year interval method of calculating time characteristic of Olympic chronometry since its revival in 1896, while the other numbered the actual games which had taken place since 1896, omitting the games cancelled by war in 1916, 1940, and 1944. Both sentences then referred to the same thing, although this "thing" was yet to be, but were not, strictly speaking, in a relation of translation with respect to each other. A similar asymmetrical construction governed the verb "to celebrate": For the French, *nous* (whether audience-inclusive or royal-exclusive) celebrate the Games in Montreal, whereas for the English it is the Games which celebrate the Olympiad. How could the Queen be so perverse? Surely, she meant to "open" the Games, if for no other reason than to see her own daughter defend the colors of the United Kingdom in the equestrian competition. Yet the whole thing had been flubbed. Confound Canadian bi-lingualism! The only solace to be found was in the decision of twenty-three nations to boycott the Games, ostensibly because of the International Olympic Committee's refusal to bar New Zealand from participation because its national rugby team was touring South Africa in violation of the international sports boycott of that country, but perhaps just because they were as bemused as the speech act theorist about the actual status of the Montreal Games: Had they actually been opened? If so, at which point?

The predicament of the speech act theorist in this example of alternating Capitolian height and Tarpeian depth could be treated as a local one and, depending upon one's predilections, it could be used either for the confirmation of a prior rejection of the theory or for the elaboration of a better apparatus which would somehow if not quite extricate the theory from this impasse at least gain the assent of others that it had done so. But to restrict the impact of this instance of royal double-talk to speech act theory, whether from complacency or defensiveness, is to blunt the seriousness of the occurrence. For what matters here is that in spite of the fact that they were not properly "opened," the Games did take place: Athletes competed, records fell, and even closing ceremonies, of equally dubious status, were held. If speech act theory were a theory at all, if a theory was at work here, then the failure to produce a correct or, as some linguists like to say, a grammatical, utterance of the "opening" should clearly have resulted in no Games at all. To be sure, one could explain the problem away by pointing out that the declaration of opening is but a ritual and that in our secularized world the outer forms of ritual suffice for its efficacy, but this merely displaces the ground of the explanation and leaves intact the problem of speech act theory.[4]

The question is of some importance because speech act theory has come to represent in contemporary thought upon language a rare bulwark against a formalism preoccupied with the internal structures and functioning of language and discourse, and against all instrumental views of language which posit it as being in a secondary relation to whatever is defined as the primary (whether it be the psychological or the social, etc.). Speech act theory has attempted to think language in a continuum with other aspects of human activity, thus providing speculative room for, among others, ethico-political dimensions of linguistic experience. The predicament raised by the opening declaration(s) of the Montreal Olympics relegates it to the status of poetry or philosophy in Aristotle's *Poetics* (§9, 1451 a36-1451 b11) where these two discursive practices are defined, by opposition to history, by their separation from the world of actuality. For any theory of language that does not start out with formalistic assumptions, this is a deadly blow for it makes language and its internal constituents the limits of its inquiry. Whether speech act theory can extricate itself from this predicament is a question best left to its practitioners;[5] what matters more to those of us concerned with the possibility of a practice of literary criticism is to understand both how such a predicament has come about and what it signifies for our own activity.

I

Followers of the recent critical scene in this country will have had no difficulty in identifying the paradigm of the predicament: Two equally well-formed linguistic entities occur in juxtaposition in such a way that they are mutually contradictory and require an interpretive decision in favor of the one or the other, yet no possibility of making such a decision exists. This is the paradigm of aporia;[6] sometimes it is identified with deconstruction, but the appropriateness of that designation is very much open to question.[7] It ought to be stressed also, and this fact is generally forgotten in discussions of aporia, that the indecision is a readerly one only, for the text, just as the Olympics in the previous example, simply proceeds along with nary a notice of the problem.

The most meticulous thinker of aporia has been Paul de Man, who, trained in techniques of close reading at Harvard and in philosophical inquiry in Europe, began to explore the possibility of a critical practice based upon its most fundamental act: reading. In a series of papers written during the sixties, de Man analyzed the reading practices of prominent critics and critical schools and, finally, upon encountering Jacques Derrida's *De la Grammatologie*, formulated the question of "the future possibility of literary criticism" (*BI*, 111). To some, it has not always been apparent what the answer to that question has been; yet the very fact that de Man has gone on to write *Allegories of Reading* since and is at work on other projects ought to serve as a clue, and, given the persistence of the question, encourage those concerned to examine his handling of the issue. I shall follow then the emergence of the question of a critical practice grounded in reading to its full discussion in the crucial essay of *Blindness and Insight*, "The Rhetoric of Blindness: Jacques Derrida's Reading of Rousseau" (*BI*, 102-41).

It is well known that in the essays devoted to American New Criticism, Binswanger, Lukács, Blanchot, and Poulet, which came to be published as a lengthy introduction to "The Rhetoric of Blindness," de Man applied his considerable exegetical powers to discern in every case a "flagrant contradiction" (*BI*, 27) between the central critical achievement of these critics and the means by which they had obtained it. A single example suffices: Examining the methodological claims of American New Criticism, de Man identifies the role played by "intentional fallacy" in the meta-practical thought of these critics. Drawing upon his ample knowledge of phenomenology, he easily demonstrates that the concept of intentionality meant to be exorcised by the intentional fallacy is a thoroughly misunderstood one, although it plays a foundational role in establishing the poem as thing, that is as an autonomous entity possessing unity. Intentional fallacy is then further seen as the very device which allows the claim to autonomy of the poem to rest upon a Coleridgian notion of organic unity. But in Coleridge himself, de Man is quick to show, the notion of organic unity requires the concomitant notion of the will which is nothing but a properly understood concept of intentionality. If, at this juncture in de Man's analysis, the New Critics appear to be in somewhat of a critical quagmire, having first misunderstood intention and then failed to grasp that organic unity required intentionality, they nevertheless go on, like the Olympic Games, to their major achievements: The application of the techniques of close reading to works assumed to be free-standing and unitary produces a plurality of significations and, against all expectations, makes of the New Critics celebrants of irony and ambiguity.

Similar patterns of a movement in the thought of the critics he reads emerge from the other analyses: An initial claim resting upon a misunderstanding or a particulary repressed content is shown to have made possible, once its full force is unveiled by de Man, the very achievements of the critics. De Man is not content merely to follow this movement; he shows not only the originating error but also whence it came: for example, the New Critics mistook their own projection of the totalization characteristic of interpretation for a property of the text which they then had to see as unity. A more dramatic critic, and one more mindful of academic power games, might have used the acuity of his analyses to invalidate the claims of his predecessors and to disqualify them. But de Man, with commendable, and characteristic, restraint, refrained from any such course and chose instead to interrogate the very recurrence of a pattern in which the best critics of the day seemed "curiously doomed to say something quite different from what they meant to say" (BI, 105-6).

Paul de Man had begun his meditation on the significance of this pattern in one of his early essays, reviewing Heidegger's reading of Hölderlin (EHH). As is his wont, de Man is quick to show that Heidegger misreads Hölderlin, yet the misreading is productive: Heidegger claims that, in conformity with his own thinking about the relation of language to Being, Hölderlin's poetry successfully 'names' Being through poetic naming; this claim is not borne out by Hölderlin's text, and in that sense Heidegger is quite wrong. What actually occurs in Hölderlin's poems is that the attempt to name Being is constantly thwarted, caught up in a series of intervening stages of mediation which not only postpone the naming of Being but deny its very possibility. Again, de Man's reading is so persuasive that his reader is a little taken aback when, in the concluding pages of the essay, de Man praises Heidegger: Heidegger may indeed have been wrong on the actual success or failure of Hölderlin's poetic project, but it is his great merit to have identified this project as the desire to name Being. And lest his reader attribute such a statement to an observance of the conventions of polite reviewing, de Man formulates this early view of the problem of reading and criticism: Error need not be fatal to the critic as long as his reading represents a grasp of the problematic at hand. Heidegger may stand at the opposite end of Hölderlin, and in that he is quite wrong; but he has gotten hold of the right vector to Hölderlin, and a second reader, in this instance de Man, can correct Heidegger's apprehension. "To say the opposite is still to be talking about the same thing'' (EHH, 809). This statement sums up de Man's early view of the dialectically productive power of error.

What is striking, yet frequently unappreciated, about de Man's procedure is its almost obsessive preoccupation with truth. It is quite clear that in the Heidegger/Hölderlin essay, e.g., de Man follows standard scientific procedure and, attempting to falsify, in the technical sense of the term, Heidegger's claims, immediately succeeds. Rigorously analyzing the scope of his falsification, he limits it to the specific evaluation of Hölderlin's project and thus shows that the discovery of the project remains as the valid part of Heidegger's claims. At this stage, de Man's conception of his own activity seems to be governed by almost Popperian concepts of truth and falsehood, and his notion of critical writing, a version of scientific theory building. Yet, as a phenomenologist rather than an analytical philosopher, de Man sees this slightly differently, or more precisely, focuses on the process rather than the result.

The granting of truth-value status to a proposition represents one's free agreement to that proposition, a free agreement which can be granted only after careful deliberation. It is the very freedom of the thinker which is implied in such a process, for to agree to a proposition under some form of coercion is to alienate oneself in the agreement. This free agreement to a proposition represents, then, the preservation of one's self, one's very own identity at the crucial moment when that self is challenged by the unknown where thought is leading it. The mechanism of the agreement is then also a mechanism for the preservation of the self as same, indeed for the reduction to sameness of all that, which in its radical otherness, would challenge the self and perhaps lead to its fragmentation or cleavage. Metacritical thought, if one is allowed this term to designate an activity, such as de Man's in the Heidegger/Hölderlin essay, thus seeks to establish truth-value testing as a means for the creation of an intellectual space in which certitude would obtain, where the self, in full grasp of the propositions to which it acquiesces, could deploy its thought freely. Metacritical thought, like philosophy, would, by reducing the other to the same, eliminate obstacles to thought and thus render thought free. Thought could roam then through the realm of being, and indeed invest more and more of it, in a process deployed in History. In this view nothing *happens* to the Self: actions take place, events occur, time passes; yet the Self remains it-self, its very own Self, same unto itself. The transitory is merely the dimension of its history.

For this type of thought, the autonomy provided by freedom is crucial.[8] The irruption of any new or foreign datum is immediately perceived as an obstacle to be overcome and integrated. Truth is the mechanism of this overcoming and integration. The potential violence of the encounter with the external is deflected by turning the external into evidentiary matter, which preserves the Self as knowing subject exercising its cognitive ability freely. External realities may threaten this freedom, but truth allows the Self to comprehend them and to contain them. As Kierkegaard had observed, this notion of truth is totally removed from that of revealed truth or indeed from any revelation or encounter with the divine. It only deals with the Socratic version of the already known which merely needs to be discovered or found (invented) in the Self, which serves as the mold of any unknown.

But a phenomenological analysis of truth opens up yet another space, the space of experience. Truth requires the thinker to enter into a relation with a reality distinct from his own. We do not gain any experience unless we are brought beyond our familiar horizons. The movement of truth requires a transportation of the Self away from its intimate surroundings, from the space of sameness, to a beyond. Truth implies then not merely an exteriority which would serve as the (necessarily temporary) boundary of the realm of the Same, but a genuine beyond, that of transcendence, which would not be content to merely challenge the Self but oppose to it its radical indifference, but threaten it with a capacity for unstoppable irruption. The transcendent remains foreign and maintains, like Hölderlin's Being, its singularity.[9]

A practice of literary criticism grounded in reading will have to have recourse, in varying degree, to both modes of conceiving of truth. Insofar as the critic's own text seeks to account for a reading, or becomes the space where a reading deploys itself, it must first command the critic's assent to the propositions he or she formulates regarding the text read. A more phenomenological criticism, such as that of Georges Poulet, e.g., will attempt to capture the experience of a radical otherness by opening itself up to the constitutive elements of the other's text. Any reflection upon the truth value of critical statements will eventually encounter these modalities, singly and in combination.

De Man's early encounter with the problem in the Heidegger/Hölderlin essay was simple enough. Entirely circumscribed within the conception of truth as free agreement, it merely had to correct dialectically Heidegger's error by reversing his assessment of Hölderlin's attempt to name Being. But in the essays of the sixties, correction through dialectics does not prove possible: The New Critics do not come to uncover ambiguity and irony in poetic texts by means of an error which can be reversed dialectically; rather, they do so by means of an 'error' which must be maintained as such, whose truth they must not recognize in order to reach their judgments. With respect to the conceptual system which establishes the organic unity of the text, the discovery of textual polysemy takes on the form of an irruption which is unexplainable. De Man can explain it by showing that the exclusionary gesture of the intentional fallacy permits the occult return of intentionality as the guarantor of organic unity and, therefore, authorizes the application of techniques of close reading, which, in turn, lead to the overturning of unity by discovering textual ambiguity and irony. This final step does not lead to the affirmation of the intentional fallacy, for it remains quite unexamined and still shrouded in misprision, nor does it lead to its renewed rejection: The inaugural gesture of exclusion is too foundational to be repeated. De Man can describe and explain this sort of pattern as he unveils it in his readings of the other critics; yet the explanations remain conjunctural, accounting for the specific form in which the problem arose. Were it random, this would be the proper way of proceeding, but the very recurrence of the pattern suggests that a more powerful explanation is to be sought, one which would attempt to account for the nature of this mechanism. De Man came upon such an explanation in Jacques Derrida's *De la Grammatologie*,[10] but its very power required a number of precautions.

II

De la Grammatologie presents itself as a book in two parts: The first, roughly one-third in length, serves as a general theoretical introduction to the problematics of logocentrism, while the second is devoted to what appears to be a more historical approach to the epoch of logocentrism, centered upon Rousseau, a writer who has held considerable interest for de Man, as part of his own project of a "historical reflection on Romanticism" (*AR*, ix). But this structure is misleading: The Rousseau section starts with a lengthy discussion of Claude Lévi-Strauss and additional theoretical considerations, the most important of which, for our purposes, occurs at the very center of the book (pp. 226-234; 157-164) under the subheading: "The Exorbitant · Question of Method." Anyone even marginally acquainted with Derrida's thought[11] will not fail to be struck by the irony of having the question of method placed under the rubric of the exorbitant, and then the compounded irony of the exorbitant occurring at the center of the book.

"The Exorbitant" is a meditation upon reading. In a book ostensibly concerned with writing, the question of reading arises in the context of a discussion of the mediations which mark the gap betwen "total absence and the absolute plenitude of presence" (*G*, 226; 157). Rousseau himself rejects explicitly the recourse to mediations; instead, his impatience at not being able to locate himself in either absence or plenitude, seeks a derivative, what Derrida, following Rousseau, calls a "supplement."[12] The supplement comes to hold the middle between total absence and presence: "le supplément tient ici le milieu entre l'absence et la présence totales" (*G*, 226; 157). External to the given of the problem, the supplement is there first to appease Rousseau's impatience and then, more importantly, to appease the concept of the intermediary: "La virulence de ce concept est ainsi apaisée, comme si on avait pu l'*arraisonner*, le domestiquer, l'apprivoiser" (*G*, 226). The translator renders this difficult sentence as: "The virulence of this concept is thus appeased, as if one were able to *arrest it*, domesticate it, tame it" (*G*, 157). Which is close enough except for the term "arraisonner," which does not mean 'to arrest', but, rather, is a naval term describing the action of boarding a suspect vessel and conducting an inspection. But it is clear that beside this seme of policing, Derrida sought to force the French language to yield a term which would describe a mode of apprehension by reason (*raison*) similar in scope and effect to the German philosophical term *begreifen*, whose role in the constitution of the concept (*Begriff*), as a seizing by reason, is well known. But, as language would have it, the term, of considerable antiquity,[13] is, in its maritime context, a catachresis; its earliest meaning had little to do with order on the high seas though quite a great deal with smuggling: it meant "to seek to persuade"[14] and designated the very project of rhetoric.

The meditation upon reading, upon "our reading" as Derrida writes (*G*, 226; 158), is thus marked from its inception by the problem of mapping that gap which is marked by the absence of the text read and its total presence. The reading, which is designed to serve as a mediation to the text's solidary conjunction of absence and presence, is itself caught between the ability to subject to scrutiny implied by the inspection which follows the boarding and the displacement effected by the rhetorical project. What is the "task of reading" then?

Reading must always aim at a certain relationship, unperceived by the writer, between what he commands and what he does not command of the patterns of the language that he uses. This relationship is not a certain quantitative distribution of shadow and light, of weakness or of force, but a signifying structure that critical reading should *produce*. (G, 227; 158)

Derrida is acutely aware of the possible misprisions which the word "produce" may engender and, therefore, attempts to foreclose them through a *via negativa* in which he rejects the reproducing commentary as well as the so-called transgression of the text toward an external referent. This leads to the famous "il n'y a pas de hors-texte" (*G*, 227; 158). The reading must remain immanent; it must not let itself slowly drift toward the uncovering of the presumed content, the transcendental signified: "Literary writing has . . . lent itself to this *transcendent* reading, in that search for the signified which we here put into question, not to annul it but to understand it within a system to which such a reading is blind" (*G*, 229; 160). The system of the writing which carries the assertory content of the writing is occulted in this content and may be, indeed generally is, at odds with it for it is caught within the closure of logocentrism. The task of reading, insofar as it is a productive one, is to spell out the relationship between the asserted and the system of the writing which asserts it: "what Rousseau has said, as philosopher or as psychologist, of writing in general, cannot be separated from the system of his own writing" (*G*, 230; 160). Reading then occupies a locus which is both necessary for the articulation of the asserted to writing, yet whose explicit articulation ruptures that first articulation, deconstructing the totality of logocentrism which guaranteed it. To the extent that such a reading traces a path around that totality according to a logic which exceeds the logic of logocentrism, it is by necessity exorbitant. In the reading of Rousseau the path of the exorbitant is already traced by the supplement which also both occupies the locus of the mediation and exceeds the system of mediation.

The reading of Rousseau remains immanent to the text insofar as the text no longer constitutes a fixedness inhabited by a transcendental meaning to be divined, but, rather, marks the space of an operativity to which Derrida gives the name of textuality. But this operativity is not simple. By virtue of its exorbitant path, which carries it beyond the laws of logocentrism (such as identity, in this instance), the supplement does not remain stable but exploits "the virtualities of its meaning" (*G*, 234; 163). The actualitization of these virtualities cannot be described by appealing to the passivity or activity, unconsciousness or lucidity of the author. These categories, foundational of metaphysics, must be abandoned by reading which must instead "produce the law of this relationship to the concept of the supplement" (*G*, 234; 163) This is a genuine production, Derrida insists, for it not only does not "duplicate what Rousseau thought of this relationship," but is rendered necessary by the fact that the relationship is never articulated in Rousseau's text:

The concept of the supplement is a sort of blind spot [tache aveugle] in Rousseau's text, the not-seen that opens and limits visibility. But the production, if it attempts to make the not-seen accessible to sight, does not leave the text. Moreover, it is only by illusion that it has ever believed that it was doing so. . . . [W]hat we call production is necessarily a text, the system of a writing and of a reading about which we know *a priori*, but only now and only through a knowledge which is no longer knowledge, that they are ordered around their own blind spot (*G*, 234; 164. Translation modified.)

I have followed Derrida's text at some length with a reproductive commentary for it is a section of *De la Grammatologie* which has escaped the attention which it deserves; moreover, and more to the point of our project, de Man's relation to the exorbitant is far from simple, even upon first examination.

The movement of Derrida's argument is caught entirely in what could be described as a diacritical gesture: on page 227 the project is formulated of opening a space of reading under the name of "task of reading": *une tâche de lecture*; seven pages later, the project is brought to its conclusion and the space of reading is opened around its ordering principle: *[une] tache aveugle*, "a blind spot." The task of reading consists, then, in opening up a space which reveals a blind spot, just like the literal losing of a circumflex accent, shaped like an overhanging roof, turns the purposeful activity of imposing a tax on the text (task derives from tax) into a blind spot. The irruption of blindness in reading is the result of Derrida's meditation, and de Man has no difficulty in recognizing in the complex interplay of blindness and insight the mechanism of the pattern which he has been encountering.

Generally unaware of the close proximity of "The Exorbitant" and de Man's own rhetoric of "blindness and insight," most readings of "The Rhetoric of Blindness: Jacques Derrida's Reading of Rousseau" have tended to valorize the second part of de Man's essay where, most brilliantly, he is seen as, at once, refuting Derrida's evaluation of Rousseau as blinded by/to his own textuality and asserting that this is but a ploy on Derrida's part to deconstruct the critical tradition of Rousseau by means of Rousseau himself. This last point is generally taken to be de Man's master stroke, for it is seen as advancing ironically a reading of Derrida to which Derrida can only assent. Such readings of the essay may not have heeded a Pascalian injunction which de Man adopts as the epigraph to *Allegories of Reading*: "Quand on lit trop vite ou trop doucement on n'entend rien."

At it most obvious, what needs to be remarked first is de Man's embrace of the logic of blindness and insight to describe the complex processes of meaning formation in the critics he studied.[15] The first ten pages of "The Rhetoric of Blindness" are devoted to a retrospective discussion of the previous essays from the vantage point of the new terminology, effectively turning them into an introduction to the essay on Derrida. Recognizing the dialectical potential of a concept such as blindness, de Man starts out with insight and formulates the nature of the mechanism that has been producing the pattern which he has been encountering:

Their [the critics he studies] critical stance . . . is defeated by their own critical results. A penetrating but difficult insight into the nature of literary language ensues. It seems, however, that this insight could only be gained because the critics were in the grip of this peculiar blindness: their language could grope toward a certain degree of insight only because their method remained oblivious to the perception of this insight (*BI*, 106).

What is immediately less obvious is that the adoption of the blindness and insight paradigm as descriptor of a structure and its operations does not imply a similar adoption of Derrida's entire theory of reading. This is particularly difficult to argue, let alone demonstrate, because Derrida's theory was already defined negatively, and de Man's treatment proceeds mainly by selective use of silence. These are not preciosities of style, but indications of the complexity of the matter.

De Man subjects to silence the guiding principle of Derrida's meditation upon reading: production. The last sentence of "The Exorbitant" bears more careful examination:

[W]hat we call production is necessarily a text, the system of a writing and of a reading about which we know *a priori*, but only now and only through a knowledge which is no longer knowledge, that they are ordered around their own blind spot (*G*, 234; 164. Translation mine.).

Production was a term very much in vogue at the time Derrida wrote *De la Grammatologie*, most notably among his early boosters in the *Tel Quel* group who used it in what they claimed was a Marxist seme. Textual production, as the origination of the text under analysis, was being defined as the project of a criticism which would move beyond the synchronic descriptive imperative of structuralism. Derrida writes of production otherwise: It is a text itself and it alters knowledge to such an extent that it is knowable to a knowledge which is no longer knowledge. In other words, production opens up the question of knowledge and, through it, the question of truth. The classical structure of knowledge is articulated around a knowing subject who, in the act of knowledge, takes possession of the object. Subject and object are both predetermined in their constitution and in their very relationship. The knowing subject encounters the object, takes hold of it through perception, formulates a proposition concerning the object, and then, in the act of judgment, freely assents to this proposition. We have seen this to be one of the modalities of truth. Derrida's critique of logocentrism deconstructs the solidary opposition of subject and object as well as the deliberative modality of truth. Rousseau's relation to the supplement is much more fluid than the subject/object relation allows, for neither "Rousseau" nor the "supplement" constitute stable entities but represent a *mouvance* capable of multiple configurations, in which the idea of one somehow seizing and possessing the other is hardly thinkable. Insofar as the operation of cognition is the experience of an otherness, it cannot be converted into a category whose recuperative movement would lead back to identity and identification. For the "knowing subject" there is no return to the point of departure. Textuality cannot be thought of as a form of energy which agitates a text but remains equal to itself.[16] Nor is it a technique for the reduction by means of a *via negativa* of the world of the Other to mine. Both of these conceptions continue logocentrism by affirming the sameness of being to itself and centering thought upon its own apprehension. The movement Derrida traced in the wake of the supplement is one which starts from the identical in the direction of the Other but never returns to the Identical. To borrow a striking contrast: "to the myth of Ulysses returning to Ithaca, we would like to oppose the story of Abraham leaving forever the land of his fathers for a country still unknown, and forbidding his servant to ever bring back even his son to the point of departure."[17]

The cognition which occurs here is of a different order from that proposed by the classical structure of knowledge. Whereas the latter had always been governed by a certain *skopia*, a sight which seizes a totality in its interpreting glance, the former resembles more a blind groping of something radically unknown.[18] Such a palpation is not gratuitous or playful; it does result in a certain kind of cognition, sometimes even in knowledge when the thing is identified, when it becomes an object. Yet what happens is that, as in the case of any radical experience, we speak more of the experience as event, as epiphany of the other, than anything else. Production begins to take on the meaning of a pro-duction, a bringing forth of the Other, of the transcendental. But the very deconstruction of logocentrism undertaken by Derrida has insisted on the solidarity of the concept of the transcendental with the other structural concepts of logocentrism, so that it is not possible that Derrida meant by production the irruption of the transcendental, at least not the transcendental as logocentrism has known it. That is why, for Derrida, pro-duction is necessarily a text, that is a mode of inscription of a transcendental, not ontological but grammatologic, which does not overhang the text in the way that, in its classical conception, the signified dominates the signifier, but rather is the disruptive operativity which, just at the moment when a hermeneutic and an exegesis have peeled away the cultural determinations of the text and begun to seize it as a totality, radically disrupts it by putting us in touch with the blind spot at its core.

Why is it that de Man does not assume, along with the blind spot, the discussion of the task of reading as production? As one might by now expect, the matter is not broached directly, but there is no lack of clues.

To begin with, even though *écriture* as advanced by Derrida is not a phenomenal entity,[19] the recourse to production permits misreadings in that direction. For de Man "a literary text is not a phenomenal event that can be granted any form of positive existence, whether as a fact of nature or as an act of the mind. It leads to no transcendental perception, intuition or knowledge but merely solicits an understanding that has to remain immanent because it poses the problem of its intelligibility in its own terms" (*BI*, 107). In other words, a text is neither a production, in the sense of the manufacture of an artefact, nor a pro-duction. De Man means to exorcise the possibility of a return to the phenomenal: "However negative it may sound, deconstruction implies the possibility of rebuilding" (*BI*, 140). Not that he misunderstands deconstruction which most emphatically does not imply, in the logical sense of the term, a rebuilding; but the dictionary term "deconstruction" inevitably suggests, by virtue of its semantic associations, the possibility of reconstruction and can, therefore, precipitate, as indeed it has, calls for a move "beyond deconstruction." It is precisely because he anticipates such calls that de Man means not to provide them with any ground for a toe-hold in his text. This raises a strategic question: how to attack logocentrism if a deconstruction can turn into a construction? Metaphysics, like a child's bounce-back dummy, is constantly being knocked down but just keeps on standing, its fundamental ballast intact. How to attempt to stand outside metaphysics when one remembers that the categories of inside and outside are fundamental to, and governed by, metaphysics? De Man's reading of Derrida's theory of reading hinges on this strategic question.

Derrida's notion of production as pro-duction, and pro-duction as text, is, for all its precautions, still formulated within the orbit of the phenomenal and, therefore, risks leading back to it. It may, like Hölderlin's text which is incessantly traversed by the impossibility of naming Being, occasion a reading like Heidegger's which sees it as successfully achieving its goal. The movement of displacement which occurs in Derrida's text at the moment when the pro-duction of the transcendental undoes the transcendental and the phenomenal by stating that production is a text, is necessarily fraught with dangers for it could be read in the mode of loss, whereby the displacement would be categorized as an effect of the transcendental, which would leave the latter intact. As de Man reads it, what is required is a more explicit focusing on the question of knowledge. Thus, in the case of Rousseau, Derrida's "structurization of Rousseau's text in terms of a presence-absence system leaves the cognitive system of deliberate knowledge versus passive knowledge unresolved and distributes it evenly on both sides" (*BI*, 118), which is in accordance with Derrida's general project, adds de Man, but may permit the kinds of misreadings we have been concerned with.

What de Man calls the "cognitive system," and I have been referring to as the two modalities of truth, has certain implications for the manner in which one conducts an argument, that is one's textual strategy. Truth as manifestation, in Derrida's argument: as pro-duction, immediately before it is asserted that it is a text, presupposes the occurrence of instances of epiphany which can be recorded. It partakes of the characteristics of a sacred history in which the irruption or the manifestation of the divine marks moments of plenitude and articulates stages in a history which holds the promise of ultimate revelation. Derrida's text follows the structure of such a movement and, therefore, adopts narrative as its fundamental device. Of course, in the end, this movement is shown to lead to production as text, and, therefore, to have been proceeding in a certain blindness, not Derrida's, who knew that this is no end, that there is no end, but for the reader who is conditioned to expect ends for narratives, even if they have to take the form of interruption.

We have seen earlier (p. 25) that the other modality of truth, in which thought invests the realm of being, is also dependent upon narrative: The progressive conquest of being by reason requires the chronicling of its expansion. History as science, what Heidegger calls *Historie*, is indeed born from the historicity of presence (Geschichtlichkeit) and, therefore, is located within logocentrism.[20] Derrida's dilemma is that to make logocentrism manifest, he must tell its history, or, as de Man, eager to stress the dependence upon narrative form, puts it, its "story" (*BI*, 119). Derrida's double dependence upon narrative permits the contamination of his deconstruction by logocentrism. Already, in his essay on Blanchot, de Man had noted that at times narrative must be held in check (*BI*, 78), not that it is incapable of insight, but, rather, that the insight it provides is brought forth in blindness. To continue to speak though of "insight brought forth in blindness" is to continue being dependent upon narrative and redoubling the process, and taking refuge in a structure of *mise-en-abyme* which in turn requires a reversal of polarities of height and depth for the illusory avoidance of new blindness. This is the path of endless repetition and regression.

De Man returns to the non-phenomenality of the text instead, for it provides not an outside to this problematic but rather a structurally indeterminate moment which is not a locus. Just as in the verb *arraisonner*, the moment of mastery by reason is profiled on the horizon, yet it has not occurred, one is in an in-between which is not a mediation, for it turns out that the bringing forth to reason, *a-raison-er*, does not obey the logic of reason but is the realm of rhetoric. Rhetoric, as hardly bears repeating, bears only a distant relationship to truth. As a technique based upon the study of causes insofar as they produce effects of persuasion, it permits the handling of words without concern for the handling of things or objects. It permits an autonomous functioning of discourse without depriving it of effectiveness. We have seen that *arraisonner*, in Derrida's text, marks the very moment when the supplement substitutes itself to the intermediary; in this metabola, it is mediation itself which is exceeded; a dimension which is no longer just an in-between is opened. The violence of the intermediary is contained, but through a violence of a different sort. Whereas the first endangered discourse, the latter preserves itself at the cost of nearly everything else. In the little allegory of the word, it is the operation of boarding the ship which smuggles in the contraband, with all the trappings of legitimacy at its disposal. It is precisely because all is confined to the discursive, that it is already in the text; no irruption takes place nor is there need to presuppose any outside. It is, at once and seamlessly, part of the discourse in which it finds itself and a subversion of that discourse, yet without any of the peripateia or agonistics of narrative. *Arraisonner* is marked by what de Man calls its "rhetoricity": "any text that implicitly or explicitly signifies its own rhetorical mode and prefigures its own misunderstanding as the correlative of its rhetorical nature" (*BI*, 136). De Man will come to claim that such a rhetoricity is at work in both Rousseau's and Derrida's texts. Tactically, this resolution, if one can call it that, emerges with some difficulty, for de Man has to introduce the question of rhetoric in his own text via Derrida's assessment of Rousseau's statements on the figurality of language.[21] But the difficulty is worthwhile, for it avoids the pitfalls of production.

III

Nicht durch Zorn, sondern durch Lachen tödtet man.
F. Nietzsche, G.W. xiii, 47 (Musarion Vlg.)

De Man is able to state that Derrida's "chapter on method, on literary interpretation as deconstruction, is flawless" (*BI*, 139) because he sees the rhetoricity of Derrida's own text as leading him to adopt the strategy of narrative deployment for his argument:

Throughout, Derrida uses Heidegger's and Nietzsche's fiction of metaphysics as a *period* in Western thought in order to dramatize, to give tension and suspense to the argument, exactly as Rousseau gave tension and suspense to the story of language and of society by making them pseudo-historical. Neither is Derrida taken in by the theatricality of his gesture or the fiction of his narrative. (*BI*, 137)

However, as de Man's "corrective" reading of Derrida's handling of figurality in Rousseau demonstrates, Derrida's procedure is not without risks. De Man may claim that the question of his own blindness is "one which he is by definition incompetent to ask" (*BI*, 106), yet we may assume that it has received his attention. An indication is provided in the only evaluative statement which does not praise Derrida in the essay: Rousseau harbors no hope that he could escape misunderstanding; "he cuts himself off once and forever from all future disciples. In this respect, Derrida's text is less radical, less mature than Rousseau's" (*BI*, 140). As the context of the discussion makes clear, it is the fact that Rousseau did not seek to "correct" those he polemicized with but rather sought to indict language itself, which earns him the accolade refused to Derrida. Derrida's deconstructive enterprise, as radical as it may seem to us, is not radical enough for de Man, for it is still inscribed within the historical fiction of the epoch of metaphysics. To treat logocentrism as an epoch, in the wake of Heidegger and Nietzsche, is to still hold out for a possibility of undeceived language. From de Man's perspective, such a possibility is still maintained in Derrida's text, however much it may be barred by the deconstructive gesture, by the structural focus upon *écriture* a focus with respect to which the question of reading is exorbitant.

Since *écriture* is not a concept, it is not amenable to dialectical 'correction' through reading, which is not a concept either. Rather, since *écriture* requires the deployment of a narrative—the story of logocentrism, only a different story—the story of reading can be juxtaposed to it. But, as de Man reminds us, "unlike epistemological statements, stories do not cancel each other out" (*BI*, 119), and he chooses not to give us this story. Since, however, his reluctance has led many to attempt to write the story of a "beyond deconstruction," I shall have no such qualms, and fewer illusions.

Philosophical thought arises historically, but, from the moment of its emergence, it seeks to define itself as a form of cognition which would be based on a first principle understood as the foundation of all forms of being and thought. Philosophical thought is thus in a quandary from its inception: It must grant the status of philosophical question to the very circumstances which gave rise to it while formulating the mode of philosophical questioning as independent of any contingent considerations. In the *Phenomenology of Mind*, Hegel proposes to address this difficulty by starting with the recognition of contingent phenomenal knowledge and contingent natural consciousness, and advancing the hypothesis that it is by the experience of thought upon the totality of the contingent that we reach the universal. In this manner the contingency of the historical is not an irreducible obstacle but a necessary stage in the constitution of the universal. This solution requires, however, the positioning or the importation of a first principle which will ground both knowledge and its object, otherwise an endless dialogue will ensue. This principle is found in the transcendental possibility, that is in the capacity of natural consciousness to transcend phenomenal knowledge. In our tradition, and at least since Descartes, the transcendental possibility has been conceived of as the subject, which constitutes the locus from which the question of the adequation of thought to elements of the world of being can be decided under the form of truth. We rejoin here the world of logocentrism equally based upon the assumption of an identity of thought and being.

But the identity of thought and being is not immediate, otherwise the problem would not have arisen immediately, nor would philosophy have had any historical roots. As Hegel thinks of mediation, it is based upon the recognition of the contingency of the contingent. The mode of my being in the world translates itself through actions which I undertake and by which I transform both the world and myself; but what matters in such a formulation is that, in each case, the instrument of the action is mediated: I am the instrument of the transformation of the world, and it is through this externality that I transform myself. Mediation is a structure of indirection. Thought proceeds in similar fashion since consciousness apprehends itself only as consciousness of something else. In ordinary thinking, natural consciousness does not keep track of this mediation. It takes itself as immediate consciousness of the external. It is only in a movement of return upon itself, that reflection, as mediated reflection upon itself, apprehends this movement. This leads to the reexamination of truth, for, if in the first instance, truth was the adequation of thought to being, but thought and being are mediations of each other, then the propositions of truth are valid only insofar as we reproduce their conditions of emergence. But, and here the paradox grows, this is nothing more than a primary utterance forgotten by simple reflection. The forgetfulness of simple reflection consists in the fact that it tends to lose itself in its object; it can regain its status as reflection only by means of a second reflection, one which can pretend to truth only insofar as it monitors its own conditions of emergence. But this, in turn, implies that propositions have only locally determined meaning, so that all that is given up is the claim to totality, universality, and transcendence. Expectations are scaled down but the basic mechanism is left intact. This possibility is already envisaged by Hegel who recognized that the apparatus of the absolute remains absolute, and that it functions no less because its *deus* has become *absconditus*. Local mediations draw their power and are authorized by absolute mediation.

This moment, which takes the form of a structured opposition between the age of the symbol and that of allegory in Gadamer,[22] immediately suggesting a historical periodization, places us in the epoch which lives in the age of the ruin of the symbolic. What then are our options? One is the Marxian, which, refusing this periodicity, proceeds from the recognition that the totalization did not in fact occur and abandons description for prescription. The identity of ontological thought has never been realized; praxis and thought have not been united. Let us seek this identity and this unity, but, in the meantime, recognize that the claim that it has occurred opens up the space of the ideological by occulting contradictory social reality.

Another avatar is the attempt through various neo-Kantianisms to reopen the epistemological question in such a way that the concept of identity becomes part of the very project of knowledge conceived of as the dimension of life (Dilthey, e.g.). This culminates in Heidegger's effort to describe understanding as the very mode of being of *Dasein*, a proposition upon which Gadamer will build his hermeneutics. In this instance, the hermeneutic moment coincides with the second reflection which redresses the structure of prejudgment (*Vorverständnis*) which has been carried in predetermined form by language, texts, and tradition. An unresolvable dialogue, rendered endless by our finitude, ensues.

But the moment that a form of prejudgment or prejudice is elevated to the rank of principle of comprehension, it permits forms of existential commitments which will require in turn a new form of enlightenment. And since the problem can now be reformulated within the framework of a communicational model which would ensure the formation of correct understanding through proper communicational procedures, then various forms of pragmatics, that is sciences of speech in action, will come to the fore, for they alone can determine the conditions of successful communication, where success is measured by the realization of the identity of the speaking subject. Thus, in order not to return to the Queen of England who also sometimes speaks as the Sovereign of Canada, we may give exemplary status to Jürgen Habermas's attempt to determine, on the basis of a second reflection, the constitutive and regulative principles of all communication.[23] Truth is achieved by discursive consensus, and its validity is assured by the invocation of an ideal communication situation which relies on the operation of contrafactual falsification to detect shortcomings in its constitution. Once again, we have truth as adequation. Once again we are locked into perpetual discussion and infinite dialogue. Once more we are in logocentrism.

My narrative is sketchy and it is built of propositions each of which would require voluminous demonstration. But it does lead us back, following the erection and simultaneous collapse of the Hegelian enterprise, to the inescapable conclusion that any history of philosophy is a philosophy of history and, therefore, also a theory of narrative. More discouragingly, it shows that the structure of logocentrism is at work more than ever in the discourse of philosophy after Rousseau, and that current attempts, including those on the so-called New Left, are mired in the same problematic, that is the problematic of the same. One indeed cannot oppose a story which could cancel the story of logocentrism.

De Man, therefore, does not write this story, nor does he seek to produce it. He reads instead, for there, in reading, is the space which renders such production unnecessary. A counter-story, an agonistics, only allows the terrible dialectic to work its wonders and to reduce to identity the seeming other. But reading, in the legitimate operation of boarding for inspection, smuggles in the contraband. But at what cost, it is now frequently asked. Derrida is domesticated by de Man's reading, tamed, and has lost his virulence. Yet, it was not long ago that he asserted:

A deconstructive practice which would not bear upon "institutional apparatuses and historical processes" (to use your terms), which would remain content to operate upon philosophemes or conceptual signified, or discourses, etc. would not be deconstructive; whatever its originality, it would but reproduce the gesture of self criticism in philosophy in its internal tradition. This was clear from the outset, from the minimal definition of deconstruction, which bore upon logocentrism, the last instance of meaning or of the "transcendental signified," the transcendental signifier, the last instance in general, etc.[24]

Is this Derrida tamed, domesticated? Only in the sense which those two terms can have in Derrida's text (G, 226), where they occur immediately after *arraisonner*. But that is another story.

NOTES

1. *Le Devoir*, July 19, 1976, p. 1.

2. *How to Do Things with Words* (Cambridge: Harvard University Press, 1962).

3. *Washington Post*, July 18, 1976, p. A12.

4. Deconstructionists and their allies ought to ponder the power of the speech act theorists' lobby which, intent upon preventing a repeat of the Montreal fiasco, managed to block any broadcasting of the 1980 "Opening" ceremonies from the Moscow Games. This must have been the meaning of the much used phrase "the symbolic significance of the Olympic boycott."

5. One may anticipate some of their reaction in John Searle's refusal to understand Derrida, who placed Searle in front of a similar instance of duplicitous duplication in "Limited, Inc." *Glyph* 2.

6. From the Greek 'poros'. passage, with preceding privative a-, meaning: without passage, blocking the flux, undecidable. Aporia has come to mean undecidability.

7. See Rodolphe Gasché, "Deconstruction as Criticism," *Glyph* 6 (1979), 177-215.

8. A more detailed analysis, which is out of place here, would show that this concept of freedom is necessarily auto-telic and must be axiomatic, independent of any justification.

9. This opposition of truth as manifestation vs. truth as adequation is well known since M. Heidegger's *Sein und Zeit* (1927).

10. Paris: Editions de Minuit, 1967. English version as *Of Grammatology*, translated and prefaced by Gayatri Chakravorty Spivak (Baltimore: The John Hopkins University Press, 1976). References will be made in the text as G. followed by page number to both versions, French first.

11. Such as the standard text by which he had been known in this country for a long time before the more recent translations: "Structure, Sign, and Play in the Discourse of the Human Sciences," *The Structuralist Controversy: The Language of Criticism and the Sciences of Man*. Eds. Richard Macksey and Eugenio Donato (Baltimore: The John Hopkins University Press, 1970), 247-65.

12. But which Gayatri Spivak curiously chooses to translate as "substitute." Cf. *G*, 226: "Je trouvais dans Thérèse le supplément dont j'avais besoin." vs *G*, 157: "I have found in Thérèse the substitute that I needed." Since the discussion which follows is concerned with the "supplement," and, indeed, the chapter is entitled "Ce dangereux supplément . . . ," this is a strange oversight.

13. The oldest attested occurrence in French dates to 1080.

14. "Comme si on avait pu l'*arraisonner*" should be rendered then as "as if it could have been brought to reason," which retains the semes of control as well as those of movement which *arrest* loses without forgoing the investment of a vehicle by reason.

15. I am not arguing from the perspective of a study of influences, and even less one of sources. I am more interested in bringing out the effects of a specific encounter.

16. Psychoanalytic versions of textuality need particularly to be examined on this point. Far too often the displacement they follow and inscribe is a surface one, caused by a cathexis which, remarkably, remains equal to itself, or at most "spends" itself, and then is unable to preserve its identity but remains within its orb.

17. Emmanuel Lévinas. *En Découvrant l'existence avec Husserl et Heidegger*, édition augmentée (Paris: Vrin, 1967), 191.

18. The blindness is marked here somatically in the straining of the eyes leaving their sockets to attempt to see, as in cartoons: ex-orbitant.

19. This point is brought out with considerable vigor and precision by R. Gasché's "Deconstruction as Criticism," which is fundamental for any discussion of this issue.

20. *Sein und Zeit*, pp. 394-95. Heidegger's argument is more complex since it is articulated around the notion of *Dasein* as possibility. History is organized around the possibility of an existence which has taken place, and it is in the name of such a project that it seeks out "data." It is not a recording of what has been, but the inquiry into the possibility of that which has taken place.

21. This is the best known part of the essay and there is no need to rehearse its arguments. Suffice it to notice that the matter of this argument is not as central as it is generally believed. De Man is uncharacteristically assertive in his reading of the passage on metaphor in Rousseau, which, interestingly enough, is read somewhat differently in *Allegories of Reading*. Within "The Rhetoric of Blindness" essay, the matter is of tactical interest, tracing an approach to the strategically more important question of reading.

22. Hans-Georg Gadamer, *Wahrheit und Methode*. 4th ed. (Tübingen: Mohr, 1975).

23. *Der Universalitätsanspruch der Hermeneutik*. (Frankfurt: Suhrkamp Verlag, 1971). Also "Was heisst Universalpragmatik?" *Sprachpragmatik und Philosophie*, K. O. Apel and J. Habermas, eds. (Frankfurt: Suhrkamp Verlag, 1976) pp. 174-272.

24. "Ja, ou le faux-bond," *Digraphe* 11 (Avril 1977) 83-121, p. 117. (Translation mine.)

Part II

Aesthetic Criticism:
Geoffrey Hartman
Michael Sprinker

"The question of style is also a question of method."

Geoffrey Hartman

Writing to Louis Colet in 1852, Flaubert envisioned an ideal work of prose fiction. This ideal has haunted European literature ever since:

What seems beautiful to me, what I should like to write, is a book about nothing, a book dependent on nothing external, which would be held together by the strength of its style, just as the earth, suspended in the void, depends on nothing external for its support; a book which would have almost no subject, or at least in which the subject would be almost invisible, if such a thing is possible. The finest works are those that contain the least matter; the closer expression comes to thought, the closer language comes to coinciding and merging with it, the finer the result. I believe that the future of Art lies in this direction. . . . This emancipation from matter can be observed everywhere: governments have gone through similar evolution, from the oriental despotisms to the socialisms of the future.

It is for this reason that there are no noble subjects or ignoble subjects; from the standpoint of pure Art one might almost establish the axiom that there is no such thing as subject, style in itself being an absolute manner of seeing things.[1]

Such passages led Nietzsche to accuse Flaubert of nihilism, but led Pater and Henry James to celebrate Flaubert's martyrdom on the altar of art. The novels eventually realized from this severe aesthetic, *Madame Bovary* and *L'Education sentimentale*, have left an indelible mark on the writing of subsequent fiction. Through the work of Ezra Pound and his formidable critical influence on several generations of poets, Flaubert's aesthetic has also made its way into modern poetry. But the passage points in other directions as well. Not only is an entire aesthetic figured here, but also a politics of art. For Flaubert's explicit linking of the history of art to the evolution of world history, his virtually Hegelian intuition about the homology between the future of art and future social formations, projects not merely the entire tradition of modernist aesthetics, of which he can legitimately be said to be one of the founders, but also a system of thought with which he was intimately connected but which only rarely has been considered germane to aesthetics at all. Flaubert's "pure Art" is but the reflex of that "value-free science" hypostatized by Weber; Flaubert's artist, inscribed in English letters by Joyce's famous image of an indifferent, nail-paring deity, bears a striking resemblance to what Lacan has termed the "sujet supposé savoir" which forms the ideological cornerstone of modern scientific inquiry. The ideology of art is entangled in the general structures of modern social formations in which social practices like science and art appear to be relatively autonomous with respect to each other, completely unmotivated by the subjectivity of those individuals and groups in whom the practices are realized.

Thus one reads at first with some astonishment Geoffrey Hartman's dedication in *Saving the Text*: "For the Subject." Barring the possibility that this is Hartman's coy way of dedicating the book to Derrida (the ostensible "subject" of the intersection announced in the subtitle between literature and philosophy), one is led to think Hartman's project archaic and nostalgic, an attempt to hold the line against the various incursions into literary and aesthetic studies by scientific method and ideology, to "save" art from the various critical machines that seem currently to threaten its survival. Despite the care and devotion lavished in *Saving the Text* on *Glas*, the final chapter, "Words and Wounds," makes "a counterstatement to Derrida" (*ST*, 121), who remains, previous attempts by Hartman to appropriate him for a "tender rather than exact . . . theorizing" (*ST*, 155) notwithstanding, an enemy to aesthetic perception and thus a threat to literature after all. Hartman nowhere says so explicitly, but one surmises that his unallayed suspicion about Derrida stems from the philosopher's allegiance to the Flaubertian-scientific ideal of style: an ideal so absolute that it is in fact no style (signature, self, subject) at all. Hence Derrida the "great amateur of Littré and Wartburg" (*ST*, 82), pioneers (along with Murray and the makers of the *OED*) of scientific language study. Style marks for Hartman the space of literature, the domain where the subject remains recoverable and alive.

But there remains a complication, one that is inherent in the paradox of Flaubert himself. The founding discourse of what has been called aestheticism necessitates, as Nietzsche believed it must, the effacement of the aesthetic, of the phenomenality of the object. Flaubertian style is thus "subjectless" in a double sense. Hartman's recovery of the subject implicitly criticizes Flaubert, but in a curious way; for in characterizing the Flaubertian ideal as no style at all, Hartman produces the very definition of the aesthetic object that has grounded the discourse of aesthetics since Kant: "To write without style, to write unseen, would be, at once, to reduce visibility and vulnerability, or to be purposive without purpose" (*ST*, 156). The question of style is indeed a question of method; literature and philosophy intersect at the point of the aesthetic.

Hartman's writing meditates the problem of style as a constitutive as well as mediatory agency in the formation of knowledge. One might attribute this concern to the influence of Hartman's teacher, Erich Auerbach, recalling in particular the minute and sustained analyses of individual texts in *Mimesis*. But to read Auerbach and Hartman together is to be struck immediately by the profound differences separating the styles of these two critics themselves. Auerbach's sober, restrained, judicious manner, characteristic of the scholarly tradition in which he was trained and whose heritage he attempted to preserve, is the very embodiment of what Hartman has called the neoclassical style in criticism, perfected and sanctified in English by Matthew Arnold and T. S. Eliot. Although Hartman honors this ideal, and although he can write with neoclassical restraint when the occasion demands, he seems in general to suspect the calm detachment and cool superiority projected in Eliot's and Arnold's criticism. His own prose often swerves toward outrageously indecorous punning and baroque involution as a defense against the scholar's native impulse to pure objectivity and impersonality. And thus in his own writing, Hartman enacts the drama of modern literature that has been his chosen subject since *The Unmediated Vision*.

The Arnoldian legacy remains powerful, as the number of reviewers who have simply called Hartman's prose "bad" will attest.[2] Hartman's critique of this legacy is not calculated to give solace to its contemporary defenders. For example, he remarks in the title essay to *The Fate of Reading*: "Criticism should be reflective vis-à-vis itself as well as vis-à-vis its immediate object, the work of art. It should reflect on its historical debts (that it may not be as distinct from religious hermeneutics as it might wish to be) and on the possibility that it is, after all, an art form— more of a *mythologie blanche* (Derrida) than it realizes" (*FR*, 271). The exemplary instance of this white mythology in modern criticism is the style cultivated by I. A. Richards in *Principles of Literary Criticism*. Despite Richards's identification of Coleridge as the ancestor of his own scientific criticism, *Principles of Literary Criticism* inhabit a Benthamite world, where Richards's stimulus-response psychology turns art into something like the game of push-pin to which Bentham unfavorably compared it:

They [the *Principles*] are written in a kind of Basic Philosphical English. Everyone with a certain level of culture can understand the terms and follow the argument. Elements are repeated till the mind behind them becomes clear through iteration and aggregation rather than absolute logical schemes on the one hand or artistic inventiveness on the other. At no point is ordinary, commonsensical experience threatened. We have entered a Normal School of discourse; and this would be all right if it were not accompanied by an artificial dignity that "levels" us in quite another way. I mean that Richards' language of description, in this early work, takes what dignity it has from a highly managerial scientific model, one that is born in the laboratory or is sustained by the ideal of controlled experimentation.

. . . In short, the base is English but the superstructure is the managerial imperative of what is now called Social Science (*FR*, 26).[3]

We understand why students and teachers of literature continue to abominate, even as they are fascinated by and often unconsciously resemble in their pedagogical practice, the figure of Gradgrind—"Satire is a sort of *glass*, wherein beholders do generally discover everybody's face but their own." (Swift).

Hartman honors the achievement of Richards, as he honors that of Arnold and Eliot and such latter-day Arnoldians as F. R. Leavis, Lionel Trilling, M. H. Abrams, and Northrop Frye, but at the same time he criticizes this tradition, which has so powerfully shaped the study of literature in Britain and America, for its having constrained criticism in questionable ways. Although justly skeptical of the various incursions of the social sciences into contemporary critical discourse, Hartman manages often enough to speak in their behalf and to salvage a measure of utility from the categories and the vocabulary they present. One is reminded of Kenneth Burke's pioneering essay, "Freud—and the Analysis of Poetry," which put clearly the limitations of psychoanalytic theory for the description and analysis of works of art while yet stipulating for the importance of psychoanalytic categories as instruments for interpreting symbolic action. Similarly, Hartman incorporates the language and the concepts of semiotics, psychoanalysis, communication theory, and even on occasion Marxist sociology, into a critical discourse that is at once rich and various without being modishly eclectic. Resistant to the totalitarian impulse in theorizing,[4] he has from his first essays been evolving a theory of literature as mediation. As he says in the opening sentences of his essay on Richards: "Aesthetics has long been linked to a study of the affective properties of art. It should really be called *psychoesthetics*, for it investigates the relation of art to the life of the mind, and particularly the affections'' (*FR*, 20). Although Hartman does not say so here (in other contexts he is well aware of the history and lineage of the concept), this theory repeats Schiller's definition of the aesthetic in the twentieth of the *Aesthetic Letters*, where the affect of art becomes the very condition of harmony among all the mental faculties.[5] Art provides what Wordsworth called "monumental hints" (*Prelude*, XIII. 352) of "a motion and a spirit, that impels/All thinking things, all objects of all thought,/And rolls through all things" ("Tintern Abbey"), harmonizing, momentarily, the discordant faculties of perception, will, and reason in Schiller's "aesthetic state" (*ästhetische Zustand*). How such a state of the soul or psyche might be attained is most readily disclosed in the reading of discrete texts. In the work of Geoffrey Hartman, no texts are more pervasive than those of Wordsworth.

* * *

Hartman's scholarly career opened with a reading of "Tintern Abbey." Several of his recent essays have dealt with largely neglected minor poems from the period of Wordsworth's post-1807 decline. Wordsworth's poetry has been for Hartman a "sounding cataract," haunting him "like a passion." It is one measure of his power as a critic that no subsequent reader of Wordsworth has been able to avoid confronting Hartman's interpretation. As will become apparent, even the strongest among current readers of modern poetry, Harold Bloom, finds himself compelled and ultimately overcome by Hartman's Wordsworth. This Wordsworth of humanized imagination and apocalypse avoided remains, today, the most seminal and least assimilable of modern poets.

In his book on Wordsworth, Hartman was willing to concede the poet's loss of imaginative power after 1807, acknowledging the comparative failure of *The Excursion* (the poem "is not successful even on its own terms") and the diminished grandeur of the River Duddon Sonnets in comparison to "Tintern Abbey." At the same time he alluded to "strange happenings in the later poetry, which has a precarious quality of its own" (*WP*, 290-91, 331). But the book halts at 1814, a self-imposed limit that in effect repeats what virtually every reader of Wordsworth from Jeffrey and Coleridge to the present has sensed: the absence of poetic intensity in the later poetry, the effective death of the poet's imagination. Hartman excuses Wordsworth by pointing to the poet's growing sense of isolation, not only from the world, but from the history of English poetry, which seemed to be leaving him behind in Shelley, Keats, and Byron, just as he himself had repudiated the poetic diction of the previous generation. In the end, Wordsworth's very uniqueness betrays him, for "despite his love for the older writers, and especially for Milton, [he] can turn to no one in the desire to save nature for the human imagination. He is the most isolated figure among the great English poets'' (*WP*, 338).

This canonical reading of Wordsworth's career has always stumbled over a curious fact: the continuing revision of *The Prelude* from 1805 until the poet's death in 1850. It is known from the scrupulous scholarship of this century that some of the poem's finest lines were comparatively late additions, but this knowledge has not yet altered the received understanding of the poems Wordsworth did publish later in life. Perhaps there is something amiss in the estimation of the later Wordsworth, a misunderstanding of his restraint and reserve. Perhaps, as Hartman has recently suggested, Wordsworth's isolation is not a sign of weakness but of a peculiar strength, of a self-sufficiency that is difficult for a modern audience to imagine:

The life of Wordsworth's lines is often uneasy and as if somewhere else: still to be manifested by the action of time and the utterance of future readers. One could apply to Wordsworth what he says of the idiot boy: ''You hardly can perceive his joy.'' We should not forget that Wordsworth's greatest poem remained hidden, and that its power and authority (in the light of which we *now* read everything else) was but alluded to in the rest of his oeuvre. . . . Keeping *The Prelude* in reserve, almost like God his own Son, Wordsworth reposed on a text-experience whose life remained with God. He delayed becoming the author of a poem so original that it could not be accommodated to known forms of Christianity. In what he does publish, then, the relation of author to poem is often the strangest mixture of knowingness and childlikeness—it is, in short, a divine idiocy. The inter-textual glitter of Milton, his blended might of Scripture and classical lore, is but undersong to Wordsworth's intratextual strain that repeats something already begotten in himself (*WWW*, 213).

One can of course think of poets for whom such an experience was less salutary—Hopkins, for example—but this only makes Wordsworth's achievement the more remarkable.

In one sense, Hartman's meditations on Wordsworth have all been of a piece. The high argument of *Wordsworth's Poetry*, Wordsworth's avoidance of apocalypse and his consequent humanizing of imagination, remains the dominant motif of the more recent essays. What troubles and exercises Hartman, as it has all of Wordsworth's most discerning readers, is the peculiarity of Wordsworth's style, its ''precarious quality'' that verges so often on bathos and almost inevitably defeats attempts to characterize it discursively. Matthew Arnold thought this indicative of a complete absence of style, while Pater interpreted it as a sign of repose, of the poet's "inborn religious placidity."[6] Hartman's judgment is more technical, but no less mindful of the strangeness of this most personal and yet most restrained of poetic signatures:

In Wordsworth's style, early or late, the fallen sublimity of classicizing or poetic diction blends with the naturalism of elemental speech-acts of wishing, blessing, naming. Faded figures, and archaic or trivialized fragments of high style are naturalized in a way that remains undramatic, and even, at times, awkward (*BT*, 200).

One is reminded of the famous Beerbohm caricature, which captures the Wordsworthian awkwardness with such cruel precision. This preeminent poet of nature seems at times so unnatural, even a bit absurd, as in "The Idiot Boy." But to Beerbohm's superior common sense, Wordsworth's reply would surely be the same he made to John Wilson's objections that an idiot "is not fit subject for poetry":

You have given me praise for having reflected in my Poems the feelings of human nature. I would fain hope that I have done so. But a great Poet ought to do more than this: he ought, to a certain degree, to rectify men's feelings, to give them new compositions of feeling, to render their feelings more sane, pure, and permanent, in short, more consonant to nature, that is, to eternal nature, and the great moving spirit of things. He ought to travel before men occasionally as well as at their sides.[7]

Rarely has the voice of the prophet declaimed in such subdued tones.

The undersong of Hartman's meditations on Wordsworth is a respectful but stubborn polemic with his colleague Harold Bloom, and not only with Bloom's reading of Wordsworth, but with the theory of poetry and influence that Bloom has gradually unfolded since his massive study of Yeats. Reviewing *Wordsworth's Poetry*, Angus Fletcher observed that "Hartman has written a book as much about Wordsworth's forerunners as about the poet himself. . . ."[8] Indeed, much of the argument of that book can be seen to anticipate Bloom's troubled broodings over the situation of post-Enlightenment English poetry. Wordsworth's relation to his precursors (principally Milton, Spenser, and the Renaissance poets, but also Collins, Gray, and Thomson, whose achievement Wordsworth's poetry brings to fruition and surpasses), the uneasy response he provoked among his contemporaries (hyperbolically in Blake), and the daunting example his poetry has presented to subsequent readers, many of them poets or would-be poets in their own right (notably Arnold, Ruskin, and Pater)—these questions circulate through Hartman's text and counterpoint the psychological theme of the drama of Wordsworth's growth into self-consciousness and selfhood. Here, for example, is Hartman on a prominent allusion to "Lycidas" in Wordsworth's early loco-descriptive poem, "An Evening Walk":

The presence of Milton is not an abstract tribute. His style is associated for Wordsworth with the supreme objectification of personal loss in pastoral and epic form. Milton's privations, including the loss of sight, served only to increase an inner brightness. The figure of the blind man, of the spirit feeding on darkness, already haunted through "The Vale of Esthwaite," and we know that Wordsworth's own loss, mentioned at the beginning of his poem, is the difficulty of taking joyous nourishment from visible nature, together with strange tidal movements of his increasingly self-aware, autonomous spirit. . . . Milton is Vision, the might of a spirit separated from nature and therefore seeing nature's truly supernatural aspect. There is a theory that two powers fought for the soul of Keats: Milton and Shakespeare. Two powers also fought for the soul of Wordsworth: let us call them Nature and Milton (*WP*, 99).

Milton was for Wordsworth the very exemplar of the poet, and his figure as well as his verse continued to haunt Wordsworth's poetry throughout his life. But this psychological burden, figured in the opposition Milton/Nature, is only part of the story, for it was also Milton's style— in "An Evening Walk" and "Descriptive Sketches" the rhymed couplets of "Il Penseroso," later in *The Prelude* the sinuous blank verse of *Paradise Lost*—which blocked Wordsworth's path to poetic originality. The psychological argument of *Wordsworth's Poetry* is thus mediated by a kind of formalism such that Wordsworth's gradually maturing poetic style becomes the focus of his inner psychic drama. *The Prelude* is as much the growth of a poet's style as of his mind: an observation that takes us to the foot of the Bloomian orrery.

For Bloom, Wordsworth stands "in the shadow of Milton," a point scarcely disputable, though in itself not particularly original or enlightening. But Bloom's genius—despite the carping hostility of some of his critics, it should be called that—is to have shown how this relationship of the great precursor to his ephebe operates in individual poems. In *Poetry and Repression*, Bloom takes as the central Wordsworthian text "Tintern Abbey" and what he calls the composite trope of memory, "a defense against time, decay, the loss of divinating power, and so finally a defense against death, whose other name is John Milton" (*PR*, 53). Memory is linked to forgetting, and what Wordsworth has forgotten or repressed in "Tintern Abbey" is Milton, in particular the invocations to Books III and VII of *Paradise Lost*, which underlie what Bloom identifies as the "Sublime tropes or strong hyperboles" of Wordsworth's poem (*PR*, 56). Bloom then goes on to cite Hartman on the absence of literary echo or allusion in Wordsworth, a point Bloom disputes by, characteristically, interpreting Hartman's argument as an unwitting anticipation of his own: "Hartman's true point is Wordsworth's characteristic internalization of allusion" (PR, 58). Bloom's reading of "Tintern Abbey" proceeds along these lines, uncovering Miltonic figures (including Milton's Penseroso in the Hermit of ll. 21-22)[9] hidden behind Wordsworth's studied anti-apocalyptic stance.

Near the end of this remarkable performance, Bloom makes the following judgment on ll. 781-94 from the fragment of "The Recluse," lines which manifest the true face of the Wordsworthian ego Bloom has uncovered in its repressed form in "Tintern Abbey":

That is Wordsworth, taking on Jehovah and Milton together only a few months before writing *Tintern Abbey*. That is not a poet whose eye and ear "half-create." *Power* is being repressed in *Tintern Abbey*, a power so antithetical that it could tear the poet loose from nature, and take him into a world of his own, restituting him for the defense of self-isolation by isolating him yet more sublimely. Wordsworth defends himself against his own strength through repression, and like all strong poets he learns to call that repression the Sublime (PR, 76).[10]

One need not quarrel with this reading of "Tintern Abbey," nor for the moment with Bloom's intuition that Milton is the perpetual *Doppelgänger* in Wordsworth's poetry (Wordsworth may well have associated the Hermit in "Tintern Abbey" with Milton, the great solitary). but it is necessary to point out that this is precisely the argument, elaborated in great detail over some four hundred pages, of *Wordsworth's Poetry*, and that Bloom has either forgotten (repressed?) this, or simply failed to acknowledge it in his zeal to establish Hartman as the canonical, idealizing reader against whom he must pit himself. Power is not only being repressed in "Tintern Abbey" but everywhere in Wordsworth's poetry, for this power is the imagination apostrophized in *Prelude* VI:

Imagination—here the Power so called
Through sad incompetence of human speech,
That awful Power rose from the mind's abyss
Like an unfathered vapour that enwraps
At once, some lonely traveller (ll. 592-96).

The lonely traveller is the poet, emblematically halted by his intimation of a power usurping the senses, blinding him to nature, which now appears as

features
Of the same face, blossoms upon one tree;
Characters of the Great Apocalypse,

> The types and symbols of Eternity,
> Of first, and last, and midst, and without end (ll. 636-40).

This is a key passage for Hartman; he comes back to it many times in the course of *Wordsworth's Poetry*. His reading of it is too complex to summarize, but it may suffice to compare his words on "The Solitary Reaper" with Bloom's on repression in "Tintern Abbey":

> The supervening consciousness, which Wordsworth names Imagination in *Prelude* VI, and which also halts the mental traveler in the Highlands, is *consciousness of self raised to apocalyptic pitch*. The effects of "Imagination" are always the same: a moment of arrest, the ordinary vital continuum being interrupted; a separation of the traveler-poet from familiar nature; a thought of death or judgment or of the reversal of what is taken to be the order of nature; a feeling of solitude or loss or separation. Not all of these need be present at the same time, and some are obliquely present. But the most important consequence is the poem itself, whose developing structure is an expressive reaction to this consciousness. . . . The Highland girl, a single, lonely figure, startles Wordsworth into an exceptionally strong self-consciousness, yet no stark feelings enter a poem which mellows them from the beginning. The poem here is on the side of "nature" and against the "imagination" which fathered it; it hides the intense and even apocalyptic self-consciousness from which it took its rise; it is generically a veiling of its source (*WP*, 17-18).

That source may be, as Bloom says it inevitably is, Milton. But it may also be, as Hartman has begun recently to insist, some others as well. Moreover, the harshness indicated by calling this denial of ancestors repression seems misleading in Wordsworth's case; the veil Wordsworth casts over his sources is rarely a shroud.[11]

Throughout Wordsworth's poetry, the imagination is represented in various guises, as the "unfathered vapour" of *Prelude* VI, as the apocalyptic deluge of *Prelude* V or "Resolution and Independence," or, in what seems at first a more Blakean figure, brightly burning fire. This last figure Hartman calls in his essay on the Devil's bridge sonnet "the luciferic moment," alluding to fallen Lucifer and his diminished brightness in *Paradise Lost*. But the Blakean force of the imagination's fire ("Tyger! Tyger! burning bright/In the forest of the night") typically is muted in Wordsworth, suggesting a less fearful, more approachable imagination that receives its full due in the later poetry: "The later poems often require from us something close to a suppression of the image of creativity as 'burning bright' or full of glitter and communicated strife. Wordsworth's lucyferic style, its discretion and reserve, appears to be the opposite of luciferic. Can we say there is blessing in its gentle breeze?" (*BT*, 202). The allu-

sion to the figure of Lucy from *Lyrical Ballads* is telling, enforcing the connection between Wordsworth's first great poems and the sup-
posedly mediocre verse written after 1807. More subtly, Hartman's closing rhetorical question challenges Bloom's claim that Wordsworth's swerve
from Milton, his "lucy-feric" rather than "luciferic" style, is inherently
a loss. Moreover, though Milton's influence is powerful in Wordsworth,
it is not exclusive.

A poem of 1816, "A little onward," provides an occasion for reflecting further on the Miltonic presence in Wordsworth's poetry. As Hartman shows, the opening lines allude to the opening of *Samson Agonistes*,
and through Milton to Sophocles' *Oedipus at Colonus*. But there is
another allusion buried in these lines ("—What trick of memory to *my*
voice hath brought/This mournful iteration?"). Surprisingly, it is to
Shakespeare, to the painful meeting between mad Lear and blinded
Gloucester in act IV of *King Lear*. One may recall the explicit linking
of the two poets in *Prelude* V—"Shakespeare, or Milton, labourers
divine!" (l. 165)—and thus assent to Hartman's recognition of their shared
place in Wordsworth's mind (along with Spenser) at the fountainhead
of English poetry. From them the poetic diction of the eighteenth century, condemned by Wordsworth in the Preface to *Lyrical Ballads* but
revived in poems like "A little onward," developed as "a compromise
with them, which incorporates in an urbane and distanced, rather than
open and creative way, many of their 'tricks' " (*DDW*, 214).

Hartman acknowledges Bloom's claim that such stylistic curtailment
is defensive, but he resists the further claim that defensiveness reveals
only comparative weakness: "Surely the Wordsworth who renews poetic
diction is on the defensive once more: cornered by the repressed strength
of the fiat in him, arrested by an image of Voice he cannot evade. Yet
it remains a strong defense, as they say in chess, because his diction is
also genuinely neoclassic, not only defensive but mediational" (*DDW*,
214-15).[12] Finally, Hartman questions the priority of Milton as precursor
in this poem. In thus proposing a revision of the intransigently exclusionary scheme of Bloom's Milton-Wordsworth filiation, he opens up once
more the vexing question of Wordsworth's poetic style:

It seems to me that Wordsworth approaches Shakespeare *through* Milton. The
overt presence, Milton's, may be the less dangerous one: it is possible that the
real block, or the poet defended against, because of the power of his word, or
the way he represents its wounding effect—wounded eyes and ears pictured by
means of brazen pun and stage spectacle—is Shakespeare. In the poem of 1816,
at least, Milton is a screen, or part of the "outwork" (Freud's metaphor) erected
by Wordsworth's imagination to keep it from a starker scene. The poet's tribute

to the "mystery of words" in the fifth book of *The Prelude*,

> There darkness makes abode, and all the host
> Of shadowy things do work their changes there,

has a Shakespearean rather than a Miltonic ring (*DDW*, 215).

Poetic tradition may offer sustaining riches as well as debilitating embarassments.[13]

* * *

Milton as mediator between Wordsworth and Shakespeare? The seeming strangeness of this genealogy is only superficial, since there is no reason, *pace* Bloom, why Shakespeare should not be as important a force in Wordsworth's blank verse as Milton, why *King Lear* might have been any less crucial a formative experience than *Paradise Lost*. Hartman's quiet polemic with Bloom betrays perhaps the temptation of the comparatist to see connections everywhere, but at the same time it suggests a more nuanced and diffuse scheme of literary history than Bloom has thus far presented. Hartman, the student of Erich Auerbach and René Wellek, preserves the heritage of the German philological tradition above all by respecting the intricate rhetorical and aesthetic structures of individual texts, structures so fine that no idea as hegemonic as the anxiety of influence can violate them.[14]

Some of Hartman's finest essays have been close readings of individual poems. In the essays on Valéry's "L'Abeille," on Keats's "To Autumn" and *Hyperion*, on Blake's "seasonal" poems in *Poetical Sketches*, and on "Milton's Counterplot," as well as in the recent pieces on Wordsworth's minor poems, Hartman has shown himself a master of *explication de texte*. Elegant and discriminating as these readings are, however, they are scarcely mere philological exercises. The broader concerns of literary history, of aesthetics, and of the theory of poetry are "endlessly elaborated"; they converge, like Stevens's poem, on a theory of life, which is cancelled yet preserved in art.[15]

To call Hartman an aesthetic critic is to recall not only Oscar Wilde but Pater's ideal of the aesthetic poet. That such a poet would also be a critic, no reader of Pater need be reminded. And so, writing of the artist in his essay on "Romanticism," Pater is at the same time describing the ideal critic, the aesthetic critic who is, as he also avers in the essay on style, necessarily a scholar:

Material for the artist, motives of inspiration, are not yet exhausted: our curious, complex, aspiring age still abounds in subjects for aesthetic manipulation by the literary as well as by other forms of art. For the literary art, at all events, the problem just now is, to induce order upon the contorted proportionless accumulation of our knowledge and experience, our science and history, our hopes and disillusion, and, in effecting this, to do consciously what has been done hitherto for the most part too unconsciously, to write our English language as the Latins wrote theirs, as the French write, as scholars should write.[16]

Pater's faith in the artistic potential of prose revises Hegel's infamous declaration in the *Vorlesungen über die Ästhetik*: "Art . . . is and remains for us a thing of the past"[17]—along lines laid down by Schiller in the *Aesthetic Letters*.[18] The death of poetry and the birth of prose announced by Hegel do not signal the end of art, but the emergence of a new art form, Pater's "imaginative prose" (*Appreciations*, p. 7).

Pater's essay on "Style" attempts to shape an aesthetic of critical prose; it is an extended meditation on and elaboration of the categories of material, medium, form, and import and of the possibility of harmonizing them in prose literature. But the essay is also, and this is what is most often left out of conventional accounts of Pater's "aestheticism," a defense of the ethical and educative function of art, for there is a fine but necessary distinction between "good art"—which manifests all those qualities of form Pater has adumbrated—and "great art"—which possesses the highest social purpose:

Given the conditions I have tried to explain as constituting good art;—then, if it be devoted further to the increase of men's happiness, to the redemption of the oppressed, or the enlargement of our sympathies with each other, or to such presentment of new or old truth about ourselves and our relation to the world as may ennoble and fortify us in our sojourn here, or immediately, as with Dante, to the glory of God, it will be also great art; if, over and above those qualities I summed up as mind and soul—that colour and mystic perfume, and that reasonable structure, it has something of the soul of humanity in it, and finds its logical, its architectural place, in the great structure of human life (*Appreciations*, 36).

Pater and Arnold have often been paired as antitheses in Victorian criticism, and in many ways they are. Nothing could be further from the meandering, sometimes ponderous style of Pater than the disciplined balance of Arnold. Nor could anything be less Arnoldian than the decadent sensuousness of the description of the Mona Lisa in *The Renaissance*. And yet Pater and Arnold share the most fundamental conviction of nineteenth-century aesthetics: the urgent necessity to preserve the highest qualities of life in art.[19] The legacy of this conviction continues to dominate contemporary criticism in a variety of modes.

Among contemporary critics, perhaps the most intransigently Paterian is Harold Bloom, whose anti-Arnoldian and anti-Eliotic diatribes have in part obscured the ways in which the Arnold-Eliot-Leavis axis in English criticism preserves Pater's conviction about the moral quality of style. The problem with this internecine conflict, as Geoffrey Hartman contends again and again in *Criticism in the Wilderness*, stems in large part from its parochialism. Although Arnold certainly understood his debt to Goethe, Schiller, and German philosophy, Eliot and Leavis tended either to conceal this aspect of their ancestry or, less pardonably, to dismiss it with contempt. And even Arnold was not as candid as he might have been, less than Carlyle or Coleridge for example, in acknowledging the mediation of his own thought by German aesthetics. For Arnold, Eliot, and Leavis, along with their contemporary scions, are all engaged in a quest for purification. Nowhere is this quest more clearly in evidence than in the prose style they cultivated and successfully legislated for the entire Anglo-American critical tradition.[20]

One of the questions *Criticism in the Wilderness* addresses is why figures like Bloom, Derrida, or even Kenneth Burke appear so heterodox. The immediate response is that they violate the decorum established for critical prose by the Arnoldian Concordat, at which neoclassical virtues of restraint, clarity, and simplicity were established as the foundation of an acceptable plainstyle for critical exposition. Its virtues are still widely worshiped among academic critics and dutifully promulgated in Freshman English, where students learn the catechism of disciplined clarity and are told that one day, if they first master the rules, they may be allowed to break them—if only occasionally and always with a somewhat guilty conscience at having violated one of the commandments. But we all know—don't we?—that the literature about which we write and which we teach our students to admire knows nothing of this restraint. To which it is often answered, yes, but criticism is not literature. In response, here is Hartman on the scandal of Carlyle's *Sartor Resartus*:

Sartor challenged the principle of decorum on which cultural commentary had proceeded: that, except for outright satire or polemics (of which Swift and Arbuthnot were the models) it should be an extension of the familiar essay or the letter to the *Spectator* or *Gentleman's Magazine*. Carlyle saw—as Proust did later in his *Contre Sainte-Beuve*—that to reduce criticism to formal conversation was to reduce literature to formal conversation, to "belles lettres" (*CW*, 137).

What gets lost in the translation of literature into neoclassical critical style is the art; literature is domesticated at the cost of its very being. We murder to disinfect.

There is more at stake here than art alone. Commenting on Eric Blackall's study of *The Emergence of German as a Literary Language*, Hartman identifies the social significance of the Enlightenment standard of intelligibility: "For language touches on practically everything in society; and Blackall shows not only the clash of ideals (of enrichment versus purification, for example), but how these were related to political and social aspirations. So the standard of intelligibility—clarity, lucidity, good sense—becomes more crucial as the middle class tries to consolidate its standing" (*CW*, 148).[21] Arnold's "prose of the center" is as much a political and social as an aesthetic ideal. There is politics in style as well as styles in politics, and Arnoldian disinterestedness is as much a "white mythology" as Ricardian practical criticism.

Hartman's praise of the heterodox figures in the critical tradition is severely qualified. As he says of Carlyle: "The link between language and terror becomes itself a form of terrorism" (*CW*, 150). The critique of humanism, now openly proclaimed in Foucault and Althusser, has its uglier side, and at moments one confesses a certain nostalgia for Arnold's sober good sense or Eliot's limpid sentences. Not merely as a relief from the strain of navigating the heavy abstraction of Foucault and Althusser, the intricate mannerism of Derrida, or the terminological eccentricity of Bloom and Kenneth Burke, but also as a reaffirmation of one's connections with a stable and sustaining culture. Although Arnold and Eliot were both capable of chilling political judgments, one can scarcely imagine either of them writing something on the order of Carlyle's "The Nigger Question." But Eliot's comment on Arnold, that he was "the poet and critic of a period of false stability,"[22] should remind one at the same time of what lurks behind the veneer of calm and order in the prose of both. As Thomas Mann's *Death in Venice* so poignantly discovers, the Apollonian surface of culture never completely triumphs over its repressed Dionysiac origins. Thus Hartman concludes on the battle over critical style:

The question of style . . . remains: How can the critic respond to the extraordinary language-event and still maintain a prose of the center? I object only to those who rule out the question, who seek to control the situation in advance. We have as yet no principled, or theoretically founded, way of dismissing the question of critical style: of Carlylese, or, for that matter, of Heidegger's and Derrida's closely written readings. If we respect the language of art, it is often because of critics whose language is but a lesser scandal (*CW*, 157).

* * *

And what of Hartman's own style? One hesitates to characterize it. Hartman has many registers, most of which can be heard in *Criticism in the Wilderness*, though it can be said that in general they are subordinated to the clarity and restraint of the book's opening sentences: "This is a book of experiences rather than a systematic defense of literary studies. The best apology for criticism (as for literature) is doing it; and, at present, reading it closely. . . . What follows is an attempt to bring together my reading of criticism with my reading of literature: to view criticism, in fact, as within literature, not outside of it looking in" (*CW*, 1). It is as if Hartman had attended to previous complaints by reviewers about the obscurity of his writing and agreed to lay his cards on the table, to capitulate to the Arnoldian Concordat and to observe a neoclassical decorum here questioned and heretofore most often shunned in his own writing. None of Hartman's previous books, with the exception of his brief introduction to Malraux, observes so judiciously the demand for plainness, lucidity, and purity of diction often made of him as does *Criticism in the Wilderness*. Having adapted a quotation from Matthew Arnold in the title, Hartman seems to have adopted Arnold as the master of his style as well. No one could with justice characterize this style as "overreaching" or "*clair-obscur.*"[23]

Still, old habits die hard, and much remains of times and texts past. Hartman has referred to *Glas* as an "epigrammatology" (*ST*, 2), a witty and self-revealing coinage, for Hartman's own style tends to produce pointed and memorable judgments that reach sharp conclusions from which there is nowhere to go but down. Hence the structure of many of his recent essays, including several of the chapters in *Criticism in the Wilderness* and virtually the whole of *Saving the Text*. They are characteristically divided into numerous sections, brief *pensées* loosely connected and, when taken together, manifesting only the most tenuous structure. Hartman's essays proceed by fits and starts, concluding customarily with a flourish, but often a somewhat gnomic one, as in the final sentences of *Criticism in the Wilderness*: "It is a mistake to think of the humanist as spiritualizing anything: on the contrary, he materializes us, he makes us aware of the material culture (including texts) in which everyone has always lived. Only the passage of time spiritualizes, that is, volatizes and deracinates; we are in transition; our life remains a feast of mortuary riddles and jokes that must be answered. In the shape of that answer everyone participates who takes time to think about time" (*CW*, 301). Strange to think of meditation—taking time—as a materializing activity, a mode of praxis. There is, of course, the notebook entry of Coleridge, cited by Hartman in his first essay on *Glas* (*ST*, 1), that links etymologically "thinking" with "thinging": "Think, Thank, Tank = Reservoir of what has been thinged." But doubts persist.

Hartman at one point demands "a theory of criticism that is not simply a new version of pastoral: a theory of the relation of criticism to culture and of the act of writing itself as a will to discourse with political implications" (*CW*, 259). A wholly admirable ambition, but one he himself has hesitated to fulfill. Hartman has only rarely in the past confronted the political dimensions of the aesthetic humanism to which he is committed. Most often, the gesture toward a politics of art has been compromised by a subordination of politics to aesthetics. For example, in his book on Malraux, Hartman apologized for not treating Malraux's politics, but then finessed the point by arguing that they are politics conducted in a different mode, the anti-politics of art: "Malraux's dedication to art is, in reality, a very special kind of politics called forth by the failure of humanistic philosphies to produce politically effective men of action. His aim is to reconstruct faith in humanism by sponsoring a new concept—a new myth perhaps—of the nature of the artist and the role of the intellectual" (*Andre Malraux*, 90). This sounds too much like the special pleading of a university intellectual, nor is Malraux's concept particularly new. It is the old Arnoldian commandment to criticism and culture that they be disinterested, that they judge the world in light of the best that is known and thought, that they divorce themselves from the immediate, the practical, the material. Whatever else humanism may do, it scarcely materializes culture.

The point is not to accuse Hartman of bad faith, but of having stumbled over a contradiction that the discourse of aesthetic humanism cannot finally resolve. Some gestures toward resolution are made in *Criticism in the Wilderness*, but with an ever-present suspicion of political solutions to aesthetic problems. Hartman is troubled by the politics of art, though more because he fears the degradation of art by politics than the aestheticizing of politics in works of art. In the chapter on "The Work of Reading," it is observed:

The notion of work introduces that of economic value and the possibility of a Marxist analysis. I am not ready to go in that direction, at least not systematically. We have seen the Critic become the Commissar, and this danger is one reason so many today prefer to see the critic subordinated in function to the creative writer, who is notoriously uncomformable. (*CW*, 162)

Hartman knows very well that Marxist aesthetics is not synonymous with socialist realism, and he ought to know as well that Marxist politics are not synonymous with the Moscow trials and the camps. His meditation on Lukács (*CW*, 191 ff.) focuses on the pre-Marxist writings, thus evading the very systematic works (the *Aesthetics* and *Ontology*) which would challenge his own humanism most powerfully. Still, to be fair, *Criticism in the Wilderness* does open the door to a theory of literature and criticism that is, if not systematic, more politically conscious than the familiar forms of academic humanism that have held sway over our literary thinking since the Second World War, forms monumentalized in such works as *The Liberal Imagination*, the post-*Anatomy* books of Frye, and *The Idea of the Humanities*.

Hartman poses the problem of art's relation to politics most succinctly in his reading of Kenneth Burke. "Great art is radical," Hartman avers, in a clause that fairly jumps off the page and rivets attention on what is to follow, though he immediately (and characteristically) qualifies this boldness: "But art's contribution to the political sphere remains difficult to formulate" (*CW*, 98).

Hartman's own formulation keys on two concepts: charisma and inner voice. Artists and political leaders share a charismatic energy, though what is admirable in the former can become dangerous in the latter. Without stating it so crudely, Hartman effectively says that art and politics don't mix. The offspring of their union are most often monsters, whose familiar modern avatar is surely Hitler. Hartman even calls upon Burke's essay on *Mein Kampf* in *The Philosophy of Literary Form* to illustrate the incommensurability of art with degraded political ends. Hitler's program was to silence the discordant voices in Germany, but it is precisely the lesson of all art that voices inevitably erupt uncontrollably from within, as in Ariel's song from *The Tempest*. Art resists and admonishes (a favorite Burkean word) against political simplifications, and Hartman in his turn reminds us of the meaning of the radicality of art:

The engagement of the Romantic artists with the French revolution—as of Milton with the Puritan revolution—can hinder our grasp of art's relation to the sociopolitical sphere if the political event is given priority or made the exclusive focus. For the radical character of art is then overshadowed by a fixed point of reference that excludes too much else in thought. What is meant by the radical character of art, in isolation or in conjunction with other types of radical activity, can only be demonstrated by a close analysis of the rhetorical and symbolic dimension. (*CW*, 100-101)

To which one might respond with Carlyle's "No man works save under conditions," or Marx's "It is not the consciousness of men that determines their being, but, on the contrary, their social being that determines their consciousness."

The difficulty with Hartman's claim for the radicality of art is the privilege it grants to ideas and their representation in art at the expense of social reality. Moreover, the position itself can be historicized and shown to be the determinate outcome of a particular social project which, as Erich Auerbach saw, was coming to a close in the twentieth century. Auerbach's recognition of his own "late bourgeois humanism" was matched by his nostalgia for the monuments of bourgeois culture. Hartman's own mission of "saving the text" attempts to preserve the *élan* of the bourgeois cultural revolution, but it is in effect a holding action. Hartman affirms culture over the conditions of the social formation, an ideological strategy analyzed most usefully by Herbert Marcuse:

[The] decisive characteristic [of affirmative or bourgeois culture] is the assertion of a universally obligatory, eternally better and more valuable world that must be unconditionally affirmed: a world essentially different from the factual world of the daily struggle for existence, yet realizable by every individual for himself "from within," without any transformation of the state of fact. It is only in this culture that cultural activities and objects gain that value which elevates them above the everyday sphere. Their reception becomes an act of celebration and exaltation.[24]

Marcuse's essay, written during the period of fascist ascendance in Germany, is a powerful critique of the impotence of bourgeois cultural theory and practice to maintain the goals of its project against the onslaught of economic and political crisis. But at the same time, Marcuse identifies the inherently utopian project of bourgeois culture as a defense against the degradation of everyday life under capitalism: "Affirmative culture was the historical form in which were preserved those human wants which surpassed the material reproduction of existence. . . . There is an element of earthly delight in the works of great bourgeois art, even when they portray heaven."[25]

Bourgeois culture, aesthetic humanism, remains the hegemonic form of critical practice within literary studies. Its utopian projection of the aesthetic as a realm apart is vitiated by its simultaneous ideological claim that this realm can only be preserved by acts of individual attention: reading, for example. Against this claim, there stands the counterstatement of Walter Benjamin at the end of his essay on "The Work of Art in the Age of Mechanical Reproduction":

"*Fiat ars—pereat mundus*," says Fascism, and, as Marinetti admits, expects war to supply the artistic gratification of a sense perception that has been changed by technology. This is evidently the consummation of "*l'art pour l'art.*" Mankind, which in Homer's time was an object of contemplation for the Olympian gods, now is one for itself. Its self-alienation has reached such a degree that it can experience its own destruction as an aesthetic pleasure of the first order. This is the situation of politics which Fascism is rendering aesthetic. Communism responds by politicizing art.[26]

Geoffrey Hartman has recalled how Wordsworth's repudiation of Poetic Diction and his project of humanizing the imagination were profound political, as well as poetic, gestures. But the power of such gestures remains circumscribed as long as art continues to be valorized over politics. Surely the problem facing contemporary criticism is not to preserve art from devastation by politics, but rather to create a politics of art that serves human and democratic rather than mechanical and totalitarian ends.

NOTES

1. Gustave Flaubert, *Selected Letters of Gustave Flaubert*, trans. and ed. Francis Steegmuller (New York: Farrar, Straus and Young, 1953), pp. 127-28. The passage is discussed in a comparison with Walter Benjamin's "Messianic politics of prose" (articulated in some notes to the *Theses on the Philosophy of History*) in Irving Wohlfarth, "The Politics of Prose and the Art of Awakening: Walter Benjamin's Version of a German Romantic Motif," *Glyph* 7 (1980): 132-34; 143-44.

2. Unfavorable estimations of Hartman's style abound: see Edward W. Said, "What is Beyond Formalism?" *MLN* 86 (December 1971): 933-45; Denis Donoghue, "Mediate and Immediate," *TLS* 3832 (22 August 1975): 934-35; William H. Pritchard, "The Hermeneutical Mafia or, After Strange Gods at Yale," *Hudson Review* 28 (Winter 1975-76): 601-610; Wallace Martin, "Literary Critics and Their Discontents," *Critical Inquiry* 4 (Winter 1977): 397-406; and Gerald Graff, "Fear and Trembling at Yale," *American Scholar* 46 (Autumn 1977): 467-78. For more positive judgments, see Angus Fletcher, "The Great Wordsworth," *Yale Review* n.s. 54 (Summer 1965): 595-98; Philip E. Lewis, "Athletic Criticism," *Diacritics* 1 (Winter 1971): 2-6; Gerald L. Bruns, "A Scrutiny of Criticism," *PQ* 55 (Spring 1976): 260-78; and G. Douglas Atkins, "Dehellenizing Literary Criticism," *College English* 41 (March 1980): 769-79. Virtually everyone on both sides of the question acknowledges the importance of playfulness and punning to Hartman's writing, more noticeable in the works following *Wordsworth's Poetry*; what divides them is a different judgment of the appropriateness of Hartman's verbal exuberance to literary criticism as a discipline. The question is dealt with in greater detail below apropos of Hartman's own meditation on critical style in *Criticism in the Wilderness*.

3. Richards began his university studies in history but switched to Moral Science under the tutelage of G. E. Moore. The lessons and manner of the British analytic tradition in philosophy, above all its attempt to promulgate a "Basic Philosphical English," remained a permanent influence on his theorizing, as on his style.

4. This aspect of Hartman's work is treated at greater length in my review of *Criticism in the Wilderness*; see Michael Sprinker, "Hermeneutic Hesitation."

5. See Friedrich Schiller, *On the Aesthetic Education of Man*, ed. and trans. Elizabeth M. Wilkinson and L. A. Willoughby (Oxford: Clarendon Press, 1967), pp. 140-43. This superb edition contains extensive explication and commentary on the history of aesthetics, particularly on the philosophical context in eighteenth-century Germany that has continued to be an important (albeit often indirect) influence on aesthetics to the present day.

6. Matthew Arnold, "Wordsworth," in *Essays in Criticism*, 2nd Series (1888; rpt. London: Macmillan, 1896), p. 155; Walter Pater, "Wordsworth," in *Appreciations* (London: Macmillan, 1889), p. 42.

7. *The Early Letters of William and Dorothy Wordsworth (1787-1805)*, ed. Ernest de Selincourt (Oxford: Clarendon Press, 1935), pp. 295-96.

8. Fletcher, "The Great Wordsworth," p. 598.

9. Citations of Wordsworth's poetry refer to William Wordsworth, *Selected Poems and Prefaces*, ed. Jack Stillinger (Boston: Houghton Mifflin, 1965). Line numbers are those given in this edition.

10. Bloom's dating of the Prospectus to "The Recluse" is eccentric in light of recent scholarship. Mark Reed places the composition of the fragment between late March 1804 and early September 1806 (see Reed, *Wordsworth: The Chronology of the Middle Years 1800-1815* [Cambridge: Har-

vard University Press, 1975], p. 37 and Appendix VI). According to the Cornell Wordsworth, the earliest extant manuscript of the Prospectus appears in a notebook probably purchased in Calais in 1802 (see William Wordsworth, *Home at Grasmere*, ed. Beth Darlington [Ithaca: Cornell University Press, 1977], p. 255).

11. Here one must demur slightly from the judgment of Jonathan Arac, who in an essay on *The Prelude* characterizes Hartman's reading of Wordsworth as "insisting upon a fierce, debilitatingly self-conflicting struggle" ("Bounding Lines: *The Prelude* and Critical Revision," *boundary 2* 7 [Spring 1979]: 42). This makes Hartman sound too much like Bloom *avant la lettre*, and though the two share a great many concerns, including an unwavering commitment to the revival of Romanticism. Hartman's emphases always temper the extremity of the Bloomian agon of poetic tradition. Moreover, as Hartman's more recent essays make clear, Wordsworth's "self-conflicting struggle"—quite as fundamental, it is true, to Hartman's reading as to Bloom's—is less debilitating than strengthening. It is this preternatural "joy" that marks Wordsworth as a poet and makes him exemplary in Hartman's continuing quest for a humanized imagination.

12. Cf. Hartman on the style of the "Ode to Duty": "The change of style [from *Lyrical Ballads*], then, is due to a poet consciously fashioning his own diction of generality. If it is asked why Wordsworth modifies his style in this way, and runs the risk of falling back into Poetic Diction, the answer is that he thinks of himself as entering a new stage of life, in which his mission is to propagate his knowledge, and draw closer to his kind. There is no change of heart, but there is a self-conscious attempt to assume that *his* truths are also *general* truths, or will be accepted as such in time, so that certain intimate features of his experience should not obtrude" (*WP*, 283). In other words, Wordsworth once more, here in a less personal and more public mode, is engaged in humanizing the imagination. As George Eliot saw so clearly, Wordsworth's moral imagination was bent on a domestication of the sublime. The "Ode to Duty" is truly a celebration of what she calls in the "Finale" to *Middlemarch* "the home epic."

13. This discussion might be usefully supplemented by Hartman's reflections on euphemism and "soft names" in "Words and Wounds" (*ST*, 122, 125, 133, 145-48). Here again the swerve from Derrida (or from de Man, for whom Derrida is perhaps merely the screen figure in *Saving the Text*) is subtly insistent.

14. In reviewing *The Anxiety of Influence*, Hartman fleetingly mentions the similarity of Bloom's revisionary ratios to the terms of Kenneth Burke's dramatistic pentad (*FR*, 56). Thus it is apposite to recall here Richard Blackmur's suspicion of Burke and of the "omnicompetent methodology" he has evolved: "The feeling of spate, or copiousness, you get in Burke is because of this abstract neutrality; he has no need to stop and there is nothing to arrest him: there are no obstacles he cannot transform into abstract or reduce to neutral terms in his rhetoric. He is a very superior example indeed of the mind in which the articulate organization has absorbed the material organized. The rhetoric is so good for any purpose that it very nearly engorges purpose. The methodology is a wonderful machine that creates its own image out of everything fed into it: nobody means what he says but only the contribution of what he says to the methodology" (R. P. Blackmur, "The Lion and the Honeycomb," in *The Lion and the Honeycomb: Essays in Solicitude and Critique* [New York: Harcourt, Brace, & World, 1955], p. 194).

15. Hartman has consistently, from *The Unmediated Vision* onward, been concerned with the relationship of poetry to philosophy, hence with theory as such, but something of a turn toward more direct confrontation with the problems of literary and aesthetic theory can be observed after the publication of *Wordsworth's Poetry* in 1964. The essays of the sixties collected in *Beyond Formalism* can be roughly divided into two categories: explications of and meditations on the discipline of literary criticism; interpretive essays of a familiar literary-historical kind on texts, authors, or entire periods. Among the latter, a number of pieces on pre-Romanticism seemed a preliminary charting of the ground for a sweeping reinterpretation of English literary history from Milton through the Romantics, the very ground Bloom would effectively anathematize in *The Anxiety of Influence*.

In *The Fate of Reading* this project is continued in the essays on Keats, Smart, and the image of the evening star in late eighteenth-century poetry. Faced by Bloom's scorn for the eighteenth century on the one hand, and Paul de Man's denial of the very project of literary history on the other, it is perhaps regrettable that Hartman has been distracted from the historical project that appeared to command much of his attention after the Wordsworth book. A careful and complete mapping of the poetic tradition between Milton and Wordsworth, with a just appreciation of the mediations worked on English poetry by French and German thought, would be a welcome addition to the current revisionist moment in literary studies.

16. Pater, "Romanticism" (1876), reprinted as the Postscript to *Appreciations*, from which this passage is quoted, p. 263.

17. G. W. F. Hegel, *Aesthetics*, trans. T. M. Knox, 2 vols. (Oxford: Clarendon Press, 1975), I:11.

18. See Wilkinson's and Willoughby's discussion of the form of Schiller's work in their introduction to the *Aesthetic Letters*, especially the concepts of "aesthetic discourse" (*schöner Vortrag*) and "thinking presentationally" (*darstellend denken*). On Pater's debt to and his patent misprision of Schiller, see Wilkinson and Willoughby, p. 256 and introduction, clx ff. This is perhaps the place to remark on the conjunction of figures and traditions that informs the intellectual background of Hartman's work. No single label is likely to capture the variety of critical practices associated with the names of Auerbach, Wellek, Pater, Goethe and Schiller, Hegel, Coleridge, Carlyle, and Arnold. Nonetheless, one is tempted by the, admittedly complex, filiation of all these thinkers with German Romanticism and its historicist tendencies to lump them together under Fredric Jameson's convenient label, "historical and cultural aestheticism," which he characterizes thus: "On the one hand, as in classical German aesthetics itself, all praxis is in this experience suspended (whence the well-known Hegelian formulas of the 'Sunday of Life,' and the dusk in which Minerva's owl takes flight). Meanwhile, the quality of rapt attention which existential historicism brings to the objects of its study—texts as expressions of moments of the historical past, or of unique and distant cultures—is essentially that of aesthetic appreciation and recreation, and the diversity of cultures and historical moments becomes thereby for it a source of immense aesthetic excitement and gratification" (Jameson, "Marxism and Historicism," *New Literary History* 11 [Autumn 1979]: 51). Any contemporary effort to rethink and rewrite literary (or cultural) history must confront the achievements of this tradition head-on. Among the signal contributions of Hartman's work is to have undertaken this task in full consciousness of the monuments of previous scholarship, whose stature he honors even as he attempts to erect a new edifice atop them.

19. See the chapter on "The Moral Aesthetic," in Jerome Hamilton Buckley, *The Victorian Temper: A Study in Literary Culture* (1951; rpt. New York: Random House, n.d.), pp. 143-60.

20. The problem is much more complex than these remarks suggest. Both Eliot and Arnold were deeply influenced by German thought and culture, though it may be argued that this influence was most often buried beneath their admiration for France, above all for the lucidity of French critical prose. Moreover, it is fair to say that Arnold, Eliot, and Leavis all partook in varying degrees of the familiar English disdain for German philosophy (epitomized in Byron's "Coleridge has explained metaphysics to the nation/Oh, that he would explain his own explanation"), and that the Anglo-American empiricist tradition guided the temper of their prose and their thought quite as much as it did that of Richards. A full consideration of these relations remains to be undertaken; *Criticism in the Wilderness* measures the cost that this repression has exacted in the past and provides a guide to some of the most fruitful directions for future studies to pursue.

21. See also Jean-Claude Chevalier, *Histoire de la syntaxe: Naissance de la notion de complément dans la grammaire française (1530-1750)* (Genève: Droz, 1968).

22. T. S. Eliot, *The Use of Poetry and the Use of Criticism: Studies in the Relation of Criticism to Poetry in England* (London: Faber & Faber, 1933), p. 105.

23. The phrases are taken from William H. Pritchard's review of *The Fate of Reading*, "The Hermeneutical Mafia."

24. Herbert Marcuse, "The Affirmative Character of Culture," *Zeitschrift fur Sozialforschung* 6 (1937); rpt. in *Negations: Essays in Critical Theory*, trans. Jeremy J. Shapiro (Boston: Beacon Press, 1968, p. 95).

25. *Ibid.*, p. 120

26. Walter Benjamin, *Illuminations*, ed. Hannah Arendt, trans. Harry Zohn (New York: Schocken Books, 1969), p. 242.

J. Hillis Miller:
The Other Victorian at Yale
Donald Pease

Several abrupt turns mark the critical career of J. Hillis Miller and withhold from his works that sense of stability and continuity that a lifelong pursuit of a single critical project might otherwise provide. They do so, moreover, because they seem precipitated more by Miller's translation and adaptation of the positions of other critics than by reversals in his own thinking. First, there was the New Critical dissertation at Harvard; then, after a one-year stay at Williams in 1952-53, the years of phenomenological criticism at Johns Hopkins from 1953 to 1972, and more recently the move to deconstruction at Yale. As if to effect a literal correlation between *topoi* and figures of thought or to suggest that academic places do indeed cast a spell over the mind, Miller has signified his changes of mind with changes of academic affiliation. It is only his more recent move, however, from phenomenological criticism to poststructuralism that has met with widespread critical resistance.

Which is not to say that his introduction of phenomenological criticism to the American critical scene went unnoticed. Some critics conceived of the phenomenological program with its re-introduction of authorial intention, its transgression of textual boundaries, and its claim to re-experience the work from the inside, as a full-scale regression, a loss of that analytic rigor and its concomitant authority only recently secured by the New Criticism. But for others this loss of rigor was precisely the attraction of the criticism of consciousness. When Miller wrote in an article on his mentor, "The Literary Criticism of Georges Poulet," "The duplication of an author's mind in a critic's mind is accomplished when the critic can, as it were, speak for the author" (p. 473). J. Hillis Miller provided a counter-language to that of the New Criticism, a counter-language whose value lay in its capacity to "re-humanize" the "discipline" of criticism. The New Criticism, after all, had won literature its new-found respectability in the university by banishing as heresies both the author's intention and the reader's response. Despite their insistence on the distinction between the truth claims of scientific discourse and the "pseudo-statements" of literature, the New Critics both explicitly and implicitly acknowledged the authority of scientific objectivity: explicitly by treating the verbal icon as an object, implicitly by casting literature in a merely compensatory, "emotive" relationship to the rational objective truth-claims of the sciences. Subordinated to yet insubordinate of the rational discourses of both science and criticism, literature was valued for a complex tensional structure which never quite evaded so much as it validated the discipline of criticism. When the Geneva critics discovered renewed value for some of the terms and practices banished from the academy by the New Critics, the newer group, in the minds of some American academics, had the effect of evening the score, of recovering a humanistic discourse not despite but *through* its opposition to the New Criticism.

Moreover, phenomenological criticism was not alone in its challenge to the authority of the New Criticism. It found an unexpected ally in the reader-oriented criticism practiced by Wolfgang Iser, Stanley Fish, and Norman Holland. In calling for a virtual communion of minds with only enough self-consciousness remaining for the critics to realize the author's thoughts as if they were their own, the phenomenological critics for all intents and purposes idealized the reading process; and the idealized process prepared the way for the reader-response critics' postulation of an informed or an implied reader, a transcendental, trans-historical ideal "interpreter," whose experience of the poem constituted both its meaning and its form. Moreover, after the author and reader, banished via the "intentional" and "affectivist" fallacies by the New Criticism, reappeared under the protection of the "ideal," it did not take long for these prodigal ideals to overthrow the New Criticism. Neither, however, regardless of all of these idealizations, and for reasons I will suggest later, did it take long for these newer criticisms to lose critics some of their authority in the academy.

Given the elevated tone, the spiritual aspirations, and the liberating effect of Miller's phenomenological criticism, it is hardly surprising that his turn from it encountered resistance. If phenomenological criticism marked a "conversion upward" of the language of criticism, deconstruction with its programmatic "de-idealization" of the critical discourse implicitly inscribed in its very advance over phenomenological criticism a fall from grace. As we begin to understand when we consider Miller's means of making up his mind in the first place, however, more is at stake in his adaption of this newer method than one critic's loss of faith. In his earlier identity as a critic of consciousness, Miller had "experienced from within" many of the masterworks of the nineteenth and twentieth centuries. In books like *The Disappearance of God* (1963) and *Poets of Reality* (1965), Miller had not merely delineated the place for these masterworks in what he as a post-structuralist would come to call the logocentric tradition, but with an uncanny sense of the interpenetrability of sacred and secular canon, he identified the mystery of the Incarnate logos as his means of sanctioning their placement.[1] In other words, he did not merely describe but actively constituted that tradition, all of which suggests that Miller's "conversion" had institutional as well as merely personal significance. Now we do not need to carry metaphorical attribution so far as to assert that Miller, as a constitutive principle of the logocentric tradition, in changing his mind changed that tradition; but we cannot fail to see that his prior act of identification with the logocentric tradition made his conversion valuable for the American post-structuralists.

Curiously, however, in much the same way that archaic religious symbols were made to serve in the sixteenth and seventeenth centuries as powerfully corroborative backdrops for purely secular ceremonies, Miller's deepest value for post-structuralism inheres not in the persuasive power of his new-found rhetoric, but in the very incompleteness of his conversion experience. Ironically, it is the insufficiency of Miller's conversion, betrayed by remnants in his discourse of his "undeconstructed" phenomenological phase, that has provided validating force for the deconstructive enterprise. In a turn governed by the logic of the uncanny, it is as if through Miller's role as its representative, the logocentric tradition had not only acceded to but empowered its own dismantling.

Furthermore, Miller has implicitly indicated his role as a representative of institutional practices rather than an arbiter of merely personal choices by his means of publicly disclosing his conversion. In place of a presentation of his "personal" reasons for shifting ground, Miller issued a series of position papers: reviews of critics still laboring under the misconceptions of logocentrism, new prefaces to his own earlier published works, revaluations of his former authority figure George Poulet, deconstructive rereadings of his own prior interpretations, and overviews of the Yale School. Several perspectives might be considered as rationales for Miller's "dissemination" of his conversion experience in these discursive practices. In these "re(-)views,"' he was freeing himself from his own prior acts of criticism; and since these acts entailed an excessive identification with the consciousness of others, Miller's liberation had to coincide with the that dis-identification from a former position implicit in any revaluation. Moreover, since Miller's former acts of identification were the equivalent at the level of consciousness of a language's representation fixation, Miller could cure his own identification compulsion through a demystification of language's referential claims.[2]

It is this last perspective, however, of Miller's former status as a victim of the "specular capture" of representation that confers authority upon his new enterprise. In these "re(-)views," Miller must "work through" his prior entanglements within the tradition of presence, but he cannot do so as a "personal" identity (for that could reconfirm his status within the tradition) but only as a series of discursive practices capable of unsettling the delusions of self-presence. This delusion of self-presence, at once the object and the means for Miller's deconstructive strategy, operates according to that same uncanny logic at work in the incompleteness of Miller's conversion; for Miller can isolate and praise, for example, an instance of this delusion as it is evidenced in Edward Said's belief in historical periodicity even as he criticizes this belief in the work of Joseph Riddel.[3]

Although I will later suggest a rationale for Miller's seemingly arbitrary judgments, for now I would like to focus attention on another of Miller's reviews—that of M. H. Abrams's *Natural Supernaturalism* ("Tradition and Difference"). This encounter did not entail a confrontation between an authority figure and an ephebe, as was the case in Miller's reviews of Said and Riddel, but a confrontation between two authority figures, one of whom had converted to a new methodology and one of whom had not. This review, moreover, although not exemplary for the rigor or force of Miller's deconstructive position, is almost a literal example of "dissemination in action," because it resulted in a session of the Division of Philosophical Approaches to Literature at the 1976 MLA convention entitled "The Limits of Pluralism," a publication of the panelists' papers in *Critical Inquiry*, and a strange second version of Miller's paper in a volume by the Yale critics entitled *Deconstruction and Criticism*.

If, as we suggested, Miller chose texts to review as a means of working through his prior entanglement in the logocentric tradition, Abrams's *Natural Supernaturalism* provided him with an ideal opportunity. As an examination of the replication of religious patterns in secular forms, Abrams's book—like Miller's earlier ones—facilitated, in its unexamined privileging of the power of metaphysical tradition to reanimate itself in other forms, an expansion of the tradition of metaphysics. Abrams, however, effected this expansion by means of a kerygmatic paradigm remarkably similar to that at work in Miller's earlier writing: He begins with an image of metaphysical unity, describes the fall into fragments and dispersal, but foresees the power to regain this unity at some point in the millennial future.

In his review, Miller first presents a lucid, even sympathetic, "traditional" account of Abrams's book, with generous praise for its achievements. He then proceeds to attack Abrams's unreflected use of four signifiers—the concept of tradition, the notion of representation, the activity of humanization, and the practice of interpretation—and faults Abrams for his consistent failure to acknowledge the heterogeneous "dialogic" power capable of unsettling the undisturbed mastery of these signifiers. While Miller based his review on the differential activity of the "heterogeneous other" at once within and without the logocentric tradition, Abrams's strategy in his response was to curtail that activity by reducing it to a function. With a lucidity and sympathy easily the match of Miller's, Abrams not only provided a cogent account of deconstruction, but "contained" the discourse of deconstruction within his own context. Abrams did not dispute Miller's implicit claim that deconstruction releases the signifier from the semantic restraints of the logocentric tradition; instead, he reduced deconstruction to a series of linguistic constraints allowing freedom to be played out as a mere language game. Most tellingly, however, Abrams used these rules not only to predict Hillis Miller's response, but to rehearse it in enough detail to make Miller's "different" discourse sound like a metaleptic repetition of Abrams's traditional one. Other innuendoes, less playful, insinuated their way into Abrams's presentation. By alluding to Miller's sympathy, generosity, and intelligibility as recognizable "humanistic" virtues not cast off in Miller's "conversion" to post-structuralism, Abrams offered a less than favorable view of Miller's "incomplete" conversion. In Abrams's view, as the adaptation of still another continental trend rather than an authentic change of heart, Miller's conversion implicitly lacked integrity.

Abrams's attack, staged as it was before a representative segment of the "profession," had the curious effect of an almost ritual "completion" of Miller's conversion experience; for if Miller had not, in his turn to deconstruction, disaffected himself from the logocentric tradition, that tradition, at least in the person of M. H. Abrams, was disaffiliating itself from him. In a truly ironic turn of events, J. Hillis Miller, who as a phenomenologist had already willingly sacrificed *his* consciousness to the logocentric tradition, had been turned into a public scapegoat by a representative of that tradition. But the ironies of this scene are not exhausted by Miller's "double" conversions; for Miller could not have deconstructed the ideal "virtues" of humanism or revealed the disruptive violence concealed within its self-justifying rhetoric any more forcefully than Abrams had in his fierce "humanistic" attack.

Several explanations, all of them inadequate, suggest means of comprehending this curious exchange. Perhaps deconstruction as a full-scale revolt against an established tradition elicited justifiable force from Abrams, the tradition's self-confessed representative. Certainly his "humanism" alone cannot account sufficiently for the vindictive, at times brutal, animus at work in his position paper. If, however, Abrams's behavior seemed out of character, Miller's paper, as a repetition of precisely the form Abrams had already outlined, seemed docile, even humane, by contrast. Curiously, however, Miller did not seem humane through the generosity or civility of his response. In fact, he did not respond to Abrams at all, but performed a series of moves with the concepts of critical and creative texts after which it became increasingly difficult to distinguish one from the other. In his response, then, Miller acted out his own effacement, dissolving himself along with every other "critic" into an interpenetrable interface between text and interpretation. In terms of his own critical biography, Miller was doing an about face, reneging on the notion of Miller the phenomenologist that the critic, through an act of consciousness, could completely identify with the authorial *cogito*. In the terms of his confrontation with Abrams, however, Miller effected neither an exemplary act of deconstructive self-effacement nor a personal about face. Instead, he lost face as Abrams's fierce countenance seemed to grow more menacing with each charge Miller failed to address.

What remains truly extraordinary in this exchange resides neither in Abrams's attack nor in the specifics of Miller's response, but, rather, in Miller's failing to respond; for Miller's deconstructive stance made a coherent point-by-point response impossible. Such a response would have truly confirmed deconstruction as just another position, maintained by still another subject within the logocentric tradition. Abrams knew this limitation in advance and exploited it to the point where, as we have seen, he co-opted and thereby neutralized Miller's potentially disruptive position. But if Miller could not appear in Abrams's context to his advantage—if Abrams had already, in effect, made Miller disappear from it—Miller could, as if in imitation of "trace" operations, instead reappear in another context. Having been expelled from the logocentric tradition, Miller reappeared in a context that in 1976 had not yet found its ultimate form, in a paper which served the double function of a rejoinder to Abrams and the last words in a volume on deconstructive criticism as practiced at Yale that would be published in 1979. Miller, in other words, did not "personally" respond to Abrams's implicitly personal attack. Instead, he responded as an institution, the Yale School.

Miller's title clarifies his strategy. In choosing to entitle his essay "The Critic as Host," Miller alludes to one of Abrams's earlier assertions (itself a citation) that the deconstructive reading of a given work "is plainly and simply parasitical" on the "obvious or univocal reading."[4] In the course of the essay, Miller, through a series of etymological cross-definitions, teases out the critic's double rose as consumer and consumed in relation to a work and "deconstructs," in the sense that he displaces and reverses, Abrams's charge. He thereby turns critics into hosts who do not deny their parasitic inclinations. By exploiting the self-divided status of Abrams's accusations, Miller, in his role not as critic or host but as depersonalized representative of deconstructive criticism, makes Abrams a victim of the limitations of a less resourceful critical discourse. Most significantly, however, Miller recontextualizes the entire exchange in an institutional form where Miller feels more at home than Abrams. He welcomes Abrams, in other words, to his "host" institution, Yale, where such uncanny reversals are familiar rather than foreign practices; and in an article that remained to be finished at the time of the 1976 confrontation and a book that would not be published until 1979, in which Miller and several of his colleagues take their turns dismantling Abrams's prior interpretation of Shelley's *The Triumph of Life*, Miller looked forward to having, quite literally, the final word in his exchange with Abrams.

But I have not lingered on this "staged" confrontation to tease out all of its subtle double ploys. Nor do I wish to judge either participant triumphant; for, if anything, Miller and Abrams do not oppose, but mirror each other, though not in their explicit positions so much as in their means of securing them. Both Miller and Abrams utilized the strategies of co-optation and containment to accommodate potentially disruptive discourses to the institutions they represent. Both of them display the assimilative, defusing power of institutional practices. What truly differentiates deconstructive discourse from other modes, however, is that it is in origin never anything but this institutional practice. Indeed I would maintain that deconstructive criticism, at least as it is practiced in these United States, served the function of recovering for literary criticism some of the institutional authority I earlier suggested it had lost. What I now wish to suggest is that criticism lost this authority during that period, prepared for by Miller's phenomenological criticism and reader-response criticisms (like Fish's affective stylistics), when many literary critics demanded that literature surrender its autonomous, independent standing within the academy so that it could "demystify" the explosive political scene.

In the turn to audience-oriented criticism, as we recall, the literary work was seen not as an expression of the depths of an author's personality or as a cultural artifact requiring understanding of or identification with the institutions of a bygone culture; nor was it seen as the paradoxical rendition of a complex, coherent allocation of textual energies. Instead, it was viewed as an experimental space where the reader's responses have been anticipated and reformulated. Consequently, the reader-response critic did not prove the power of his personality by mastering a difficult text, but rather by finding the text *to be his personality* projected into an objective form. When he reads a text, a reader-response critic looks forward to the pleasure of witnessing the dissolution of the distinction between himself and the work; the text embodies his personality as if it were its form. Through his critical activity, the reader-oriented critic looks forward to converting the form back into his own personality.

The polemical equation of the form of the work with the anticipated response of its readers undermined more than the New Criticism's definition of the work as an object in and for itself. By eradicating the distinction between the work and the subjectivity of not simply a single "informed" reader but a community of readers bound together through personalities shaped by common interpretive strategies, affectivism transformed literature into one more social institution, not fundamentally different in its effects from any other social expression. As a result of the leveling activity secured by the polemics of affectivist criticism (as well as the persistence of the Vietnamese War), it took little time for literature, once considered a power of language in excess of the coercive capacity of society's dominant discourse, to justify itself through a "relevant perspective" on the political news. This call for relevance, however, concealed dual demands. On one hand, arising as it did at the very moment the reader gave himself the illusion of absolute coincidence with the text, relevance seemed to be the final "democratization" of literature, its assimilation into all other forms of public opinion (for *relevance* is public opinion disguised as the truth; it is not a wish to attain uncommon knowledge, but to make all forms of knowledge speak a common language, namely, that which is already known). On the other hand, since this call for relevance occurred at a moment in the nation's history when it was looking for some moral center to legitimate a national foreign policy in direct contradiction to the nation's moral self-image, the demand for relevance concealed a wish for literature to disrupt the nation's habits of self-explanation with more radical speculations. However urgent this second demand may once have seemed, with the passing of the war the call for a literature of relevance only betrayed the suspicion that literature was not a privileged perspective but just one more aspect of the depressing news.

Ironically the literature of relevance produced an effect precisely the opposite of what might have been expected. Instead of transforming the elite institution of literature into a popular subject, relevance only disenfranchised literature of the popularity it may once have enjoyed; for relevance made literature seem less challenging to the assertive and appropriating demands of the student body. Consequently, the literature intended to provide a timely perspective on social problems of the day instead literally became a social problem itself, a pocket of economic depression offering a surplus of professors far beyond the demands of an every-diminishing classroom.

In this highly condensed, admittedly schematic, and more than somewhat polemical history of recent American criticism, I am suggesting that our critical project was directed upon a self-destructive course. Beginning with the wish to be equal to a demanding text methodized into the practices of the New Criticism, we had succeeded in equating the text with the reader's response. This action not only increased the always present danger of solipsism, with the attendant hypertrophy of the critic's self-consciousness, but it also relinquished the critic's fundamental mode of justifying his place within society. When a text is defined as only a consolidation of a community's subjective response, it does not challenge a social model for coherence enough to require a critic to coerce it back into a society's pre-existent constitutive schemata. Since reader-response criticism presupposes linguistic competence of all readers, it denies the critic the highly refined powers of clarification, discrimination, and expansion of a significance he was used to imposing on a potentially unstable text.

If the "work" of literature lost some of its standing because of a threat to its "autonomous" status partially secured by Miller's earlier displacement of the literary with the authorial *cogito*, Miller recovers that autonomy by revaluating the authorial *cogito* not as an external cause, but as itself an effect of literature's capacity to "demystify" in advance every correlation between literary representation and the "real" world. And the control over politically disruptive texts engendered by this apolitical demystification partially accounts for Miller's means of praising Edward Said's book *Beginnings*. In contrast to Miller, Said has an interest in textuality which includes a program whereby the text is relieved of its hermetic claims and permitted to assume its "affiliation" with institutions, agencies, classes, and ideologically defined professions. Unlike the post-structuralists[2], Said's description of a discourse attempts to redefine the particular interests that texts serve. Miller, in his review, isolated a particularly complex passage in which Said works out the tangled interrelationship between the events constitutive of an author's history and the history the author made of those events. In his handling of Said's discourse, however, Miller ignored the political implications in this textual statement by attending instead to the purely textual operation of a "double scene" he found at work throughout the text, thereby leading to the politically neutral conclusion that "Said is caught in one important version of the universal impasse of every deconstructive discourse" ("Beginning with a Text," p. 4). In praising Said's discourse as an "example" of a discursive practice repeated often enough in deconstructive criticism to assume shape as its crucial means of dismantling the text, Miller effectively defuses the political power of Said's statement. By using the review as a pretext to assimilate a potentially disruptive text, Miller verges dangerously close to conscripting deconstructive strategies as forms of what Herbert Marcus earlier referred to as "repressive tolerance."

Moreover, in revaluating his own pre-deconstructive criticism in terms that never stray from post-structuralist formulations, Miller doubly undermines any "political" retrievals of it. Having in his own earlier criticism reduced the problematic to be demystified to one of *mimesis*, Miller does not need to subject any of his earlier presuppositions about the "Real World" to radical question. Instead of conceiving of "the real" as a historically produced, socially organized complex of ideologies, institutions, and intersubjective relations, Miller relies on the rather archaic philosophical notion of the Real as a stable object of perception.[5] Furthermore, while Miller's reduction of history to a group of teleological prejudices and diachronic sequences certainly facilitates his deconstructive discourse, it simply disregards the complex interplay between subjectivity and history implicit in Edward Said's work, to name but one example.

But I have not paused over the confrontation between J. H. Miller and M. H. Abrams to grow nostalgic over the lost battles of the sixties. To do so would ascribe to the discursive practices of the time a theoretical and practical sophistication they sorely lacked. Nor have I lingered over this scene to deconstruct the later Miller in terms provided by the earlier. To do so would only neutralize and co-opt the power of Miller's turn to deconstruction and abjectly corroborate his interpretive strategy by helplessly miming it. In what follows I do not wish to defuse the power of Miller's transfiguration, but to discern it. I can begin to discern some of the power Miller has invested in transfiguration when I acknowledge his reappearance in his response to Abrams on another scene, as an instance of transfiguration at work. This "other scene" was not, however, subject to the uncanny logic of Derrida's "double scene" with its "supplemental" ability to disrupt the security of settled referents by signifying in excess of the captivating power of referentiality. Instead, as has been mentioned, it derived its power from an affiliation with an already established practice—deconstructive criticism—at an established academic institution, Yale. To show how Miller helped constitute this other scene, even as he was constituted by it, I intend to bring Miller's earlier incarnation as a phenomenological critic on this scene as a means of setting the stage for Miller's dramatic reappearance. In doing so, moreover, I hope to clarify the "principles of deconstructive practice." As a technique for overcoming the delusion of self-presence, deconstruction, through the temporal deferring and spatial differing qualities of the play of *différance*, releases a self-erasing mark, what we might call an underdetermined indetermination. To intimate the otherwise inconceivable force of this indetermination, the deconstructive critic must stage a powerful opposition, say between deconstruction and the entire logocentric tradition; or, as in the case of the Yale School, a rebellion of the "creative" critic against the artist. In other words, to signify the force of this indetermination, the deconstructive critic must *over*determine an *under*determined practice. Ironically, however, the very scene capable of signifying the disruptive power of the practice is also able to displace a resolutely non-conceptual practice (the play of *différance*, we must remember as that which has already been and yet is always about to be, "is" always before and after every scene intended to signify it, and consequently never quite takes place as such) with the staged scene.

So again, in the case of the Yale School, the rebellion of criticism against literature has the effect of validating and conserving the "institution" of literature (and implicitly criticism) as the scene wherein language exempts itself from any referential claims, even though *différance* as imaged *through the aporia* has always already "purified" itself of just this coercive situation. In the hands of the Yale School, then, deconstruction *in* its very demystifying procedure has been used to remystify or defamiliarize a literature that previous acts of criticism had made too familiar, which is to say that the recent assertion by the Yale School of criticism's right to cross over into the domain of literature is not a renewed display of critical power, but a repetition of the wish to experience literature *as* a power—a power experienced by the critic in the form of anxiety over crossing a sacred threshold. In other words, the conversion of the critic's translating, transitional, and *transitory* activities into full-blown transgressions against the realm of literature only betrays the critic's wish to participate in a newly affirmed "mysterious" power of literature, even as the Yale doctrine of the anxiety of influence is a way of recovering power for an original in an age of mechanical reproduction.

As already discovered, Miller, in his role as phenomenologist, was instrumental in securing some of this mysterious power for literature. But even as a phenomenologist, Miller was never quite converted. Indeed it is clear from Miller's essays on Georges Poulet that Miller strove to attain

Poulet's process of identification as an "ideal" rather than a practice. From the very beginning, Miller never adequately represented Poulet so much as he exploited a formal element missing from Poulet's discourse, the opacity rather than the transparency of language. As Miller wrote in his preface to his *Charles Dickens: The World of His Novels*:

A poem or novel is indeed the world refashioned into conformity with the inner structure of the writer's spirit given, through words, a form and substance taken from the shared solidity of the exterior world. It is in this sense that the words of the work are themselves the primary datum, a self-sufficient reality beyond which the critic need not go. (p. x)

That the "recalcitrance" of Miller's "formalism" prepares the way for his "conversion" to post-structuralism seems obvious enough; that this recalcitrance signals a "return" of the apparently "transcended" New Critical principles "in the form" of Miller's attention to language perhaps needs to be remarked upon. but once we duly appreciate the significance of these observations for Miller's later practice, we should not fail to notice the *force* and *character* conferred on Miller's phenomenological project through the very insufficiency of this earlier conversion. While in our preceding analysis, we noted the "authorizing" value in Miller's insufficient conversion to post-structuralism, we did not focus on another of its rhetorical resources—its power to coax out the conversion of the critical community in terms of its dominant language, in the instance of this quotation the language of the New Criticism, later the language of the logocentric tradition. Indeed, we might interpret the power of Miller's entire career as a phenomenological critic in terms of his repeated efforts to come to terms with his unredeemed formalism; for when we do so, we can begin to understand two peculiar elements in his phenomenological criticism: Miller's analogical correlations of his inability to identify with the authorial *cogito* and the opacity of language, and his use of the "transcendent" power of language—its alterity to the world it would ostensibly represent—as a means not of negating but of stabilizing existent orders. In Miller's elaboration of Dickens's world, language, in its arbitrary, purely conventional status, becomes Dickens's means of partaking of and thereby validating the process of social formations which structures itself "like a sentence." In his implicit emphasis on the institutionally stablizing value of language, we can begin to discern a repetition of Miller's accommodation to, rather than total revolution from, the already existent "New Critical" canon. But it is Miller's second equation that deserves reflection, because in this implicit linking of the opacity of language with the resistance of the critical consciousness to total submission, Miller begins to draw a connection between the self-consciousness of the critic and the self-reflexivity of the text.

During Miller's tenure as a phenomenological critic, the latter term of the equation, the self-reflexivity of the text, was effectively silenced by the first, the self-consciousness of the critic; but not before this "critical" self-consciousness transformed Miller's problems of "incomplete identification" into a spiritual history of mankind. Indeed we might argue that in *The Disappearance of God* and *Poets of Reality*, Miller's "progressive" arrangement of the "spiritual" projects of select writers has more to say about the consciousness of the critic than about any of the writers. Significantly enough, it is Matthew Arnold, out of all the critics discussed, who best reflects the dilemmas of Miller's own method. For Arnold, like Miller, "remains withdrawn from life . . . things present themselves to him never as something he has experienced from the inside, but as a spectacle to be regarded from a distance. . . . He seeks rather to understand than to sympathize" (*DG*, p. 243). As it turns out, this Arnoldian alienation, rather than undermining the critical project entirely, is rhetorically heightened (in the alienation of God from the world), then healed. Again, however, it is Miller's process of healing which must give pause. Just as, through his equation of language and society, Miller was earlier able to evaluate the *imposed* social order as an *opportunity* for man to *choose* his social situation, so he is now able to re-read a *forced* disconnection from meaning (as in the case of Conrad) as an opportunity for a decisive emptying out of all referential indices and a recovery of the "imageless essence" of Being. In *Poets of Reality*, in other words, that "space between" critical and authorial consciousness, word and thing, God and world, which earlier signified despair, alienation, and anomie, turns out to be, through its very absence of meaning, a source of revitalization, the place where everything gets derealized into interpenetrable energies.

This plot should not surprise anyone. It follows the Hegelian pattern of Being and the loss of Being through its alienation into alternate manifestations, followed by the inevitable recovery of Being *through* this very alienation, a metaphysical paradigm Miller is later to condemn in Abrams's *Natural Supernaturalism*. What is important to note here, however, is not that Miller followed this pattern through its various manifestations from the nineteenth century to the present, but that by attending with remarkable discrimination to the convolutions of this pattern, he exhausted its dialectical resources. Having brought the history of consciousness, from deQuincey to William Carlos Williams, to its end, Miller did not take very long in putting an end to history.

Putting an end to the literary history he had helped establish, however, meant securing a fresh start for Miller's critical project. Since we now find ourselves in that "space between" Miller's phenomenological and deconstructive projects, perhaps we may best delineate Miller's move from one to the other by calling attention to his deconstructive re-reading of the final poem in his history of consciousness. In his earlier reading, Miller found that Williams "solved" for him the sense of alienation engendered by the disappearance of God. In Williams's dematerialization of both world and word, spectator and spectacle, into interpenetrable energies, his poetry short-circuits the sense of alienation endemic to any intentional or representational project, as everything in this poetry participates in the sense of reciprocal presence released by a "process" of wording. In Miller's deconstructive re-reading, however, Williams's "presencing" turns out to be figural rather than literal, the demystification of the "final" refuge of *mimesis* (in the guise of making a world rather than being about one) by anti-mimetic impulses. "Like Aristotle's mimesis, Williams' is both part of and more than nature, both immediate revelation and creation at once. Like the long tradition he echoes, Williams remains caught in the inextricable web of connection. ("Williams' *Spring and All* and the Progress of Poetry," p. 428).

Many reflections could be brought to bear on this re-reading, but in terms sanctioned by our discussion thus far, I wish to suggest only two. Through the notion of the inevitability of mimetic contamination, Miller does not need to banish but can conserve the traditional canon. Moreover, through his undermining of all representational urges, Miller has, using the alibi of textual demystification, justified his earlier "critical" failure to re-present completely the consciousness of the author.

Having reached that point in our discussion where the deconstructive project turns out upon reflection to involve Miller in an act of "saving face," we inevitably find ourselves back in that "other scene" where Miller quite literally lost face in his confrontation with M. H. Abrams.

Consequent to the foregoing survey of Miller's critical career, we cannot return to that other scene without renewed recognition of its significance. One of the previously unnoticed ironies in the "dialogue" with Abrams was Miller's apparent loss of the power of identification, the vaunted mainstay fo the phenomenological method. In replacing capable dialogue with the "dialogic" power of radically heterogeneous signifiers, Miller implicitly disconfirmed the phenomenologist's claim that reading involved an act of identification in which the text was virtually displaced by a resounding union of the authorial and critical consciousness. One unmentioned motive for Miller's refusal to engage Abrams in spontaneous dialogue, then, was to reassert the supremacy of the text that Miller in his offices as a phenomenologist had almost lost sight of. As Paul de Man has suggested in his dazzling article on Poulet, the prospect of losing sight of the priority of language through a self-consuming act of identification should strike fear in the heart of every phenomenological critic. As we have suggested, however, the case with Miller is significantly different from that of the "traditional" phenomenologist. A New Critical bias intervened between him and the authorial *cogito* and deposited a formalist residue, formerly identified as a sign of Miller's "partial" conversion from New Criticism to phenomenology. If Miller, the phenomenologist, exploited this formal obstacle in the free passage between the authorial and the critical *cogito* by celebrating this communion of minds as an ideal from which, consequent to the "disappearance of God," the critic as well as the author must forever feel alienated, the formalist remnant in Miller's phenomenological project enabled him to take advantage of the dialectical resources implicit in the interplay between his *distance* from the authorial *cogito* and the resultant intensification of his desire for union with that *cogito*. In short, he converts what could have been a critical failure into a "principle" of his practice and, as a fringe benefit, generates a phenomenological criticism different enough from Poulet's to merit Miller a distinct place in the Geneva School.

In his turn from phenomenology to post-structuralism, Miller manages utterly to reverse the valences of his former conversion. As a deconstructive critic, he no longer needs to pretend to pay lip service to the one critical ceremony he never quite managed to observe. Nor does he need to continue to justify his inevitable critical impurities through the dialectical interplay of distance and desire. Fortified by the post-structuralist dogma, *différance*, Miller can re-read the phenomenologist's consciousness of consciousness as a textual delusion, an idol waiting to be breached. Through *différance*, Miller marks quite literally the partiality of his earlier conversion; and in his deconstructive practice, he re-cognizes his failure to coincide with the authorial *cogito* and the resultant unreliability of his interpretive mechanisms as "principles" of his new methodology. Or rather, to avoid the attribution of self-presence implicit in a re-cognition scene, we might say that Miller does not recognize this lapsed union as a failure but rather "acts out" these earlier failures in critical strategies that make earlier failures unrecognizable. Put still differently, we might after consigning *différance* the duty of signifying the instability and unreliability of all mediations suggest that Miller has not lost the power of sympathy he should have possessed as a phenomenologist, but, instead, in his role as a post-structuralist critic has learned to identify not with another human consciousness, but with the play of *différance* itself. Indeed he seems to have learned to identify enough with *différance* to have himself *become*, not merely in his partial conversions but in his representations of his positions, *a figure of critical instability*. This line of argument, in terms authorized by Miller's habitual conversion of loss into freedom, could lead us to maintain that Miller in his two versions of "The Critic as Host" retroactively chose Abrams's public disfiguration as an inevitable effect of the "disfigurement" implicit in all rhetorical tropes. Such a perspective, despite its deconstructive ingenuity, would not, however, account for Miller's attempt, in a section of "The Critic as Host" absent from his MLA speech though elaborated in *Deconstruction and Criticism*, to "legitimize his deconstructive project by explicitly addressing some of Abrams's attacks in language borrowed from that used in traditional ethics:

The ultimate *justification* for this mode of criticism . . . is that it works. The hypothesis of a possible heterogeneity in literary texts is more *flexible, more open to a given work*, than the assumption that a *good work of literature* is necessarily going to be "organically unified." . . . It does not *claim* [its presuppositions] as universal explanatory structures. . . . Deconstruction attempts to *resist* the *totalizing and totalitarian tendencies* of criticism. It attempts to *resist its own tendencies* to come to rest in some *sense of mastery over the work*. It resists these, moreover, in an uneasy joy of interpretation, beyond nihilism, always in movement, a going beyond which remains in place. (*DC*, 252-53; italics mine)

One reason, and certainly not the least important, for my inclusion of this rather lengthy citation is Miller's explicit use within it of the discourse of legitimation which has underwritten our consideration of Miller's work. In the language prescribed by that discourse, I "should" now judiciously consider Miller's claims. But since an inclusion of Miller's defense within the "traditional" discourse of legitimation might silence the peculiarities of Miller's ethical stand, I choose instead to re-activate the strategy of the "other scene" and review the case Miller establishes in this "trial" scene by reading it through still another scene—one, however, which bears directly on this one in that it seems to violate the ethical principles enlisted in Miller's defense of deconstruction.

If earlier we suggested that Miller could not respond to Abrams's attack without turning deconstruction into a mirror image of the unified, monologic reading it exists to unsettle, we nevertheless find such a reply in "Theory and Practice: Response to Vincent Leitch." Now the "intertextual" implications of Miller's response to Leitch are rich enough to merit a separate paper. This response refers to Miller's earlier confrontation with Abrams in *Critical Inquiry*, cites the second version of this article, and implicitly responds to Abrams's charges *through* the figures in Leitch's article. In Leitch's case, however, Miller responds "directly" to a critic's assertions, even though in this favorable article there are no explicit charges to address. Curiously, Miller chooses Leitch's essay, which, as a series of citations gleaned from several of Miller's articles and deployed around multiple and often contradictory perspectives, "dutifully" obeys the logic of deconstruction. Miller's initial response to this self-consciously detotalizing perspective on his work reverses his response to Abrams. There he divided the critic's role. Here he feels divided arbitrarily, for "no man finds his picture entirely like, however flattering it may be, or however carefully made by the cutting out of his shadow. The shadow seems strangely alien" ("Theory and Practice," p. 609). Miller's basic complaint about the article is that it does not replicate the critic/artist, host/parasite context that formed the "grounds" for Miller's "response" to Abrams. This complaint leads to a plea that Leitch "might, perhaps, have said something about particular readings that are associated with the general statements. At any rate he might have raised the question of the relation between the two." Had we been persuaded by the contentions in "The Critic as Host," such a plea might leave us wondering about the pertinence here of "particular readings" and "general statements" to a deconstructive rhetoric which formerly overruled their "definitive" distinctions. We could, of course, justify Miller's rhetoric here by subsuming it under that same uncanny logic at work in the Abrams piece. According to that logic, Miller's reduction to a series of detotalized fragments would enable him to speak from a totalizing context, always already demystified as illusory. We could offer this defense, that is, if Miller had not clearly subordinated the logic of the uncanny to what he calls an "ethics of reading."[6] When we read Miller's response in ethical terms, however, what Leitch or we might do quickly gives way to what we *must do*, since "one cannot make ethical statements or perform ethical actions, such as teaching a poem, without first subjecting oneself to the words on the page, but once that has happened the ethical operation will already necessarily have taken place." As it happens, this "ethical operation" turns out to be the repetition of "the resistance to a monological reading, which is present in any literary work." Curiously, however, when fidelity to a "dialogic" principle results in a reading of Miller, as "simultaneously a ferocious nihilist and a conservative elite lamb," Miller does not praise but condemns the reading, claiming "both names are ways of reduction and neutralization." This charge of neutralization and reduction should be familiar enough by now; and following our previous discussion of the Miller-Abrams debate it should not be surprising that Miller levels this charge at precisely the moment deconstruction demands to be taken "seriously" as an institution.

Given Miller's previous practices, neither is it surprising that he presents the "choice" of a "coercive situation" as a sign of ethical respectability.

The conversion of compulsion into a free choice is, as we have seen, one of Miller's recurrent tactics. What remains surprising, however, is that Miller, in his "humanistic" recuperation of deconstruction as an ethical activity, seems, in his very exposition of that activity, to violate his code of ethics. In Miller's rendition, a critic must follow a "linguistic imperative" and through readings "coerced by the texts themselves" free himself from an earlier practice subject to "the willful imposition by a subjectivity of theory." Clearly, however, Miller ignores the "linguistic imperative" "coerced" by Leitch's text by responding to "attitudes" which are "beyond" it, "abroad in the land." In other words, Miller, by using Leitch's article as a pretext for his elaboration of an "ethics of reading," breaks his fundamental rule of ethics; for he responds to an "external," "implicit" reaction to his deconstructive method that the "figures" in Leitch's article do not coerce but merely "make explicit." Far from constituting a "choice" of a "coercive" "linguistic imperative," then, Miller's response exemplifies a "willful imposition by a subjectivity of theory" on to Leitch's text. The rationale for this violation by Miller of his own ethical principle is not difficult to discern. In this response, he is motivated less by "his" need to activate mutually contradictory textual positions than "his" wish to represent divergent hostile attitudes he can effectively expose.

I suppose that through sufficient reflection on Miller's contradiction of his own ethical position, I could, according to the terms provided by deconstruction, resolve even this contradiction as still another example of the inevitable rhetoricity of every apparently constructive utterance; but if I did so, I would only prove how inflexible, closed, monologic, and totalizing—in a word "unethical"—the rhetoric of deconstruction really is. So instead of doing so, I will take seriously enough Miller's contention that his deconstructive readings constitute an ethical act to elaborate on the "ethical implications" of Miller's conversion from phenomenological to deconstructive criticism. In doing so, however, I will permit myself to be guided neither by Miller's early phenomenological criticism nor by his "realized" post-structuralist position, but by still another transitional text, this one authored not by the critic of consciousness, but by that "other" Victorian consciousness silenced by the phenomenologist's desire to identify himself with another mind from the inside.

In *The Form of Victorian Fiction* (1968), this "other Victorian" utterly reverses the operating procedure in Miller's earlier work. If in that work the "other" was the figure with whom the critic could identify, here the "other" is the figure through whom the critic can celebrate his failure to identify as a recovery of his self-consciousness, and thereby bring into the open the correlation between alienation and self-consciousness. In a compelling series of substitutions, *The Form of Victorian Fiction* equates this alienation not only with self-consciousness but with a demystification indistinguishable from an act of writing which at once reflects, creates, and distances the Victorian world. Here, however, the world of words is not the mere effect of subjective consciousness; it is itself a "transindividual mind," an "ideally illuminated inner space," with which the critic can identify. We need only remind ourselves that this space achieves ideal illumination through its reflection upon and demystification of language's claim to represent a world before we realize that *The Form of Victorian Fiction* effects the transition from phenomenology to post-structuralism by completing the equation of the critic's self-consciousness formerly registered as a failure in representation with the self-reflexivity of the text.

In *The Form of Victorian Fiction*, then, Miller not only converted his failure to fulfill the demands of his former method into a gain in self-consciousness, he also used this renewed self-consciousness to effect the *conversion* of his critical interest from the consciousness of the author on to the form of fiction. When we further consider that this form is itself elemented of the never quite complete transformation of the critic from the position of a reflection upon others to the position of the figure reflected upon from the position of others, we realize that *The Form of Victorian Fiction* anticipates in an uncannily precise way the self-division of the critic into host and parasite constitutive of Miller's defensive reply to Abrams. When we further recall that in this book Miller characterizes writing as a way for a character to "re-enter the social world from which he had been excluded" (p. 63), a re-entry assuming the form of an identification not with the hodiernal space of Victorian England, but with the "ideally illuminated space of demystified language occupied by a structure of minds related through their shared sense of alienation from and demystification of society, we discover that Miller had already "played out" the later scene with Abrams in an earlier book, which not only made possible his conversion from phenomenology to deconstruction, but demanded it as a new ideal.

Despite all Miller's idealization of this scene, however, we cannot fail to recognize its other less mystified functions; for in displacing Miller's potentially disruptive self-consciousness on to merely formal considerations, has not this scene also reduced and neutralized that self-consciousness? Has it not reduced and naturalized Miller's sense of loss, frustration, and dispossession and then re-articulated them not into one form among others, but into the basis for this "ideal space" of illumination? Indeed, we might say that the significance of Miller's return to formalism inheres less in his re-discovery of its significance in and for itself, or its relation to his needs or desires, than in its power to dispossess him of this sense of his frustration, its ability to make him re-read this act of dispossession as the institutionalized form of an ideal society.

Perhaps this act and the society it forms will become clearer when we offer a final reflection on Miller's response to Abrams. The context of Miller's reply, as we suggested, had already been prepared for as a space ideally illuminated by the demystifying practices of other Yale critics. The overall rationale for their procedure, however, was that their practice enabled the critic to rebel against the tyranny of the artist, thereby disarticulating the distinction between artist and critic. Miller in his formulation of the self-division of critic into host and parasite certainly honored this paradigm. When, however, Miller revealed both critic and artist to be effects of the text's power to demystify itself of all referential tendencies, he exposed the rhetoric of rebellion as merely rhetorical, and the rebellion as merely staged. The form that the rebellion assumed was only the modernist dogma of the self-referentially of the text *charged* with a borrowed rhetoric of rebellion. Deconstruction, as we have seen, has always needed to pre-empt such "charged" rhetoric whether of oppression, ethics, or psychology, in order to confer the illusion of force upon a practice whose true function inheres in defusing and neutralizing. The presence of Miller, for whom deconstruction was *never a romantic rebellion but always a Victorian form*, on the scene at Yale, however, allows for a surprising authentication of their rhetoric. For deconstruction appeared precisely at that moment in his career when Miller felt oppressed by the very criticism he was practicing. Instead of freeing him from this oppression, however, deconstruction elaborated it into a new practice and a "new" career at Yale.

Miller, then, in his serial adaptation of significantly different critical positions never completely coincided with any one critical position. Thus in place of a coherent development of a critical project, we find in his career a curious asymmetry, discernible most clearly in the disjunction between the critical position he claims to represent and the language he uses to describe that project. Throughout Miller's "later" criticism we find traces and remnants of his earlier positions. Unlike those dangerous supplements Jacques Derrida is fond of locating in traditional texts to unsettle their apparent coherence, remnants of Miller's earlier postions, functioning as if they were the return of repressed elements from what we might call the critical unconscious, confer a sense of coherence and integrity upon Miller's later criticism. Indeed, these remnants allow Miller to ensure the claims of newer criticisms by drawing on the "principles" of outmoded critical positions.

Of course, Miller in his more recent criticism does not always draw directly on his former critical principles. Instead, he marks them as points of
departure. Through a series of complex meditations on the interconnec-
tions between topographical and topological textual markings, Miller
redefines "presence," direction," and "consciousness" as mere figures
of textual relations, thereby emptying them of any substantive content.
Having converted the text into the uncanny relationship between host
and parasite in his crucial exchange with M. H. Abrams, Miller, in three
recently completed books, displays his remarkable fidelity to the implications of that conversion. In *Ariadne's Thread*, *Fiction and Repetition*,
and *The Linguistic Moment*, Miller explores the labyrinthine ways in which
critics get entangled in the narratives and poems they would define.

A moment's reflection on even the most recent of Miller's critical turns
exposes unacknowledged motives for his newly discovered critical focus.
Despite his former piety for such terms as "presence," "duration," and
"consciousness," Miller always had trouble negotiating the critical exchange these terms ensured. Even as a phenomenologist Miller approached
the celebrated communion with the authorial *cogito* with anxiety. In place
of Poulet's identification with the author's consciousness, Miller made
estrangement and the accompanying dialectic of distance and desire his
true subject. but when the post-structuralist in Miller suffers the
breakdown in the distinction between the critical text and the text criticized, he loses the anxieties over insufficient identification once harbored
by Miller the phenomenologist.

Given the source of his anxiety, it comes as no surprise that Miller cures
it by returning, in his post-structuralist phase, to those writers he never
completely identified with as a phenomenologist. In *Poets of Reality* and
The Disappearance of God, Miller had already staked the
phenomenologist's claim to such writers as Dickens, Hardy, Thackeray,
Eliot, Conrad, Williams, Yeats, and Stevens; *Fiction and Repetition* and
The Linguistic Moment "recover" that old ground by mapping out a
new topography for those writers. By repeatedly relocating the critic's
wish for a line *on* the text to a line *in* the text, Miller crosses up any attempt at a definitive distinction between literal and figurative language,
text and extra-textual reality. In "Ariadne's Thread," the seminal essay
for this shift in critical maneuvers, Miller traces the lineage of such nar-
ratological concerns as character, mimesis, narrator, intersubjectivity, and
theme to their roots in what he calls the sheer linearity of the textual
line: Ariadne's thread marks the origin for all textual concerns, but instead of functioning as a stable, ontological ground, this mythological
beginning, a metaphor for an origin that does not exist except as a
figurative relation, recrosses and entangles in labyrinthine alliances

whatever definitive line would untangle the lineage of these concerns. According to the workings of Ariadne's thread, every attempt to disentangle a text only retraces another labyrinth. Consequently, whatever trouble Miller once may have had getting *inside* the authorial *cogito*, his more recent critical pronouncements offer him no way *out* of textual entanglements.

What remains truly fascinating about Miller's recent critical practice, however, inheres less in his effort to recast Arachne's web over all the masterworks of the Western tradition than in his means of discovering formerly unacknowledged textual entanglements. For those recurrent moments when Miller records "the story's allegory of its own unreadability" or "the invasion of the text by an illogic it cannot master" should restore the anxiety Miller's conversion to post-structuralism seemed to assuage. Curiously, however, Miller does not register anxiety so much as triumph when he describes these moments of textual undecidability. Indeed, he invokes these moments of undecidability as definitive marks of great literature.

Miller's means of unlocking these undecidable moments may shed some light on his attitude of mastery. For unlike his new mentor Paul de Man, Miller does not stage the scene of undecidability around the conflict between such abstract registers as the constative as opposed to the performative function of language. Instead, in essays like "A *Buchstäbliches* Reading of Goethe's *The Elective Affinities*,"[7] Miller meditates on the co-presence within the novel of two different notions of interpersonal relations. One sees "selves" as inalienable pre-existing substances securely grounded in transhuman "being," for example in the Being of God. the other "sees selves as nothing or as nothing but a locus traversed by fleeting elements which have the sad nature of signs, to be indications of absence rather than presence" (pp. 11-12). These two different notions should be familiar to any reader of Miller in his phenomenological phase. Indeed, their opposition informs the dialectic Miller works out in *The Disappearance of God*, but we can discern an important difference when we reconsider these two different notions in the context of "partial conversion" that has been the subject of this essay.

As it happens, these conflicting notions of intersubjectivity rehearse the methodological choices that formerly confronted Miller the phenomenologist. In fact, the first notion (that each self "can function as the ground for the other") recalls Poulet's vision of identification Miller never could quite achieve. And the second notion (that selves "seek to ground themselves in others . . . but each self succeeds only in experiencing its solitude") reactivates the discourse of distance and desire that distinguished Miller's phenomenological readings from Poulet's ("A

Buchstäbliches Reading," p. 22; p. 12). In Miller's latest version, however, these solitary selves do not suffer from metaphysical malaise as they did in *The Disappearance of God* but are effects of the groundless letters, the senseless matter deconstructionists tell us comprises all written language. In discerning the ways in which each version inhabits the other, Miller provides a definitive example of textual undecidability. But the anxiety disappears when we realize that in this case, undecidability releases Miller from his former decision to choose *his* version of phenomenology over Poulet's. Moreover, if Miller's phenomenological readings were always already effects of the deconstructive letter, he not only did not undergo but he did not *need* to undergo the anxieties attendant on a conversion experience. Miller registers triumph rather than anxiety not because he cannot decide between these two notions but because he no longer needs to decide between them: By staging these crucial moments of undecidability in the context of his partial conversions of Poulet's phenomenological method, Miller at once works through conversion anxieties and uses his outmoded critical practice to elucidate and *justify* his post-structuralist readings.

Should we condemn Miller for the contradictions in his partial conversions, we will fail to understand the institution he never quite adequately represents. So instead of identifying with M. H. Abrams's public attempt to deface J. Hillis Miller or siding with those resourceful strategies of self-effacement Miller deploys in reponse, we might reflect on the inadequacy inherent in both the choice offered by the public scene. At a time in the academy when the critic's options are exhausted by the choice of sides represented in this critical debate, we can begin to understand an unforeseen advantage not in Miller's defense, but in an "attitude" implicit in the deconstructive position. For a profession whose disheartened members are subject to the anxieties provoked by the increased competition for an increasingly reduced number of jobs, a method able to re(-)read their competitive anxiety as a fundamental basis for interpreting canonical texts and able to revaluate their disillusionment with both their logocentric culture and their profession as the prerequisites for entrance into the "ideal space" of a society of intellectuals related through their shared sense of alienation seems a compelling if not an inevitable choice. Although deconstruction cannot now be viewed as the implicit recovery of a single critic's self-consciousness *through* the self-reflexivity of the text, through the increasing popularity of deconstruction for a generation of disillusioned young critics, this post-structuralist strategy will have the effect of legitimizing their common sense of powerlessness, insignificance, and instability by leveling all of these moods into effects of the "free play" of *différance*, the only viable counter-discourse to the "mastery"-oriented discourse of the logocentric tradition. Through its spontaneous conversion of alienation into a pretext for a display of methodological inventiveness, deconstruction as the only established means for a "critical" expression of self-consciousness leaves no room for cultural *anomie* to become conscious at all.

Perhaps we might conclude this discussion of Miller, then, by revising the description of him that served as our point of departure. For as it turns out, Miller's career has not been marked by several abrupt changes, but by a progressive re-orientation around its point of origin. For if Miller began his critical career by rebelling against the New Critics' dogma of the self-contained text, he ended it by, in effect, "justifying" that containment as the "demystifying" struggle between referential and anti-referential elements in a text. If in the course of that career he has failed to identify completely with any single critical position, this very failure turns him into an adequate representative of a profession of critics trying to make sense of its loss of conviction. Should we conclude this discussion of Miller's career by recalling his justification of the critical act as "an uneasy joy of interpretation, beyond nihilism, always in movement, a going beyond which remains in place," however, some of the joy of diminishes and the uneasiness increases with the renewed sense of just what "place" is at stake when Miller moves in place.

NOTES

1. Throughout his earlier work, Miller draws relationships between the role of Christ as mediator and the mediatorial functions of the artwork.

2. In this way, Miller's criticism seems to have effected a transformation of the critic from the specular captivity of the "imaginary" to the metonymic displacements of the Other characteristic of the Lacanian symbolic. In his case, however, the discourse of the Other seems to speak with institutional force.

3. See "Deconstructing the Deconstructors," review of *The Inverted Self: Modernism and the Counterpoetics of William Carlos Williams*, by Riddel; and "Beginning with a Text," review of *Beginnings: Intention and Method*, by Said. Miller's deconstruction of Riddel may have micro- rather than macro-political implications, for through this review Miller discriminates between Riddel's work and the exemplary practice of the Yale critics.

4. Wayne Booth, "M. H. Abrams: Historian as Critic, Critic as Pluralist," *Critical Inquiry*, 2 (1976), 441.

5. For a much fuller analysis of the implications of deconstruction for the social text to which I am indebted, see John Brenkman, "Deconstruction and the Social Text," *Social Text*, 1 (Winter 1979), 186-88.

6. Here we should mention that Miller's use of the term the "ethics of reading" is not arbitrary. The phrase appears in an article by William E. Cain critical of Miller's turn to deconstructive criticism ("Deconstruction in America: The Recent Literary Criticism of J. Hillis Miller," p. 374). As has been suggested, Miller's co-optation and neutralization of the language of his critics constitutes his characteristic form of critical response.

7. This entire essay recalls in an uncannily precise fashion the terms and moves Miller earlier used to accommodate Georges Poulet's phenomenological method to post-structuralist strictures.

Error in Paul de Man
Stanley Corngold

> *Pardon me the joke of this gloomy grimace and trope.*
>
> Friedrich Nietzsche, *Beyond Good and Evil*

> *We all give credence to ideas in which truth is bound up with falsity, and allow our conviction to carry over from the former to the latter. Conviction diffuses, so to speak, from the true to the false associated with it, and protects falsity, even if not so unvaryingly as in the case of madness, against justifiable criticism.*
>
> Sigmund Freud, "Der Wahn und die Träume"

Paul de Man was born in 1919.[1] This fact will come as a surprise, I think, to many of his readers. Many will have begun reading him about 1971, with the publication of *Blindness and Insight* and his increasing conspicuousness in the new critical journals *Diacritics, New Literary History*, and *Glyph*. They will have taken him to be a "strong" writer, perhaps in his thirties, on the basis of marked anomalies of his exposition: a drive toward the boldest and least cautious form of a position;[2] a taste for the jargon of foreign schools imported but not naturalized; an untroubled bravado in asking from his readers a suspension of incredulity, that is, a quite unilateral generosity, in the face of odd philology, nihilistic *pronunciamenti*, and a forbidding denseness of argument which he himself proffers with an air of total conviction. Finally, and what appears most distinctively youthful, is de Man's incessantly polemical stance: the attack attitude, which helps explain the tone of urgency and superiority; the invariable choice of texts and writers like Hölderlin and Mallarmé, Nietzsche, and, par excellence, Rousseau, already in the mainstream of controversy; and, with these, the move to heavy guns whenever the polemical case grows critical—to the European-sounding diction of "philosophy" ("totalization," "mediation," "melocentrism," "rigorous description," "constitutive activity of the sign"). This, at its most amiable, is the tone of the *Dozent* preaching impatiently in the American wilderness. Where a playful remark by Mallarmé on English versification and the figure of Natalie's aunt in *Wilhelm Meisters Lehrjahre* need to be understood through Husserl, and Rousseau's admittedly "very minor" short play *Narcisse* needs to be understood through *Sein und Zeit*, such impressions are unavoidable. Or one can avoid them if one will take literally de Man's advice in "Criticism and Crisis": "in the language of polemics the crooked path often travels faster than the straight one" (*BI*, 14).

The extremity, the provocative display, the rush to the apodictic, the modish polemical tone—these qualities so evident in de Man's work of the '70s are indeed scandalous; but misleadingly so. For it is not true that the de Man note in literary theory was first struck in the early '70s by a young man. In fact, de Man had been writing critical essays for twenty years before that, and it is only in the perspective of his genuinely youthful work that one can appraise the ungainly severity of the later style.

De Man published literary essays in Paris as early as the late '40s but comes into his own as a critic in the reviews he wrote for *Critique* in the mid '50s—among the most important of which are "Les Exégèses de Hölderlin par Martin Heidegger" and "Impasse de la critique formaliste." In these we do find in abundance the qualities we expect from the essayist's art: high polish, a certain brio, a moody clarity, musical form—and they are in evidence not only because they are written in de Man's native language. These essays are also driven, as is the later work, by a bold metaphysical thrust, an uninhibited readiness to pronouce on the first and last things in the life of the mind. The continuity of the central attitude—de Man's sense of literature's mission to *unsettle* every axiom of mental life—urges the assumption that the asperity of the later style is itself the result of meditation. What we see in the later work is not, therefore, the fierceness of youth but the final stylistic consequence of a resolute anti-aestheticism. De Man, hard foe of metropolitan meliorism, is so intent on driving the act of reading off the sofa and out of the ivory carrel into the dusty arena of combat, where sunlight and shadow perplex contestants and judges alike, that he has forsaken all mere politeness and can no longer allow the consolations of a style that could by any stretch of the imagination be called natural, pleasurable, or beautiful.[3]

The essay is de Man's form; that he collected virtually without change his earlier essays from the '60s in *Blindness and Insight* and those of the '70s in *Allegories of Reading* has to do more with the exigencies of academic maintenance and resettlement than with an elective sympathy with the book format. The essay for him is a polemical instrument; it has the capacity for defiance, though at times an insistent, dogmatic, even prophetic tone leads him to defy even the "trial" character of the essay. Above all, the essay has for him, it seems, a special aptitude for the critical act as an act of separation, of forcing crises, and of devastating horizons: it functions, that is, as rapier, saber, or poleax.

* * *

The power of literature to resist "totalization," to divide and oppose whole meaning, to separate Being from the word, or to name Being as itself divided—this is de Man's oldest and best-defended idea. Behind its deconstructionist and semiological variations in the recent work is a long genealogy of such insistence.[4] This "genealogy" (the metaphor is abhorrent to de Man) contains instructive continuities and aberrations. The continuities tend to show de Man to an extraordinary degree the captive of his beginnings. The aberrations pose a threat to the very criterion of rigor which he makes the touchstone of his position. I will restrict myself here to an account of what is coherent and what is incoherent in de Man's treatment of the category of error.

"Cette perpétuelle erreur, qui est précisément la 'vie' . . . ": this quote from Proust is the epigraph to *Blindness and Insight*. The term "error" has for de Man a furious conceptual energy: it determines a good many of his arguments, if not indeed the fundamental complex of his arguments. Error functions as a movement informing both human existence and the thought adequate to existence that is literary language. The notion of error is implicated in the very definition of the trope. The strongest source of this insight is almost certainly de Man's reading of late eighteenth-century German writers. "In the eighteenth-century," writes Baulduin Schwarz, "concern for the phenomenon of error reached a quantitative maximum."[5] Error as ineluctable deviation from originary being or authentic insight—a deviation nonetheless having exemplary value—informs Hölderlin's philosophical anthropology (especially in Heidegger's readings of Hölderlin).

Error is not *mistake*. The concept of the mistake is usable, perhaps, within the restricted teleology of pragmatic acts or within the quasi-rigorous language of scientific description. Mistakes (or what de Man sometimes calls "mere error" [see, e.g., *BI*, 109]) are without true value: trivial, in principle corrigible according to a norm already known. But the skew of error implies a truth. Furthermore, the concept of error supplies to the categories of blindness and insight as much coherence as they are able to achieve. As we shall see, it brings together the constituents of the *essential* ambivalence of all literary and at least some philosophical language (see *BI*, viii).

Looking back in *Blindness and Insight* over his deconstructive readings of such critics as Georg Lukács, Maurice Blanchot, and Georges Poulet, de Man registers the illumination he has obtained of

the distinctive nature of literary language . . . but not by way of direct statement, as the explicit assertion of a knowledge derived from the observation or
understanding of literary works. It is necessary . . . to read beyond some of the
more categorical assertions and balance them against other much more tentative
utterances that seem to come close, at times, to being contradictory to these
assertions. The contradictions, however, never cancel each other out, nor do they
enter into the synthesizing dynamics of a dialectic. No contradiction or dialectical movement could develop because a fundamental difference in the level
of explicitness prevented both statements from meeting on a common level of
discourse; the one always lay hidden within the other as the sun lies hidden
within a shadow, or truth within error. (*BI*, 102-3)[6]

As soon enjoy the illumination of pure sunlight (Faust could not) as
truth without error. More severely still, insight arises from that writer's
vision which "is able to move toward the light only because, being already
blind, it does not have to fear the power of this light" (*BI*, 106). Error
names the wavering movement of the blind man toward the sun, a light
the observer could not approach except by taking shelter in the shadow
produced by the writer's groping steps.

The complex of insights produced within the horizon of this understanding itself partakes of the part truth of error. There is no place here for
mistakes. These belong to the antipodean orders of mysticism and scientism or to discourses unaware that they are inspired by axioms of these
orders—those discourses which are excluded from the insight of literary
language. For "fiction . . . knows and names itself as fiction." "The self-
reflecting mirror-effect by means of which a work of fiction asserts . . . its
separation from empirical reality . . . characterizes the work of literature
in its essence" (*BI*, 17, 18). Separated from "empirical reality," "a literary
text is not a phenomenal event that can be granted any form of positive
existence, whether as a fact of nature or as an act of the mind" (*BI*, 107).
It cannot respond to "a science of criticism that would exist as an
autonomous discipline" nor indeed to any alleged empirically founded
psychology or psychoanalysis. "Literature, unlike everyday language,
begins on the far side of this knowledge [that sign and meaning can never
coincide]; it is the only form of language free from the fallacy of
unmediated expression" (*BI*, viii, 17). Faced with the discourse of edifica-
tion, it scatters the mystic bond of word and being. "It leads to no
transcendental perception, intuition, or knowledge but merely solicits
an understanding that has to remain immanent because it poses the problem of its intelligibility in its own terms" (*BI*, 107). These terms, it
need hardly be stressed, are themselves figurative and bring in the further bias of their own tropes.

Working from within this circle of ideas as yet inexplicitly formulated, de Man was able, in the '50s, to perceive other critics' mistakes regarding poets especially alert to the privilege of literary language: the English metaphysical poets, Hölderlin, Rousseau, and Wordsworth, for example. The hunt for mistakes guided him to incisive close readings. In "Impasse de la critique formaliste," for example, he shows the philosophical fault at the foundation of New Criticism which ultimately aligns it with the mysticism of an unmediated (or insufficiently mediated) experience. In I. A. Richards's *Principles of Literary Criticism*, you find the prospect of literature elaborating a starting point in experience. Literary polysemy is then responsive to an abundance of experience at the origin. An act of reading sufficiently sensitive to nuance, even to paradox and irony, could then be supposed able to recover this originary experience. Literature would then be a medium of *Bildung*, and criticism an educative instrument in the service of a moral order, a large hierarchical "life." But this view ignores the constitutive ambiguity of the poetic world, suppresses the non-self-identical, plural, future-oriented, actively dispersive element of "poetic language." Its philosphy of literary *experience* is mounted squarely on a contradiction, a mistake; indeed, in "the world of Richards . . . there are never errors but only mistakes" (ICF, 493).

Later, in the *Blindness and Insight* essay "Form and Intent in the American New Criticism," de Man attempts to discover and dialectically elaborate the truth inside this mistake. I see the venture as a little false, as inspired by something between intellectual panache and politeness to the host climate. The circularity (implying organicism and unity) which the New Critics posit as residing in the literary work de Man detects residing instead in the act of interpreting the text. "The circle we find here and which is called 'form' does not stem from an analogy between the text and natural things [read "living organism"], but constitutes the hermeneutic circle mentioned by Spitzer of which the history has been traced by Gadamer in *Wahrheit und Methode* and whose ontological significance is at the basis of Heidegger's treatise *Sein und Zeit*" (BI, 29). In de Man's earlier essay, however, the New Critical mistake—to the extent that this criticism is faithful to its "master," I. A. Richards—can generate no such dialectical movement; there it is consistently identified as an "impasse."

De Man arraigns another version of the same mistake in his essay on Heidegger's readings of Hölderlin. Heidegger reads Hölderlin's hymn "Wie wenn am Feiertage" so as to suppress every sign of its "failure": that as the enterprise of naming Being, the hymn cannot be completed; moreover, it speaks of the very impossibility of this enterprise. (Indeed, Heidegger shows just what "reading" might do in the way of falsely *establishing* the poem when he writes: "the text which shall serve as a basis . . . is [itself] based on the following attempt at an interpretation"!)[7] De Man enlarges Heidegger's foreclosed text with sections from an earlier prose draft of Hölderlin's hymn. These passages describe the anxiety and sense of shortcoming of the poet-persona who has assumed the misguided task of bringing sacred Being to his fellow men. This perspective of failure, established by Hölderlin, allows de Man to articulate a number of negative moments in the poem blurred or discarded in Heidegger's exegesis. These establish the poet-persona as in *error*. Extravagant exaltation, masked horror (at the incendiary death of Semele), and contradictory accounts of poetic activity mock the persona's claim to conceive poems holding "the spirit of divine powers"; yet these bright claims cast a sort of shadow script that states the truth of the case—the ineffability of Being—a truth which Heidegger, in credulously adopting only the boldest, most deluded stance of the persona, is bent on hiding. Where there is "poetic naming," writes de Man, it is not Being that is named but rather mediation, the negation and endless postponement of Being (EHH, 812). That Heidegger denies to Hölderlin's poetry the ability to gainsay its major premise (of naming Being) seems to de Man, in the light of Heidegger's dominant procedure as a reader of the metaphysicians, an uncharacteristic mistake.

In this essay, too, de Man attempts to energize Heidegger's "mere error" as something between mistake and error and hence as capable of dialectical development. Heidegger, he sees, has made Hölderlin a spokesman of Being (precisely what Hölderlin par excellence is *not!*) because he needs someone who by his own example will justify Heidegger's enterprise of "establishing his thought in *parousia* and dwelling in it, inhabiting it"; and because, even though Hölderlin, in fact, speaks antithetically to Heidegger's project, he nonetheless speaks *about* it: "Heidegger and Hölderlin are talking about the same thing. . . . The great merit . . . [of these commentaries] remains that of having identified with precision the main 'concern' of Hölderlin's *oeuvre*" (EHH, 809). It is not, therefore, so immediately reprehensible to have made one's chief adversary one's chief spokesman. But just as in "Form and Intent in the American New Criticism," de Man at once generously and violently found intellectual good in the mistake of conceiving literature on an organic, experiential model, so here too the defense of Heidegger's mistake seems specious. Not everyone will agree that "to say the opposite is still to be talking about the same thing although with the opposite meaning; and it is already quite something when, in a dialogue of this order, both interlocutors succeed in talking about the same thing" (EHH, 809).

The riddle of Heidegger's divinization of Hölderlin persists, even for the reader who discovers in Heidegger's commentaries a great many counterstatements to those with which de Man sums him up (just one instance: Heidegger writes, "The immediate can never be experienced [*vernehmen*] immediately").[8] Still, Heidegger's monotonous exaltation of Hölderlin is at last intolerable; and de Man's odd justification of Heidegger's procedure can hardly mask his own distress as one who, in so many other ways, is still in the thrall of the perspectives and rhetoric associated with *Sein und Zeit*. When Heidegger adheres to the perspective of a speaker in error, he does not at any rate commit an *error*: he makes a mistake. And to give an accounting of a mistake, as de Man does, is not at the same time to give it the status of productive error. In a methodological passage concluding the essay, de Man actually terms Heidegger's reading of Hölderlin "blind and violent" (EHH, 817).

Finally, in his essay "Structure intentionelle de l'image romantique," de Man addresses another version of this mistake: the delusion that the poetic image of a natural object can somehow attain the "ontological stability of the natural . . . object," that the activity of a poetic imagination, animated by "an intention aiming at such an [external] object," can somehow anchor or appease, situate or duplicate that very restless poetic consciousness (SI, 73, 83). This is the first of many of de Man's attacks on a canonical American criticism of Romantic poetry, organized around the history of ideas associated with intellectual historians like Ernst Cassirer and A. O. Lovejoy, the major articulation of which is a putative Romantic longing for the coalescence of "subject" and "object," of consciousness and nature conceived as a unity of terrestrial objects. Instead de Man proposes a type of "self-sufficient poetic consciousness" subsisting "independently of all relation with external objects," attached entirely to itself in a precarious hovering ascension always eluding embodiment. Such a self comes to light only as the intention of a poetic figure striving for "another nature" and "associated with the limpid, diaphanous, immaterial character of celestial substance"—a striving which, aware of the extreme fragility of its victory, finally figures forth not meaning but its own endlessly frustrated intention of meaning (SI, 83, 81). Romanticism becomes the occasion of an epochal revelation of poetic possibility demystified of all nostalgia for everything not itself—a fragile pulsation of insight into the immaterial nature of poetry as such. This nonentity is not, of course, the trivial emptiness that might be produced by removing a physical body from its place (or an "intention" aimed at such a body); it is, rather, the constitutive nonentity engendering the ecstatic time of human imagination.

Throughout these essays, de Man reproves a certain mistake about the nature of poetic consciousness—the mistake that defines the integrity of poetic consciousness by its likeness to a natural organism—and puts an altogether more "advanced" conception of consciousness in its place. This consciousness, that in no way excludes the persistence of self, is emptied of all "characteristics," corresponding in this respect to the self to which Nietzsche opposes the ego. Where in Nietzsche, however, that self is intuited in the metaphors of bodily life, for de Man the self is produced in the register of vacuity: it is a void (that is just able to know itself as such), an absence, a nothingness. But it would be a sheer mistake, at this point, to dispense with the category of the self, which is more than a metaphor and certainly privileged. This is the self evoked again in *Blindness and Insight* apropos of Rousseau: "Here the human self has experienced the void within itself and the invented fiction, far from filling the void, asserts itself as pure nothingness, *our* nothingness stated and restated by a subject that is the agent of its own instability" (*BI*, 19).[9]

We pass, with *Blindness and Insight*, into a more devastating perception of the universal adhesion of error in literary and critical texts—to a negativity more radically pervasive. This perception comes with de Man's discovery of the insistent error of the *reading* process, a discovery provoked by an ideological shift from phenomenology to rhetorical analysis, from continental philosophy to the semiotic and speech-act theory of Anglo-Saxony.

All literary language, asserts de Man—the language of poets and novelists, but also the language of all serious critics, and indeed the language of the social sciences, but not "social language"—affirms general propositions about the nature of fiction and literature. Certain conclusions ought to follow with consequences for the way these authors understand specific texts, but the insights that emerge are in fact, according to de Man, different from their theories. Yet these insights are "authentic": they would modify or usurp the theoretical statements even if a certain constitutive blindness in such writing prevented the disparity from being explicitly recognized. Other critics could presumably demystify these texts in pointing out that not the general statements but the specific "poetic" text being examined is the source of these insights. On the other hand, these critics would be entirely vulnerable in turn to demystification. Hence literature can *never* be perceived to be the source of valid insights by the critic whose text is producing these insights.

The source of insight is less a subject or a consciousness than a text. "True" texts (literature) produce "true" texts (criticism) across the consciousness of the critic. The "place" in which successive mystifications and demystifications are inscribed is not history, which might be defined as the medium enabling and homogenizing integrations performed by a subject.[10] That place is instead a logical, putative time in which textual moments of insight and blindness succeed one another in an only illusory way since they were originally snarled together in a disparity instituted, but somehow also reflected, in literature. "The positing power of language," as de Man writes later, "cannot be part of a temporal sequence of events." De Man's way of accentuating the scheme of his essays was stimulated by his readings of Derrida.

"The Rhetoric of Temporality" (1969) extends the intuitions of *Blindness and Insight* into the order of literary genres; here, too, history is suppressed in favor of the space of constitutive "divergence" (void, nothingness) which situates both the genres of irony and allegory. I cannot feel, however, that the slide in polemical attention, from the subject to a void whose only correlative is the figure, and the parallel substitution of the term "textuality" for that of "temporality" (which had been described, tautologically, as a sort of thrown understanding), represents a decisive articulation in de Man's career of thought.[11] There hovers even over the later work in *Allegories of Reading* a real indeterminateness in such matters. On the question of the self, for example, de Man offers an exemplary text of Nietzsche's which shows

that the idea of individuation, of the human subject as a privileged viewpoint, is a mere metaphor. . . . But the text that asserts this annihilation of the self is not consumed, because it still sees itself as the center that produces the affirmation. The attributes of centrality and of selfhood are being exchanged in the medium of the language. Making the language that denies the self into a center rescues the self linguistically at the same time that it asserts its insignificance, its emptiness as a mere figure of speech. It can only persist as self if it is displaced into the text that denies it. The self which was at first the center of the language as its empirical referent now becomes the language of the center as fiction, as metaphor of the self. What was originally a simply referential text now becomes the text of a text, the figure of a figure. The deconstruction of the self as a metaphor does not end in the rigorous separation of the two categories (self and figure) from each other but ends instead in an exchange of properties that allows for their mutual persistence at the expense of literal truth. . . . By calling the subject a text, the text calls itself, to some extent, a subject. (*AR*, 111-12)

Once the self has been identified as a figure, that textual identification cannot avoid "to some extent" assuming the characteristics of selfhood. I cannot see how this position (which de Man shares with Nietzsche) differs from that of Julia Kristeva, who writes, "Far from being an 'epistemological perversion,' a certain subject is present from the moment that there is the consciousness of a meaning."[12] Nor, indeed, does this position differ, finally, from Dilthey's: "Every individual *Erlebnis* occurs in relations to a self."[13] De Man's essay on *Pygmalion* shows

Rousseau's text actively undermining all assertions of privilege for the "metaphor" of the self. And yet "the discourse by which the figural structure of the self is asserted [or, indeed, evaluated] fails to escape from the category it claims to deconstruct. . . . There can be no escape from the dialectical movement that produces the text"—the essential movement of which is "that this radical negation of the self is in fact its recuperation" (*AR*, 187, 186). This knowledge protects de Man from the consequences of too unwary an assimilation of his wild surmise, that "far from seeing language as an instrument in the service of a psychic energy, the possibility now arises that the entire construction of drives, substitutions, repressions, and representations is the aberrant, metaphorical correlative of the absolute randomness of language, prior to any figuration or meaning" (*AR*, 299). A "randomness" that also generates "metaphorical correlatives" of itself re-creates that system of kinds of formal purposiveness that takes one right back into the benign Self-tolerating universe of Kant's *Third Critique*.

Equivocations similar to those concerning the death of the self attend the shift from temporality to textuality, from history to synchronicity. This is because de Man's conception of time has always been that of a "fundamental" time engendering and sustaining an interminable movement of interpretive mind, whose topic and occasion is a moment of disappearance, of void experienced. Whatever comes under the heading of vulgar conceptions of history—national and cultural emergences and traditions, the circulation of wealth, the struggle for institutional power, even the effects of ideologies—has never figured directly in de Man's earlier work, so that the later work's focusing on the aporias of textuality can hardly be registered with a sense of nostalgia for something major lost.

The oeuvre shows an extreme degree of repetitiveness, though it is to de Man's credit that in this matter he does not pull his punches. He never fails to implicate in the nature of interpretation a kind of "repetition," never fails to declare that the essential statement of all great writers has been the same, that the essential knowledge derived from both the great "genres" of irony and allegory has been the same, and so forth.[14] It may not be appreciated, however, to what extent de Man's rhetorical strategies are themselves determined by a simple, even mechanical inversion of the famous mistake which literature at once attracts and, rightly understood, annihilates: its supposititious power to produce integrations. This mechanical inversion deserves a close look.

In his essay on Rilke in *Allegories of Reading*, de Man identifies and attacks "the most classical of metaphors, conceived as a transfer from an inside to an outside space (or vice versa) by means of an analogical representation. This transfer then reveals a totalizing oneness that was originally hidden but which is fully revealed as soon as it is named and maintained in the figural language" (*AR*, 35). This description of metaphor is loaded. What will seem to the new reader an attractive, plausible, or at least time-honored thesis can only invite the derision of the initiate. "A transfer from an inside to an outside space"? Heidegger annihilated this distinction in his critique of Descartes in *Sein und Zeit*. The figure as "representation"? Representation of what? What could not fail to be mediated, if not indeed metamorphosed, by the act of so-called verbal representation? "Analogical"? As between what and what? The natural organism and the self-reflective void of consciousness? "Totalizing oneness"? "Fully revealed"? But Being conceals itself in its revealment. And being "named . . . in the figural language"? To train our scorn, we need only return to de Man's essay on Heidegger's readings of Hölderlin. "Maintained"? In the vertiginous, near vanishing vibration of the textual aporia? Such a valorization of metaphor is a sheer *mistake*. It has no dialectical energy, it could not lead to a revelation.

The grounds for undercutting this straw rhetorical figure—the metaphor—all go back to a "truth" plainly enough set forth in the '50s. For the delusion of "totalizing oneness," read, the delusive experience of parousia attributed to Hölderlin by Heidegger; for "maintained in the figural language," read, whole meaning maintained in the polysemy of the symbol. The pattern of substantive negations is familiar as a repudiation of mistakes. If this move holds, we can expect de Man will never again assert these statements as positive knowledge. And, indeed, saving minute occasional lapses against which no critical vigilance would be entirely proof, we do not find him knowingly maintaining distinctions between physical and psychic "space"; asserting, as Kafka was alleged to assert, that the poet is that being "strong in metaphors," or suggesting the consolations of oneness.[15] De Man does not make these mistakes; they have no place in his writing; his is the fertile order of part truths drawn from writers who are "already demystified" in regard to such mistakes.

It therefore comes as a surprise when again and again in *Allegories of Reading* that "most classical of metaphors," extended through its moments of deceptive illumination, nonetheless directs the production of "authentic" insights. The metaphorical vision appears to have an insistent power, which, as a mistake, it is not supposed to have. Yet de Man's procedure, like Rilke's procedure, is invariably, first, to call attention to, establish, or otherwise mark a difference, a line distinguishing an inside from an outside—between, for example, ordinary language and "literary language" (*AR*, 10), "grammatical (especially syntactical) structures . . . [and] rhetorical structures" (*AR*, 6), and metaphor and metonymy (e.g., *AR*, 67). This refined distinction, however, is no sooner formulated than it is taken away, the opposition tampered with and effaced. The specific difference creating the exclusion is shown to be untenable. "The couple grammar/rhetoric," for example, is "certainly not a binary opposition since they in no way exclude each other" (*AR*, 12). When a binary opposition is eliminated, an area of resemblance is uncovered. When dichotomies are undercut, characteristics flow across the bar of their distinction. "Our reading of the Proust passage," writes de Man, "shows that precisely when the highest claims are being made for the unifying power of metaphor, these very images rely in fact on the deceptive use of semi-automatic grammatical patterns"—that is, on contiguous, metonymical patterns. Claims made on behalf of metaphor, therefore, to the same extent belong—and do not belong—to metonymy. At first there seems to be a difference between "the rhetorization of grammar (as in the rhetorical question) and the grammatization of rhetoric, as in the readings of the type sketched out in the passage from Proust" (*AR*, 16). But this difference, too, does not last.[16]

This is where the third stage of the triad comes in. The tattoo concludes on a nihilistic beat. The effacement of specific differences points not, as in Rilke, to a totalizing oneness but to universal indetermination. It is not so that *only* the "rhetorization of grammar," as in the rhetorical question, leads to "indetermination, . . . a suspended uncertainty that was unable to choose between two modes of reading, whereas the latter [the grammatization of rhetoric] seems to reach a truth" (*AR*, 16). This difference cannot be maintained with any rigor. "We end up," by the close of the essay, de Man tells us, "in the case of the rhetorical grammatization of semiology, . . . in the same state of suspended ignorance" (*AR*, 19).

Parallel three-beat movements abound in *Allegories of Reading*. Some examples: "The disjunction between the aesthetically responsive and the rhetorically aware reading [of *A la recherche du temps perdu*], . . . designates the irrevocable occurrence of at least two mutually exclusive readings and asserts the impossibility of a true understanding." But the ostensible distinction does not strictly speaking hold and points only to an abyss of indetermination. "*A la recherche du temps perdu* narrates the flight of meaning, but this does not prevent its own meaning from being, incessantly, in flight" (*AR*, 72, 78). Nietzsche's *Birth of Tragedy* reveals equally "the endless tension of a nonidentity, a pattern of dissonance that contaminates the very source of the will, the will as source" (*AR*, 99).[17]

Finally, the refined distinctions required for a criticism adequate to Romanticism automatically call forth an effort of analysis able to annihilate those distinctions as, in other important respects, unfounded. While it is true, de Man writes, that "ways of reading better attuned to some of the intricacies of figural language" have revealed in Romantic texts "areas of signification that had remained invisible, . . . there is so much minute detail, the distinctions become so diversified, that no discussion of [Romantic] generations, movements, or specific experiences of consciousness is any longer conceivable." The outcome, for a vigilant critical intelligence, must be the need to show reductively, in any particular case in which either tropes are distinguished or a discussion of "specific experiences of [Romantic] consciousness" is conceived, that the distinction or the conceptions cannot hold. No further project is imaginable for genuine criticism.

More and more radically, de Man registers the principal undoableness of all distinctions, whether because, finally, there are no simple, nonfigurative category words or because the grammatical and rhetorical, the performative and constative, dimensions of such utterances are a priori at odds.[18] Whatever the motive, the deconstruction of a difference is never allowed to remain a local instance. De Man reads all local instances of indetermination only to point to a universal void of indetermination. The audacious surmise arises that de Man-ian rigor is not at all proof against (metaphysical) pathos—a pathos that appears to owe more to Schopenhauer (at least in Nietzsche's polemical assault on him) than it does to the historical, social, rhetorical tradition of Aristotle, Hegel, and Nietzsche.[19]

De Man's demolition of metaphor as a vehicle for mistaken substantive implications cannot defend against the persistence of the extended metaphor as an inverted figure of his own thought. A "rhetorical analysis" of the kind de Man invokes discloses the peculiar tenacity of structures he calls "mistakes." These are supposed to lack any speculative interest, any dimension of potential unfolding or usurpatory energy, and must, therefore, be distinguished rigorously from error. Yet it is this simultaneous persistence at tentative unspoken levels of the text which is precisely supposed to mark the character of *error*. In the very vehemence of de Man's repudiation of this "mistake," we perceive, in fact, a helpless reflex of the tenacity with which *the* mistake par excellence—the postulate of continuity—inheres in his text . . . as error. In the very motion of eliminating the structure of the extended metaphor, he confesses to it: we have this structure repeatedly in a movement of thought which adduces distinctions, disturbs their difference, and makes this abolition prove the void of indetermination—a void, we remember, which in early versions stands explicitly as a substantive ontological assertion; de Man "needed" this void as the self-defining experience of the ontological subject.

"A cage went looking for a bird," wrote Kafka. The goal persists; the avenues to it vary. The system changes; the void remains the same.

If it appears, then, that what is in fact an error can function as a mistake, it will appear, too, that what is in fact a mistake can function as an error; in short, that it is not possible to discriminate between these categories, with what dire effects, however, we shall presently see.

We have noted that for de Man the pattern of blindness and illumination, of the dependency of truth on "the recognition of the systematic character of a certain kind of error," replaces, as a figurative account of philology, any more "scientific" and, therefore, less "rigorous" description. Philological rigor requires the boldness and clarity of acknowledging the inherence of error in reading.

What does this point of view (*prise de conscience*) mean for the sensibility educated to protect philology from error? De Man addressed the question directly in 1955 in his essay on Heidegger and Hölderlin. There he wrote, apropos of the problem "of elaborating a language capable of handling the tension between the ineffable and the mediate," that

every exegetical method . . . finds itself confronted with the same problem. . . . The ineffable requires direct attachment, the blind and violent passion with which Heidegger treats texts. Mediation implies a reflection which tends toward a critical language as rigorous and systematic as possible, but which would do well to avoid passing too swiftly to pretensions of certainty to which it cannot be entitled except at some time long hence. As a discipline of control, which condemns arbitrariness as much as false science, philology represents an acquired knowledge. Passing beyond it—supposing such a thing were possible—would be of no value whatsoever. That elaborated act of reflection, which is forced on it by its negation—by a mysticism or by a scientism equally excessive—leads to methodological movements at the very interior of the discipline which can finally only strengthen it. (EHH, 817)

Can de Man's own work, centering as it does on a theory of error, be understood as "methodological movements at the very interior of the discipline which can finally only strengthen it"? Or is it fundamentally "contaminated" precisely by that species of mistake he calls "arbitrariness," "passing beyond" philology—a "negation" of philology? Evidently, there is a kind of blindness which is born not of fearlessness of the light but of a violence which aims to take the light by storm. Here an implicit imagery of the direct path identifies not error but rather . . . mistake; it is the mistake of an uncontrollable longing for coincidence of the critic's perceptions with the "truth" of the text. But what happens when the critic's a priori perception of the text is essentially of error, of irony? He may be inclined to an unironical and sheerly mistaken violence.

To illustrate this, I turn to the conclusion of de Man's essay of "Genesis and Genealogy" in Nietzsche's *Birth of Tragedy*:

> For if genetic models are only one instance of rhetorical mystification among others, and if the relationship between the figural and the proper meaning of a metaphor is conceived, as in this text, in genetic terms, then metaphor becomes a blind metonymy and the entire set of values that figures so prominently in *The Birth of Tragedy*—a melocentric theory of language, the pan-tragic consciousness of the self, and the genetic vision of history—are made to appear hollow when they are exposed to the clarity of a new ironic light. (*AR*, 102)

The "new ironic light" is, of course, de Man's reading, which is ironic in more senses than one. It was necessary for de Man's argument that he have the evidence of one of Nietzsche's aphorisms written during the time of the composition of *The Birth of Tragedy*. This is what Nietzsche literally writes: "Intelligence can exist only in a world in which something can go amiss, in which error takes place—a world of consciousness."[20] If one wanted to profile an implication in what Nietzsche says so as to respond to de Man's special concerns, one could render the phrase "a world in which something can go amiss" as "a world in which mistakes can occur." And if one wanted to translate this sentence so as to make its meaning as plain as possible, one could write: "Intelligence can exist only in a world in which mistakes can occur, in which [such a thing as] error [can] take place—a world of consciousness." On no account, however, could one translate the passage as de Man does: "Intelligence can only exist in a world in which mistakes occur, in which *error reigns*—a world of consciousness." The words of Nietzsche which de Man translates as "in which mistakes occur, in which error reigns" are "wo etwas verfehlt werden *kann*, wo der Irrthum *stattfindet*."[21] De Man's "translation" allows him to conclude that "Dionysos, as music or as language, must now belong . . . to the teleological domain of the text and then he is *mere error* and mystification . . . (*AR*, 100; my italics). But here the "insight" produced by the mistranslation is not simply "owed" to the error, as in the best manner of the operation of blindness/insight ("critics . . . owe their best insights to the assumptions these insights disprove" [*BI*, ix]). Rather, it is contaminated by the error which is merely a mistake. The "insight" is not valid. Nietzsche does not say that intelligence is a domain of *mere error*. And why, indeed, would de Man want him to say this unless he now believes that "mere error," or mistake, is all that governs intelligence? Nietzsche is, in fact, much more faithful to the potentially instructive distinctions of the early de Man than de Man will now allow him to be.

In what Nietzsche really says, consciousness is the order in which such a thing as a mistake could occur and such a thing as an error could occur, and it is at least arguable that they are different. In de Man's translation, it would be impossible to see how mistakes, as distinct from errors, could occur, since "error reigns"! But in his explication, error has become mere error—pure mistake. It would be troubling enough to have this reading of Nietzsche in print, since it is mistaken. It is even more troubling to have it in print as error, an epistemologically interesting case: as if mistakes in translation, in a world of pure mistakes, can have a special authority. The latter proposition is dubious, of course, on sheerly logical grounds: it at once confirms and disproves itself. We have here an evident variant of the aporetic abyss exactly as interesting as the proposition "All Cretans are liars, quoth the Cretan." The idea is especially troubling, however, for the shadow it casts back on de Man's entire enterprise of founding literary language on *rhetoric*, to which logic and grammar are subordinate but not irrelevant.[22] The authority of literary discourse depends on the *difference* between error and mistake and the primacy of error over mistake.

De Man's mistaken reading of Nietzsche may, however, be due finally to a curious return of the methodologically repressed, a compulsion to enjoy the temptation which a younger self rejected. Observe the arresting parallel between de Man's reading of Nietzsche and Heidegger's reading of Hölderlin. Indeed, de Man's "mistake" is one which he has had the impressive audacity to italicize for us.

If this is a mistake of the Heideggerean order, then two possibilities suggest themselves, both in fact disengaged for us by de Man from Heidegger's readings of Hölderlin. Briefly: (1), de Man is offering a certain reading of Nietzsche *which he needs*, just because Nietzsche—about whose intellectual authority as ironist and deconstructionist there can be little doubt—said in innumerable passages throughout the axial period of his published writing precisely and plainly the *contrary* of de Man. He spoke, in fact, not on behalf of a pan-ironic, pan-textual conception of consciousness but on behalf of a deep self for whom irony was only a mask. This matter would take us far afield, undoubtedly in the direction of an act of reflection here forced on philology "by its negation—by a mysticism or by a scientism equally excessive." Or (2), de Man knows very well what Nietzsche means and here *makes* him say what he "really" means, on the strength of many passages elsewhere that would serve equally well if they were somehow handier, notwithstanding the fact that *here* Nietzsche said something different from what de Man needs him to say.

Neither possibility is auspicious. De Man's final confusion of the terms "error" and "mistake" occurs through his pretending to truth in the mode of error. The usefulness of the concept of error as distinct from that of mistake disappears utterly. What is at least of cautionary value here is the ready parallel between a metaphysically based literary criticism, however beyond good and evil it pretends to be, and a fateful European metaphysics in this century. It gave philosophy a bad smell, invited a brash scouring of the stables, and eventually forced a stunting of both horses of the soul. The consequence of this "reflex of the discipline" was to turn philosphy into a reticent, irritable, and minor discourse.

NOTES

I am grateful to David Bromwich for suggested revisions. I leave out of this account my indebtedness—and that of many others—to Paul de Man as a teacher.

1. De Man was born in Antwerp. He is a nephew of the Belgian Socialist Hendrik de Man, at one time titular leader of the Belgian labor party. But "in 1941 [Hendrik] de Man retired from public life and left Belgium to lead a solitary existence in an Alpine hut on Mont Blanc, where he devoted himself to reflection and to writing. . . . In the end he concluded that the Socialist movement unavoidably participated in the decadence of the capitalist world order, and the best the responsible individual could do was to cultivate his garden" (Peter Dodge, *A Documentary Study of Hendrik de Man, Socialist Critic of Marxism* [Princeton: Princeton Univ. Press, 1979], p. 16).

2. De Man wrote in 1962 of Harold Bloom's criticism in *The Visionary Company*: "It is the product of a genuine intellectual passion which actually has little patience with balanced judgments and strikes out for absolute positions" ("A New Vitalism," p. 620). Bloom was then in his early thirties.

3. In his essay on de Man in *After the New Criticism*, Frank Lentricchia alludes (rightly, I think) to de Man's early indebtedness to a Sartrean metaphysics and anthropology, especially in *L'Imaginaire* and *L'Être et le néant* (see pp. 285-89). An indebtedness to Sartre shows up even in de Man's most recent writing. Here it is Sartre's deliberate antibourgeois refusal to write well (as in the last works, *Critique de la raison dialectique* and *Flaubert*) that has proved congenial to de Man.

4. In 1956, for instance, in a review of Nathalie Sarraute's *L'Ère du Soupçon*, de Man offered his reading of "the central moment of *Ulysses*, the carefully prepared encounter between Bloom and Stephen Dedalus": it "indicates, surely, the total impossiblity of any contact, of any human communication, even in the most disinterested love" (*Monde Nouveau*, 11 [1956], 59).

5. Balduin Schwarz, *Der Irrtum in der Philosophie* (Munster: Afchendorffschen, 1934), p. 275. He continues: "At no time either previously or since were so many attempts made to investigate the conditions of human error. . . . Kant [e.g.] studies the way in which the error of the entire metaphysical tradition must arise as a necessity of the human spirit" (pp. 275-76).

6. Cf. the much earlier statement of 1955: "[The New Criticism] is also instructive for ontological criticism, because it proceeds in an especially clear way from a theory which is based on philosophical presuppositions more or less unconscious and hidden. By its own inadequacy, it makes them appear at the surface and therefore leads to authentic ontological questions" (ICF, 486).

7. Heidegger, *Erläuterungen zu Hölderlins Dichtung*, 4th ed. (Frankfurt: Klostermann, 1971), p. 51.

8. *Ibid.*, p. 71.

9. An excellent joining text (which I will not discuss here but which deserves study) is "Wordsworth und Hölderlin," de Man's inaugural address on assuming a professorship in comparative literature at the University of Zurich in 1965. De Man here stresses the fragility, anxiety, and mortality of the "privileged moment" in Romantic poetry and splits it into components of act and interpretation. The moment of interpretation, of "reading," is shown to be itself textually enacted. The stability of "insight" is developed not in the field of self-consciousness but in the field of reading.

10. In Shirley Hazzard's plain words about one of her characters in *Transit of Venus*: "Grace had discovered that men prefer not to go through with things. When the opposite occurred, it made history" (New York: [Viking, 1980], p. 328).

11. According to de Man, Wordsworth represents in book 6 of *The Prelude*, through the Convent of Chartreuse, the "most universal form of Nature . . . that principle in which Time is preserved without losing the passing [*vergehende*] movement *which defines it for those subject to it*" ("Wordsworth und Hölderlin," p. 1148; my translation and italics).

12. Julia Kristeva, "D'une identité l'autre," *Polylogue* (Paris: Seuil, 1977), p. 149; my translation.

13. Wilhelm Dilthey, *Gesammelte Schriften*, vol. 7, *Der Aufbau der Geschichtlichen Welt in den Geisteswissenschaften* (Leipzig and Berlin: Teubner, 1927), p. 195; my translation.

14. On the subject of "our task as critics," de Man said: "It is a task which we can only do empirically, by exercising it upon particular forms among different authors, knowing that they are 'windowless monads' and that basically they are all saying the same thing" (*Les Chemins actuels de la critique* [Paris: UGE, 1968], p. 86; my translation).

15. Franz Kafka, quoted by John Urzidil, "Recollections," in *The Kafka Problem*, ed. Angel Flores (New York: New Directions, 1946), p. 22.

16. Indeed, there appear throughout de Man's writings, with a more than random frequency, general propositions attesting to the difficulty and danger of sustaining valid distinctions, dyadic or otherwise, whether at the order of experience, ideas, or rhetoric. One example: at a sufficiently "deep" level of thought "it is difficult to distinguish between a proposition and that which constitutes its opposite. To say the opposite is still to speak about the same thing even with the opposite meaning" (EHH, 809). Or again, Rousseau rarely makes "distinctions between particular tropes or [gets] involved in the pitfalls and refinements of such distinctions" (*AR*, 163-64). Examples of this kind are legion.

17. It needs to be pointed out that this reading is quite inaccurate to the sense of Nietsche's jottings surrounding the composition of *The Birth of Tragedy*. There Nietzsche speculates on an "innermost being," a world "core," which is "wholly indecipherable." This is that "power" out of whose "womb a visionary world is generated in the form of the 'will.' " This womb is the "origin of music . . . and lies beyond all individuation" (*Gesammelte Werke* [Munich: Musarion, 1920], 3, 341-45; my translation). For additional discussion, see my "The Question of the Self in Nietzsche during the Axial Period (1822-1888)," *boundary 2*, 9, no. 3—10, no. 1 (1981), 55-98.

18. De Man likes to claim that his unspecifically differentiated distinctions are no less rigorous for being nonbinary and nondyadic. He prefers to define their unstable difference through their effect their power, namely, to upset equally all ordinary, intelligible, dyadic inner/outer distinctions and, with them, the potential for impermissible syntheses.

When, e.g., the binary oppositions between "the couple grammar/rhetoric" is denied, the unstable opposition that results "disrupts and confuses the neat antithesis of the inside/outside pattern" (*AR*, 12). Similarly, the disjunction between purely aesthetic and rhetorically alert readings (of *A la recherche du temps perdu*) undoes nothing less than "the pseudo-synthesis of inside and outside, time and space, container and content, part and whole, motion and stasis, self and understanding, writer and reader, metaphor and metonymy, that the text has constructed" (*AR*, 72).

One may wonder whether this omnipotent disjunction is itself dyadic or not. If dyadic, then it belongs among those always deconstructable "neat antitheses of the inside/outside pattern." If nondyadic, then it, too, in the course of confusing (destroying, effacing) the antithesis of inside/outside, time/space, container/content, etc., effectually brings about, at least intermittently or in part, their juncture, their "synthesis." Whatever answer is provided to the question of whether so-called nondyadic differences at work in literature can cause to cleave or join time/space, container/content, etc., is in my view, in the last analysis, an arbitrary dictum.

19. Nietzsche writes: "What was especially at stake was the value of the 'unegoistic,' the instincts of . . . self-abnegation, self-sacrifice, which Schopenhauer had gilded, deified, and projected into a beyond for so long that at last they become for him 'value-in-itself' on the basis of which he *said No* to life and to himself. But it was against precisely *these* instincts that there spoke from me an ever more fundamental mistrust, an ever more corrosive skepticism! It was precisely here that I saw the *great* danger to mankind, its sublimest enticement and seduction—but to what? to nothingness?—it was precisely here that I saw the beginning of the end, the dead stop, a retrospective weariness, the will turning *against* life, the tender and sorrowful signs of the ultimate illness . . . —nihilism" (*On the Genealogy of Morals, Basic Writings of Nietzsche*, ed. and trans. Walter Kaufmann [New York: Modern Library, 1966], p. 455).

20. Nietzsche, *Gesammelte Werke*, 3, 239; my translation.

21. *Ibid.*

22. See Newton Garver's account of Derrida's comparable project in his preface to Derrida's *Speech and Phenomenon,* trans. David B. Allison (Evanston, Ill.: Northwestern University Press, 1973).

The Genius of Irony:
Nietzsche in Bloom
Daniel O'Hara

Nietzsche, until he went mad, did not confuse
himself with his own Zarathustra.

Bloom, *Poetry and Repression*

A poet writes always of his personal life, in his finest
work out of its tragedy, whatever it be, remorse, lost
love, or mere loneliness; he never speaks directly as to
someone . . . there is always a phantasmagoria. . . .
He is never the bundle of accident and incoherence
that sits down to breakfast; he has been reborn as an
idea, something intended, complete.

Yeats, "A General Introduction For My Work"

I
Parables of the Demon: Understanding Irony

Twin epiphanies conclude Joyce's story "Eveline." The initial epiphany
concerns Eveline's mother's fate and her own possible future:

As she mused the pitiful vision of her mother's life laid its spell on the very
quick of her being—that life of commonplace sacrifices closing in final craziness.
She trembled as she heard again her mother's voice saying constantly with foolish
insistence:
—Derevaun Seraun! Derevaun Seraun!
She stood up in a sudden impulse of terror. Escape! She must escape! Frank
would save her. He would give her life, perhaps love, too. But she wanted to
live. Why should she be unhappy? She had a right to happiness. Frank would
take her in his arms, fold her in his arms. He would save her.[1]

Eveline senses in her mother's last craziness an intimation of the life to
come for her if she remains in Ireland as housekeeper to her irresponsi-
ble and vindictive father and as surrogate mother to the younger children
of her family. Her mother's tortured Gaelic refrain, though semantically
unintelligible to Eveline, is clear enough emotionally. In Ireland "the
end of pleasure is pain."[2] So Eveline, quite naturally, yearns in despera-

tion for the opportunity to realize her dream of escape, and she sees in Frank, her romantically envisioned sailor-boy, the lineaments of the saviour who would rescue her from "paralysis."

The second epiphany, more familiar perhaps, shows Eveline clutching the iron bars of the dock gate, refusing to answer the entreaties of her lover to join him on the ship that will take them away from the repressions of Irish culture to a new life in Buenos Aires. In this posture of the terror-stricken animal that prefers the security of the cage to the unknown, Eveline becomes the perfect emblem of the "paralysis" that is Joyce's theme in *Dubliners*. Apparently fear of her own sexuality and guilt over leaving her family in the lurch prevent her at last from even acknowledging her lover's frantic injunctions:

No! No! No! It was impossible. Her hands clutched the iron in frenzy. Amid the seas she sent a cry of anguish!
—Eveline! Evvy!
He rushed beyond the barrier and called to her to follow. He was shouted at to go on but he still called to her. She set her white face to him, passive, like a helpless animal. Her eyes gave him no sign of love or farewell or recognition.[3]

A powerful "nausea" has her in its grip. It is a dread of the unknown so strong that it is as if "all the seas of the world" menace her. Frank, she now feels, "would drown her." So, like an Eve who would remain in a familiar Eden, no matter how hellish it is now, rather than risk starting a new life, Eveline refuses her saviour's hand. Apparently, her saviour would plunge her beneath, rather than lift her above, the murderously innocent waves.[4]

I begin with this conclusion to a story by Joyce not out of perversity, but because it is a powerful modern example of the genius of irony at work. No matter how many times and how closely one reads the story, one cannot help but feel that the lucid formulation of her mother's fate must compel Eveline to leave Ireland at all costs. Yet Eveline does not leave. She cannot leave. Fear of the overwhelming unknown and guilt at breaking the promise she made to her now dead mother, to keep the family together whatever the price, seize her just as she would be drawn by her girlish love for a carefree sailor out of her "hard life."[5]

However, what finally keeps her in Ireland is not simply fear and guilt in any ordinary sense. Rather, it is primarily, I think, the inexorable attraction of that image of her own potential fate—"that life of commonplace sacrifices closing in final craziness"—which captures and imprisons her imagination. Eveline, for a moment, sees into the life of her mother as her creator and the reader to see into her life. Joyce even allows Eveline to think to herself this magic formula for what, if she stays at home, must become her own mode of paralysis. Such insight and articulation would seem to be beyond the capacity of a nineteen-year-old Irish girl in turn-of-the-century Dublin who can still think of her lover's face as being one "of bronze" and can still speak of her father's occasional patronizing gestures of tenderness and concern as signs of his being "very nice."[6] Yet in saying this, I do not simply mean to imply that Joyce is violating the realistic conventions of his story. Rather, I want to suggest that he has Eveline think the story's marvelously apt motto or "touchstone"—"that life of commonplace sacrifices closing in final craziness"—because he wants the reader to understand how the forms of language can take on, even for such a one as Eveline, a self-induced hypnotic power which, ironically enough, the meanings of those forms are often meant to dispel.

The irony of the conclusion to this story, then, resides not only in the disjunction between reader expectation and final catastrophe. It resides primarily in this insight into the paradoxical operations of guilt on the imagination. For it is her promise to her pathetic old mother that grants a safely familiar local habitation and a name to her anxieties: her father's house, her future of commonplace sacrifices. In our culture one is schooled in such images as that Eveline conjures up as she recalls her mother's dismal end. We are taught to love the forms of our own self-victimage. Self-sacrifice is noble, and tragic, even as we are also reminded that it is so terribly wasteful. As Joyce puts it in the mind of the boy-narrator of "The Sisters," the first, programmatic story in Dubliners, the "paralysis" that devastates lives and empowers memory and desire with the most awesome of phantasms is like "the name of some maleficent and sinful being." This "paralysis" is the demon or "genius" of irony. It is as if the sharp differences between rhetorical figures and between these figures as literary and ideological codes are staged by the text as traces of a repeatedly grimacing smile in the mind. This is why one longs so strangely to be near the "deadly work" of "paralysis," even as one fears the fatal contamination:[7] What Joyce has written in Dubliners are parables of the demon, ironic exorcisms of his own possession by the "genius" of irony, by that particular form of Irish life as it has been shaped by the uncannily destructive influences of family, church, and nation on the imagination, and as these influences are in turn produced by the various discourses of his time. This irony is as much Harold Bloom's theme as it is Joyce's. Bloom argues that a "philosophy of composition" is necessarily a "genealogy of the imagination" and thus "a study of the only guilt that matters to a poet, the guilt of indebtedness." For Bloom, "Nietzsche is the true psychologist of this guilt" (AI, 117).

The genealogy of irony's destructive influence is, of course, Nietzsche's major topic, especially in the splendid polemic *On the Genealogy of Morals*. The vision of cultural formation and cultural history offered there is anything but comforting. For Nietzsche, "the entire history of a 'thing'," whether an object of knowledge or art, a custom or an institution, or even a bodily organ, is nothing but "a continuous sign-chain of ever new interpretations whose causes do not even have to be related to one another but, on the contrary, in some cases succeed and alternate with one another in a purely chance fashion." A will to power repeatedly rises up and imposes ever new characteristics on "a thing, a custom, an organ," making each object of this will over into yet another serviceable type or antitype in the ruling interpretation of a culture.

The 'evolution' of a thing, a custom, an organ is thus by no means its *progressus* toward a goal, even less a logical *progressus* by the shortest route and with the smallest expenditure of force—but a succession of more or less profound, more or less mutually independent processes of subduing, plus the resistances they encounter, the attempts at transformation for the purpose of defense and reaction, and the results of successful counteractions. The form is fluid, but the 'meaning' is even more so.[8]

Whether the ruling interpretation or ideology is the creation of aristocrats or plebians, the strong or the weak, conservatives or radicals, does not, in the final analysis, really matter. The hermeneutical practice of the will to power of a self-selecting group functions, according to Nietzsche, to establish its "hegemony," to use the current formulation for mastery, and the servitude of other groups.

But what is particularly apropos in Nietzsche's analysis for my purposes here is his subsequent description of the typical form in which the will to power manifests itself in Western culture, thanks to the centuries-long hegemony of the priestly class and its ascetic ideal over the natural aristocrats and their noble values. I quote now the relevant passages in full, which Bloom abridges in discussing "Askesis" (*AI*, 118):

The conviction reigns that it is only through the sacrifices and accomplishments of the ancestors that the tribe *exists*—and that one has to *pay them back* with sacrifices and accomplishments: one thus recognizes a *debt* that constantly grows greater, since these forebears never cease, in their continual existence as powerful spirits, to accord the tribe new advantages and new strength. In vain, perhaps? But there is no "in vain" for these rude and "poor-souled" ages. What can one give them in return? Sacrifices (initially as food in the coarsest sense), feasts, music, honors; above all, obedience—for all customs, as works of the ancestors, are also their statutes and commands: can one ever give them enough? The suspicion remains and increases; from time to time it leads to a wholesale sacrifice, something tremendous in the way of repayment to the "creditor" (the notorious sacrifice of the first-born, for example; in any case blood, human blood). The *fear* of the ancestor and his power, the consciousness of indebtedness to him, increases, according to this kind of logic, in exactly the same measure as the power of the tribe itself increases, as the tribe itself grows ever more victorious, independent, honored, and feared. By no means the other way around! Every step toward decline of a tribe, every misfortune, every sign of degeneration, of coming disintegration always *diminishes* fear of the spirit of its founder and produces a meaner impression of his cunning, foresight, and present power. If one imagines this rude kind of logic carried to its end, then the ancestors of the *most powerful* tribes are bound eventually to grow to monstrous dimensions through the imagination of growing fear and to recede into the darkness of the divinely uncanny and unimaginable: in the end the ancestor must necessarily be transfigured into a *god*.[9]

Self-sacrifice is thus the devotion of oneself to the work of paying back to the ancestors the debt one owes them for existence itself. This primitive guilt and fear, Nietzsche contends, continues to haunt the religious, moral, scientific, and even aesthetic values of modern culture. For Nietzsche, this ascetic ideal is not weakening because Christianity is dying. It has only become associated more intimately with science and art. What the meaning of this ascetic ideal is could not be clearer. It means that one would rather have the void of self-destruction for an ultimate purpose, through the mad devotion to one form of socially sanctioned work or other, than to be void of all useful purpose and so be compelled to invent one's own purpose for one self. Nihilism is only the growing communal recognition of the suicidal essence of the ascetic ideal, which so far has been the only (ironic) meaning that humans have given to existence. "We can no longer conceal from ourselves *what* is expressed by all that willing which has taken its direction from the ascetic ideal: this hatred of the human, and even more of the animal, and more still of the material, this horror of the senses, of reason itself, this fear of happiness and beauty, this longing to get away from all appearance, change, becoming, death, wishing, from longing itself—all this means—let us dare to grasp it—*a will to nothingness*, an aversion to life, a rebellion against the most fundamental presuppositions of life; but it is and remains a *will*! . . . And, to repeat in conclusion what I said at the beginning: man would rather will *nothingness* than *not* will."[10]

To summarize: One could say that the gist of Nietzsche's critique of values in most of his writings from 1882 to 1888 is that, despite the many different attempts at revising the ideals of Western culture, the will to power over the past in setting up new ideals to propitiate the increasing demands of the ancestors inevitably takes the form of self-sacrifice, even if the meanings of each new set of ideals do in fact shift and seem to represent a liberation from guilt and fear. Like a script composed by an unknown ironic author, the tragedy of Western culture claims Nietzsche himself, of course, when, in the end, he knowingly and with demonic laughter, embraces in *The Antichrist* and *Ecce Homo* the vision of a new aristocracy of warrior-philosophers who would put down decadence by elevating the noble values Nietzsche celebrates: "Have I been understood?—*Dionysus versus the Crucified*!"[11] Thus Nietzsche becomes a prime example of his own theory of revisionism. To revise the past in the interests of the present inevitably results, it seems, in one becoming like the latest Sancho Panza who would also see, out of a desperately guilty emulation, the jocular windmills of some master's gigantically tragic romance. All the parables of the demon, irony, then, appear necessarily to be variations on this Quixote Syndrome.[12] Harold Bloom, like Nietzsche before him, will both critique and fall victim to the demonic form of revisionism.

Before turning to Nietzsche's current influence on postmodern critics, and particularly on Harold Bloom, let me digress briefly on this notion of "parables of the demon." It is perhaps Shelley in his *Defense of Poetry* who most succinctly expresses what I intend by the term. (Bloom follows Yeats in judging the *Defence* "the most profound discourse on poetry" in English.) Commenting on the power of poetry to "enlarge the circumference of the imagination," Shelley remarks that the thoughts provoked by the poetic phantasmagoria are those "which have the power of attracting and assimilating to their own nature all other thoughts, and which form new intervals and interstices" in the grand cyclic poem to which all writers are contributing. These "new intervals and interstices" form a "void" that "forever craves fresh food." Commenting a few pages earlier on what Nietzsche will call "the gay science" of the Provencal troubadours, Shelley gives an even clearer statement of his idea: "It is impossible to feel" the spell of their verses "without becoming a portion of that beauty which we contemplate."[13]

What Shelley is saying is that the new poem disrupts the configuration of texts in the tradition as it overturns, so as to revise, the habitual patterns of thinking, those personal "touchstones" of perfection we all carry around with us in our heads. Yet this process is not simply a joy, as Shelley's poem *Alastor* can attest. For the new configuration that results from revisionism is a realignment of "intervals and interstices whose void *forever craves fresh food*," or new revisions—an image of the "god" of poetic creation that does suggest the more unspeakable rites of sacrifice.

In any event, this "void" is given a local habitation and a name by each writer. Each writer's "feary father" or "familiar compound ghost," whether Rousseau/Nietzsche, Yeats/Stevens, Hardy/Heidegger, or Wordsworth/Pater, comes to stand for that insatiable void of the revisionary impulse of the will to power. And those portions of a writer's texts that, whether openly or not, attempt to revise the void by installing there one's favorite demon by displacing from its center the favorite demon of another writer, such writings are "allegories of reading," as Paul de Man would say, that tell the story of irony. This is in part what I mean by "parables of the demon."

But I also mean something much more, and a passage from Longinus on the Sublime can help to illustrate what I am after. (For Bloom's relation to Longinus, see Arac, "The Criticism of Harold Bloom.") In chapter IX, section 13 of "On the Sublime," Longinus tries to explain his sense of *The Odyssey* as a work of less magnitude than *The Iliad*. Unable to do anything more than repeat his assertion of the difference, Longinus must resort to figures of his own invention intended to persuade the reader of Homer's failing in *The Odyssey*. As he attempts to represent, by staging, his understanding of the defect or privation that haunts Homer's later epic, that unfortunate rhetorical disjunction between heroic and fabulously comic figures and scenes, Longinus begins to use language that is an instance of the apocalyptic discourse he has claimed is one of hallmarks of the grand style as it appears in Homer's *Iliad* or Plato's *Republic*:

Accordingly, in *The Odyssey* Homer may be likened to a sinking sun, whose grandeur remains without its intensity. You seem to see henceforth the ebb and flow of greatness, and a fancy roving in the fabulous and incredible, as though the ocean were withdrawing into itself and were being laid bare within its own confines.[14]

As the writer looks into the web of the tradition, whose strands are like spun glass, the figures of speech that he would use to cut out his own space and to reshape the web invariably catch him up in the web, so that he produces texts that show him becoming, in turn, a tragic demon to the next generation of readers, because his texts, too, contain voluptuous "intervals and interstices" that seduce one into attempting to replenish the beauty of the void by renewing one of the archetypes of the literary universe, which necessarily means that one must sacrifice one's imagination to assume representative or "typical" status. In reading texts and revising the tradition according to one's own designs, then, one is always in danger of becoming what one beholds: the brilliant creator of one's own shiny prison, whose writings are "parables"—"superhuman mirror-resembling dreams"—that recount what has become since Shelley's time the demonic nightmare of revisionism—or what Nietzsche might characterize as the guilty hermeneutics of power. By a logic as apparently inescapable as it is certainly perverse, a writer who would re-interpret the past in terms of the needs of the present seems inevitably to become a self-caricature, the comedian of his own ideal, the monstrous puppet of his own creation: a divine void. Such seem to be the contours of the romance of interpretation. For who else can Longinus be ironically referring to in the above passage but himself wearing the sublime mask of his failing Homer?

If we return now to the story "Eveline," we can see how this process of self-victimage works out. The image of her mother "saying constantly with foolish insistence Derevaun Seraun! Derevaun Seraun!" ("the end of pleasure is pain! the end of pleasure is pain!"), operates like a curse on Eveline's life. This image installs itself, as it were, at the center of the disjunction between her fear of repeating her mother's fate—"the pitiful vision of her mother's life laid its spell on the very quick of her being"—and her desire for "Escape! She must escape!" The result is that she remains in Ireland held captive by a mediating phantasmagoria of her own fitful production: "that life of commonplace sacrifices closing in final craziness." (With this formulation Eveline "authors," as it were, her one and only "epitaphic" text). So, too, Joyce seems to be saying, the writer who would break out of the tradition by reformulating the sacred hollows of his literary idols must end up repeating the void of that tradition in its most regressive forms by his installing there images of his own private hell, that "agenbit of inwit," that broken tooth of conscience, Bloom's "sufferings of history," which under the guise of the loftiest and most impersonal of rhetorics, sweetens time with self-destructive, Nietzschean revenge.

II
The Master of Creative Parody: Approaching Bloom

The irony of revisionism, then, is my theme. But let me illustrate how this irony works more particularly with an example from Nietzsche:

Epicurus.—Yes, I am proud of the fact that I experience the character of Epicurus quite differently from perhaps everybody else. Whatever I hear or read of him, I enjoy the happiness of the afternoon of antiquity. I see his eyes gaze upon a wide, white sea, across rocks at the shore that are bathed in sunlight, while large and small animals are playing in this light, as secure and calm as the light and his eyes. Such happiness could be invented only by a man who was suffering continually. It is the happiness of eyes that have seen the sea of existence become calm, and now they can never weary of the surface and of the many hues of this tender, shuddering skin of the sea. Never before has voluptuousness been so modest.[15]

Nietzsche reads into the figures of Epicurus here a disjunction between the tragic need that inspires the hedonic philosophy and the serene and happy vision recommended and produced by it. A potentially paralyzing insight into the continuity of suffering creates an unwearyingly happy regard for the shuddering skin of the sea of existence. Pain has become pleasure; Dionysus has invented Apollo out of the void of pure need to transfigure existence.

What Nietzsche has done is to project this disjunction between need and vision onto Epicurus in the form of an ironic antithesis, a Dionysian commentary, arising out of Nietzsche's own need, on the Apollinian process of transfiguration. Nietzsche has recreated the void out of which Epicurus as a figure projected by his own philosophy has emerged, and so, Nietzsche has completed Epicurus by remaking him in his own image of the suffering philosopher who would transfigure need into vision by means of his "gay science." Thus, in revising the past, one becomes *like* the figure one would understand as one revises that figure. Like a passive-aggressive magic mirror, the irony of revisionism reconstructs and projects the very things it says it would represent and reflect, or renew and supplement.

But, clearly, the materials for my interpretation of the irony of revisionism are self-consciously planted in Nietzsche's own text. The framing statements from the above passage tell the tale of how we are to understand Nietzsche's studious wink: "Yes, I am proud of the fact that I experience the character of Epicurus quite differently from perhaps everybody else" and "Never before has voluptuousness been so modest." What could be more voluptuously modest that Nietzsche's singular pride here?

By such ironic remarks Nietzsche breaks the illusion of serious critical representation and nods in our direction to indicate that, of course, he knows that what he is saying of Epicurus here is also being enacted by the imitative form of his text as a kind of creative parody of himself, a reflexive shadow of the need out of which he has created this bright vision of a kindred spirit, a need that is, perhaps, his and his alone. As Nietzsche puts it in a later aphorism from *The Gay Science*: Out of the deceptive chaos of space, "I want to create a sun of my own."[16]

But in the process of such self-creation, the irony of revisionism subverts the project from within. One is defined by that which one would revise. Nietzsche's Epicurus is defined by the tradition Nietzsche would reverse.

Similarly, Nietzsche's vision is defined by his need, and so, his art of transfiguration is defined by the vision of guilt and nihilism found in the *Genealogy of Morals*. To put it in even more graphic terms: Eveline's dream of escape, though hopelessly banal and virtually unselfconscious, in being defined by the paralysis she senses, is essentially no different from Nietzsche's powerfully sophisticated vision. The only difference is that Nietzsche knows the shape of his determination and would joyfully affirm it:

I walk among men as among the fragments of the future—that future which I envisage. And this is all my creating and striving, that I create and carry together into One what is fragment and riddle and dreadful accident. And how could I bear to be a man if man were not also a creator and guesser of riddles and redeemer of accidents. *To redeem those who lived in the past* and to turn every it was into a thus I willed it—*that alone should I call redemption.*[17]

So, one could say, Nietzsche would transfigure every Eveline into the Joyce of her own situation, and every Epicurus would become another mask of the tragic god who laughs at himself and all existence as he is being torn to pieces once again. One must become the artist of one's own fate, the stylist of one's own demise—or at least one must create the fictions that enable one to claim such status. The aim is to become the master of creative parody, even as one knows that the origin of that aim is the irony of revisionism, which consists of the knowledge that one knows such mastery must become one's greatest creation.

I think that it is due to Nietzsche's exemplary irony, his playing Joyce to his own Eveline, as it were, knowing all the while that both master and slave are captives of a fate they cannot escape—I think it is this "tragic knowledge" which has made Nietzsche an influence on American criticism again.

In fact, Nietzsche's influence on American literary criticism has never been greater than it is now, not even in the heyday of James G. Huneker and his *Overtones*.[18] The chief conduit for this influence is undoubtedly Jacques Derrida. Bloom, de Man, Hartman, and Miller, among the Yale critics, have particularly attempted to assimilate and to turn to their own purposes the inspired Nietzschean clowning of the frivolous trace.[19] For Derrida and through him, for the Yale group of critics generally, Nietzsche becomes the genius of irony, the self-cancelling simulacrum of an authority figure (a trace) that occupies even as it discloses the places in their texts where rhetorical discontinuities and conceptual aporias threaten to explode these texts from within, shattering them into fragments as openly meaningless as "I have forgotten my umbrella." The work of revision is thus undermined as it gets underway. The tower of vision is deliberately built on sand, out of sand, at high tide.

Like Joyce in "Eveline" or Nietzsche himself in the passage on Epicurus, the deconstructive writer would turn the irony of revisionism back on itself. By staging parodies of his own parables of the demon even as he writes them, such a critic would subvert all movements to posit a single, final value, ideal, or style in place of the predicament of "paralysis" or "need" or "textual" implication in the web of tradition. Like Joyce and Nietzsche, this critic refuses to identify with the simulacra of his own tracing. He thereby refuses to become simply an unwitting character in his own play. Or at least that is the announced strategy or style so far: "if there is going to be style, there can only be more than one."[20]

Let me try to summarize my position here: There are places in a text of rhetorical disjunction, conceptual contradiction, and ideological conjuncture, such places of ironic representation as "the tender, shuddering skin of the sea" from Nietzsche's revision of the figure of Epicurus cited earlier. That passage is an ironic representation because it echoes, thematically and formally, the very idea of "continual suffering" it is meant to repress and transfigure. I say "formally," and mean by the term "structurally." The metaphor, "the tender, shuddering skin of the sea," revises the words "a man who was suffering continually," which, for Nietzsche, is itself a metaphor that appears to be purely literal, a "dead" metaphor which we have forgotten. The result of the resurrection of this metaphor as metaphor, and its continued life in the grand tomb of "the tender, shuddering skin of the sea," is not a dialectical sublation of antithesis, but an emerging blankness, a spectral smile haunting the most serious work of transfiguration. Such spots of apparent and momentary indeterminacy, such "intervals and interstices" whose "void forever craves fresh food," draw out a writer's revisionary tendencies and define the scope and the master-figures of the interpretation he would impose upon that void. This is why Derrida, like Nietzsche and Joyce, attempts to disrupt this process repeatedly, to keep it going, to keep flushing out the hollows of the text with figures of his own that parody the revisionary impulse in the act as it were. If the irony of revisionism can be compared (as Harold Bloom has compared it) to Milton's Satan copulating with his own offspring, Sin, to produce the horrible giant, Death, then Derrida's Nietzschean or Joycean deconstructive project—the irony of irony as it were—can be likened to a simulated coitus interruptus, after repeated artificial stimulation of an eccentric kind.

III
The Vision of the Riddle: Nietzsche In (to) Bloom?

With these words we at last approach Harold Bloom, who, as it turns out, was in our midst from the outset. For Bloom, unlike Derrida or *his*

Nietzsche, believes that the writer, if he is to become creative, and a source of influence for later generations, must periodically repress his self-consciousness and identify with the redemptive imagination of a precursor, if only so he can ransack the tomb and gnaw on the bones of the dead. Bloom's project is to murder and (re-)create:

Uncovering the Cherub, as Yeats momentarily sees, can be accomplished by the act of becoming one with the redemptive imagination of the precursor. . . . [Thus] the imaginative gift comes necessarily from the perversity of the spirit, and so the living labyrinth of literature is built upon the ruin of every impulse most generous in us. So apparently it must be.[21]

For Bloom, the irony of revisionism appears as the anxiety of influence rather than as "allegories of reading" or as the play of "differánce." The ephebe, to become strong, must repress his knowledge of indebtedness for a moment and assume the stature of his poetic father by revising his images, defenses, and rhetorical patterns in ways that make the belated poet the ancestor god, and the precursor the heir apparent burdened by the overwhelming riches of the ancestor: "Every forgotten precursor becomes a giant of the imagination" (AI, 107). That is, every would-be Aeneas has heavier and many more fathers than he can possibly bear to admit.

Bloom's topic, then, is the sublime and how one would compose a counter-sublime of one's own to best the precursor at his own game, in the endless agon of poetic history, a contest in which the later poets, like the guilt-ridden descendants in Nietzsche's portrait of cultural history from the Genealogy of Morals or like the failing genius of Longinus in his revision of Homer, can never win. One can only learn how to lose with a greater degree of nobility or honesty; and, in the end, self-conscious self-caricature, the fictions of the self that result from the feeling for the lost sublime, can be the only result:

There are no longer any archetypes to displace: we have been ejected from the imperial palace whence we came. . . . For us, creative emulation of literary tradition leads to images of inversion, incest, sado-masochistic parody, of which the great, gloriously self-defeating master is Pynchon. (MM, 31)

Like a band of little Satans, each of us would mate with our own Romance-daughters, and so, mock our loves by the production of our own deaths. Pynchon's only rival, in such a romance, besides Bloom himself perhaps, is, as we shall see, Nietzsche.

Surveying the ways in which Bloom has revised and plotted the figure of Nietzsche for his own purposes over the course of his career tells us a great deal about Bloom and the irony of revisionism. In the essay on

Walter Pater's career collected now in *Figures of Capable Imagination* but written and revised in the early 1970s, we see enshrined Bloom's very early swerve away from Nietzsche's influence. Bloom essentially sees Nietzsche at this stage in his career as an aesthetic critic of our culture who, like Pater and Emerson, longed for a creative renaissance that never quite came, a Scholar-Gipsy of philosophy whose spark from heaven came in the parodic form of the "mocking laughter of Zarathustra," which smacked, for Bloom at this time too much of *hysterica passio*: "The aesthetic man, surrounded by the decaying absolutes inherited from [the tradition], accepts the truths of solipsism and isolation, of mortality and the flux of sensations, and glories in the singularity of his own peculiar kind of contemplative temperament" (*FCI*, 29).

But in the production of the tetrology, Bloom's view of Nietzsche begins to shift radically and repeatedly. In *The Anxiety of Influence* (1973) Bloom sees Nietzsche as a genealogist of the imagination and a critical historian of the anxiety of influence:

Nietzsche and Freud are, so far as I can tell, the prime influences upon the theory of influence presented in this book. Nietzsche is the prophet of the antithetical, and his *Genealogy of Morals* is the profoundest study available to me of the revisionary and ascetic strains in the aesthetic temperament. . . . Both Nietzsche and Freud underestimated poets and poetry, yet each yielded more power to phantasmagoria than it truly possesses. . . . Nietzsche was a master psychologist in seeing that poets are far more intense in their Dionysian self-deceptions than in their share of our common Promethean guilt. (*AI*, 8)

Then in *A Map of Misreading* (1975) Bloom declares that Nietzsche is the prophet of deconstruction and the prototype of Paul de Man's "Überleser" (over-reader), that is, Nietzsche now is no longer the flawed but great ancestor; he is now in part a comrade in arms, in part an Esau whose legacy one can usurp for one's own purposes if one is resourceful and deceptive enough:

This fictive reader simultaneously somehow negatively fulfills and yet exuberantly transcends self, much as Zarathustra so contradictorily performed. Such a reader, at once blind and transparent with light, self-deconstructed yet fully knowing the pain of his separation both from text and from nature, doubtless will be more than equal to the revisionary labors of contradiction and destruction, but hardly to the antithetical restoration that increasingly becomes part of the burden and function of whatever valid poetry we have left or may yet receive. (*MM*, 5)

Not unsurprisingly, *Kabbalah and Criticism* (1975) discovers Bloom reading Nietzsche as the secret heir of Kabbalah and Gnosis, as Bloom himself now revises them:

For Nietzsche, every trope is a change in perspective, in which outside becomes inside. . . . [In this light] poetic language makes of the strong reader what it will, and it chooses to make him into a liar [against time and its "it was".] (*KC*, 120)

Finally, in *Poetry and Repression* (1976), Nietzsche has become for Bloom a master of "creative parody," that is, a master of the unwittingly self-caricaturing effects of poetic language, who, unlike Emerson and Stevens but like Blake and Yeats, never *fully* identifies himself with his own creations—never does so, that is, until he goes mad:

I myself, perhaps wrongly, tend to read *Zarathustra* as a highly deliberate Nietzschean parody of the prospective stance that frequently distinguishes the High Romantic poet. . . . Like Emerson and Whitman before him, Stevens persuades himself by his own rhetoric that momentarily, in his poem, his ontological self and his empirical self have come together. Nietzsche, until he went mad, did not confuse himself with his own Zarathustra. . . . Yeats, like Nietzsche, implicitly decided that he too would rather have the void as purpose than be void of purpose. (*PRR*, 113, 292, 234)

Bloom's point is simply this: Nietzsche, rather like Yeats and Blake, and unlike Emerson, Whitman, and Stevens, refused to identify himself permanently with the phantasm of the precursor's imagination as revised and projected by his own defensive rhetoric. Consequently, Nietzsche becomes a master of creative parody, but cannot become, in Bloom's scheme of things, a sublime creator in the grand style of Milton or Whitman.

I have rapidly sketched the descent of the Nietzschean demon in Bloom's writings in a way that I hope suggests that Bloom's six-fold pattern of revisionism is in full operation. For early in his career, Bloom swerved from Nietzsche's influence by seeing him as a version of Pater and Emerson as seen through the eyes of an antithetical Arnold figure. Nietzsche was an aesthetic critic in need of the redeeming poet who is yet to come. Then, rapidly in the tetralogy, Nietzsche is, first, a precursor whose insights into critical history Bloom would complete by his own antithetical theory of influence. But then Nietzsche becomes a brother who one claims is greater than one in certain ways, only so such self-humbling may win one the fruits of the other's labors. Next, Nietzsche's sublime intuitions concerning the will to power as "the necessity of misreading" are put into their proper light by Bloom's own hyperbolic counter-sublime of Kabblah and Gnosis. Finally, however, Bloom sees Nietzsche as the master of creative parody, the giant of irony who dwarfs de Man and Derrida and whom Bloom knows best. This Nietzsche can hollow out any pose, shift to any new perspective, in an endless round

of ironic self-cancellings of the ruling metaphors of the Western tradition of philosophical discourse. Nietzsche thereby becomes as formidable
and as graspable as the smile of the cheshire cat.

Thus, clinamen, tessera, kenosis, daemonization, and askesis do in this
way truly describe the irony of revisionism as it works itself out in Bloom
with regard to Nietzsche's influence. Bloom has, therefore, striven mighti-
ly, with this one figure at least, to exorcise the demon by creating a multi-
textual heterocosm to contain him. This version of Satan—this concre-
tion of error—must have a Hell of his own, and Bloom has assumed the
role of the divine architect who, ironically enough, would build for him
over the void of critical substitutions that stretches between ironic reduc-
tionism and mythic representation Nietzsche's own Pandemonium. With
this demon, Bloom is of God's and the Covering Cherub's party, and
knows it full well.

But, naturally, the question arises: What about the final turn of the
revisionary screw? Where is the apophrades? Or has Bloom, like Ashbery
in relation to Stevens, only managed to become yet another instance of
some giant shadow's last embellishment?

Nietzsche does make one last major appearance in Bloom's writings.
In *The Flight to Lucifer: A Gnostic Fantasy* (1979), Nietzsche shows up
momentarily under the guise of Valentinus, who, having forgotten his
original need and his intended vision, seeks advice on the matters of origins
and aims, from Olam, the Gnostic Aeon, whose wisdom echoes Nietzsche's in the Vision and the Riddle chapter of *Zarathustra*, but does so
in the prophetic tones of Bloom's own most recent esoteric rumblings:

The vision faded away again. Valentinus looked hard at Olam, who was impa-
tient to depart. "Aeon, if error and the failure belong to the truth itself, then
what is divine is degraded. How will going back to the origin restore me, or
even you?"

Olam would not answer. Valentinus went on, but speaking now more to himself.
"Or, is this the measure of our strength? That we admit to ourselves, and without
perishing, that the world of original being had ceased to be true?" Olam, provoked to a reply, seized a stone and threw it, underhand but with amazing force,
far into the sky. It did not descend. He grinned cheerfully and spoke with
assurance: "You are a stone of wisdom, and I sling them. We are both star-
destroyers! You threw yourself so high, when first you found me! But every
thrown stone—must fall! The aim is not to return to the Pleroma as it was, at
the origin! For that All was less than All, that Fullness proved only an emptiness. The aim must be to gain a past from which we might spring, rather than
that from which we seemed to derive."[22]

As we shall see in some detail, this scene derives from Nietzsche's chapter,

"Of the Vision and the Riddle," in Part Three of *Thus Spoke Zarathustra*. Ironically enough, the mocking reductive discourse of the Spirit of Gravity, Zarathustra's enemy, is staged in Bloom's text as the wisdom of Olam. Bloom has striven to become one of his own critical fathers here by staging a scene of instruction for Nietzsche, a scene that would instruct Nietzsche in the wisdom he has repressed and that Bloom has single-handedly resurrected. In the passage from *The Flight to Lucifer* Bloom aims to give birth to himself as an authentically creative writer by representing Nietzsche as a worn-out master of creative-parody who needs the Gnostic wisdom, that spark from heaven, which only Bloom can provide. But in the process Bloom recreates himself as another, later version of the Spirit of Gravity, Nietzsche's figure for what Bloom himself earlier derided as the Covering Cherub. What a comedy of errors.

We have all seen this irony of revisionism before in Bloom, in connection with Yeats. Bloom argued in his book on *Yeats* (1970) that the Irish poet had sought to correct the vision of his imaginative fathers, Blake and Shelley, by supplementing their "naive" prophetic humanism with his own more "mature" tragic vision of the irremedial evil of human existence. But in the process of working out this vision of evil, Yeats, Bloom contends, ironically becomes the antithetical fulfillment of that humanism with his embrace of a Gnostic Sophia—in Celtic garb—thirsty for the blood of Jerusalem and Asia.

But, as we now see, Bloom has now become a living example of his theory of the anxiety of influence. In the name of the aesthetic humanism of Blake and Shelley, the supposed naturalistic "morality" of Stevens and Freud, and the mystical existentialism of Martin Buber, Bloom criticized severely Yeats's supernatural hijinks in *A Vision* and in the great poetry written in its baleful light as "the worship of the composite-god of historical process."[23] Yet by decade's end Bloom himself became an academic revision of what he had beheld in Yeats: a "professor" of humane letters espousing what according to Bloom in *Yeats* is the modern form of Gnosticism: historical determinism. For Bloom's theory calls for the growing solipsism of the poet and so, in the final analysis, for the "death" of poetry in the "birth" of "poetic" criticism. It seems that, as Oscar Wilde might say and the work of Cervantes and Flaubert or Joyce might demonstrate, life does truly imitate art far more than art imitates life, and in more complex and paradoxical ways than any writer can begin to imagine. For the final danger of the irony of revisionism is, of course, that one will become the antithetical image of all that one originally held dear.

This question of revisionary irony haunts Nietzsche's *Zarathustra*, and particularly its centerpiece, "Of the Vision and the Riddle." Not the least of the difficulties of this chapter is the impossiblity of deciding wherein lies the vision, wherein the riddle.

There are two clearly defined parts to this chapter. Both are sections of Zarathustra's address to the sailors on board the ship that is taking him from the Blissful Isles to his lost companions on the mainland. The first half of his address recollects his bitter vision of the Spirit of Gravity, Zarathustra's devilish nemesis, who appears to him as demon, part dwarf, part mole, that perches on his shoulder. From that position the Spirit of Gravity mocks Zarathustra's every effort to affirm life, especially his heroic posture that would seem to exclaim homerically, " 'Was that life? Well then! Once more!' " One cannot very easily dance up to the sublime heights from which even tragedy appears comic, when the Spirit of Gravity hangs on one's shoulder and pours into one's ear the mocking remark: " 'You stone of wisdom! You have thrown yourself high, but every stone that is thrown must—fall' ".[24] (I would recall to you the passage from Bloom's *Flight to Lucifer* cited previously and as well the central image of the goal of Nietzsche's revisionary project, viz., that of becoming like a new star in the cultural firmament: " 'You must be full of chaos to give birth to a dancing star!' "[25]) Thus the Spirit of Gravity mocks Zarathustra's every effort to become himself, to transfigure himself into a living touchstone, a living philospher's stone of creative health.

The second part of this chapter concerns Zarathustra's hypothesis of the Eternal Recurrence and its riddling illustration. At the gateway of the "Moment" an eternity rolls out behind and an eternity rolls on ahead—a notion that the Spirit of Gravity immediately parodies with his sing-song vision: " 'Everything straight lies,' mimics the dwarf-mole-demon disdainfully, 'All truth is crooked, time itself is a circle.' "[26] But their spat is interrupted by a dog howling nearby which recalls a time from Zarathustra's past, from his childhood in fact, when he heard a similar howling and he was moved to pity for a dog so fearful of the ghostly moon. But when Zarathustra looks up now from his reverie, the dwarf and the gateway of the moment—all the former visionary and mock-visionary scenes are gone, vanished enigmatically. He tells the sailors that it was as if he had been dreaming and had then awakened, or perhaps it was just the opposite? For all at once, Zarathustra reports, he was standing between wild cliffs, alone, desolate in a most desolate moonlight.

What follows is the riddling allegorical vision of the most solitary man, the ironic illustration of the visionary hypothesis of the eternal recurrence that has just been articulated and mocked earlier in the chapter. I quote this ironic allegory at length because paraphrase cannot convey its terrible dramatic effectiveness:

But there a man was lying! And there! The dog, leaping, bristling, whining;

then it saw me coming—then it howled again, then it *cried out*—had I ever heard a dog cry so for help?

And truly, I had never seen the like of what I then saw. I saw a young shepherd writhing, choking, convulsed, his face distorted; and a heavy, black snake was hanging out of his mouth.

Had I ever seen so much disgust and pallid horror on a face? Had he, perhaps, been asleep? Then the snake had crawled into his throat—and there it had bitten itself fast.

My hands tugged and tugged at the snake—in vain! they could not tug the snake out of the shepherd's throat. Then a voice cried from me: 'Bite! Bite! Its head off! Bite!'—thus a voice cried from me, my horror, my hate, my disgust, my pity, all my good and evil cried out of me with a single cry.[27]

What are we to make of this vision, so riddling, so clear? That's what Zarathustra now asks the sailors as he concludes his account.

You bold men around me! You venturers, adventurers, and those of you who have embarked with cunning sails upon undiscovered seas! You who take pleasure in riddles! Solve for me the riddle that I saw, interpret to me the vision of the most solitary man!

For it was a vision and a premonition: *what* did I see in allegory? And *who* is it that must come one day? *Who* is the shepherd into whose mouth the snake thus crawled? *Who* is the man into whose throat all that is heaviest, blackest will thus crawl?

The shepherd, however, bit as my cry had advised him; he bit with a good bite! He spat far away the snake's head—and sprang up.

No longer a shepherd, no longer a man—a transformed being, surrounded with light, *laughing!* Never yet on earth had any man laughed as he laughed!

O my brothers, I heard a laughter that was no human laughter—and now a thirst consumes me, a longing that is never stilled.

My longing for this laughter consumes me: oh how do I endure still to live! And how could I endure to die now! Thus spoke Zarathustra.[28]

Thus, also, spoke the vision and the riddle. But what does it still say to us? Well, Nietzsche's translator, R. J. Hollingdale in this case, in a footnote to the section informs the reader that this scene incorporates some of Nietzsche's own personal memories of and fantasies concerning the time his father was found lying unconscious on the ground after a fall from a horse, a fall which turned out to be the occasion of Pastor Nietzsche's death. In addition, the conjunction of imagery here can suggest the retelling of several myths: that of Christ's death and resurrection, that of Ulysses' return to Ithaca, that of Hamlet's speculation on the poisoning of his father by Claudius. And more contexts could be adduced, but to what end?

Such contexts cannot, I think, account for the powerful, unceasing reverberations of this passage. How are we to interpret this desire on Zarathustra's part for such demonic laughter? What weight are we to give to his questions which besiege the sailors to solve, if they can, this riddle for him? Why is the act of biting off the snake's head so decisive? And so easily accomplished? Does it suggest that the ideas of the eternal recurrence, whose traditional symbol is the uroborus; the will to power over the past (time and its "it was"); and the *Übermensch*; do not cancel each other out, leaving one with the sense that time is only the medium for the repeated disclosures of human impotence? How does this unnatural act relate to Nietzsche's assertion that man has unwittingly killed God and so made possible a Dionysian appreciation of the innocence of becoming? In short, can the critic really make a significant difference, for himself, for his discipline, for his culture, by means of his provocative, riddling questions and allegorical visions, that are truly open-ended and not merely rhetorical, that are like Nietzsche's riddling vision here, and unlike Bloom's self-indulgent revision of Nietzsche? Can the critic's self-conscious reflections on his unknown fate actually educate others? Can the fictions of the critic, like those of the poet, make a difference by reshaping the very being of others?

As we have seen, of all the Yale critics only Bloom in Chapter 39 of *The Flight to Lucifer* has confronted this central scene of instruction from Nietzsche's *Zarathustra*. But his confrontation is in the form of a reductive, antithetical condensation and gnomic abstract formulation of Nietzsche's riddling vision. Bloom would simply incorporate Nietzsche into his own critical romance, but he does so in a way that explodes Bloom's inadequate discourse and shows Nietzsche *in full Bloom*: "The aim must be to gain a past from which we might spring, rather than that from which we seemed to derive." Bloom's invented past, his adopted Gnostic heritage, dissolves here to reveal Olam as a belated revision, not of Zarathustra or of Nietzsche but of The Spirit of Gravity. Bloom's revisionism invariably appears as the antithetical reduction and inversion of the vision of his fathers, a process that judges Bloom even as he would judge others. Bloom becomes what he beholds—not Blake's Los, but his Spectre, not the Real Man the Imagination, but the Covering Cherub: "Literary tradition . . . is now valuable precisely because it partly blocks, because it stifles the weak, because it represses even the strong. To study literary tradition today is to achieve a dangerous but enabling act of the mind that works against all ease in fresh 'creation'. Kierkegaard could afford to believe that he became great in proportion to striven-with greatness, but we come later. Nietzsche insisted that nothing was more pernicious than the sense of being a latecomer, but I want to insist upon the contrary: nothing is now more salutary than such a sense. Without it, we cannot distinguish between the energy of humanistic performance and merely organic energy, which never alas needs to be saved from itself'' (*MM*, 28-29). What might Nietzsche's rejoinder be to this paralyzing gloom? ''Bite! Bite!,'' I think.

I will not attempt to answer the questions raised by Nietzsche or dodged by Bloom. I want to propose a certain perspective to adopt for discussing how Bloom, at the moment when he appears to have most successfully internalized and reversed Nietzsche by having him in *The Flight to Lucifer* return as a spokesman for Bloom's own antithetical wisdom, has in fact been reduced by the influx of Nietzschean vision. This makes Bloom's text just another riddling commentary on a problem given classic formulation by Nietzsche. To answer the question why is it that Bloom cannot successfully negotiate the turn of apophrades, or the return of the dead in our own colors, when this passage announcing the eternal recurrence is involved, requires that we see clearly what the romance of interpretation and the irony of revisionism necessarily entail.

Northrop Frye characterizes Romance as a narrative genre in which an idealized hero, associated analogically with a Messiah figure, engages in a quest for redemption from the sterility that is afflicting him and the land of his adopted people. This quest involves a ritualized contest with all the enemies of fresh creativity, a confrontation with death, and the virtual apotheosis of the hero. Frye goes on to note that Romance thus idealizes the rites of initiation of a ruling class group, presenting in the best possible light all those conventions and disciplines that determine the ideological justification for why some are assimilated into and many others are excluded from the ''best'' society. Only those, whatever their origins, who buy the favored story of the ruling group, who are willing to invest belief in a heroic dream known to be only a dream, will be admitted into the ranks of the group:

The romance is nearest of all literary forms to the wish-fulfillment, and for that reason it has socially a curiously paradoxical role. In every age the ruling social or intellectual class tends to project its ideals in some form of romance, where the virtuous heroes and beautiful heroines represent the ideals and the villains the threats to their ascendency.[29]

In short, like Eveline, we work at learning our roles in such a self-victimizing romance. For this formulation of Romance holds true, I believe, even for our modern culture of suspicious unbelief and the facile fictionalization of reality, since that culture promotes the ironic and parodic re-enactment of all past mythic forms as the primary means for maintaining at least the perverted semblance of intellectual order and social cohesion. The result is rather naturally bizarre, a comic spectacle to end all comic spectacles, as if a host of Touchstones who would each be Tiresias turn out to be all playing, badly, the role of Oedipus all over again, in productions staged for our amusement by the various disciplines, discourses, and media of our culture.

What I want to suggest here, in closing, is that both Nietzsche and Bloom, throughout their writings but particularly in *Zarathustra* and the tetrology and *The Flight to Lucifer*, are engaging, one knowingly and creatively, the other reductively through his "creative" parody of Nietzsche, in the ironic repetition of the central plot of the romance of interpretation for the critic of our culture. This plot is the one that tells the story of how modern humanity would save the appearances of the religious representation of reality by seeing it once again in a new way as a regulative fiction: a text. In this light, the critic replaces the priest as mediator of a (now) humanistic vision that portrays humans becoming their own gods through the power of their imaginative productions:

Humanity (as an idea), in its complete perfection, implies not only all essential qualities belonging to human nature, which constitute our concept of it, enlarged to a degree of complete agreement with the highest aims that would represent our idea of perfect humanity, but everything also which, besides this concept, is required for the complete determination of the idea. For of all contradictory predicates one can only agree with the idea of the most perfect man. What to us is an ideal, was in Plato's language an *Idea of a divine mind*, an individual object present to its pure intuition, the most perfect of every possible being, and the archetype of all phenomenal copies.[30]

What Kant is arguing for here is the revision of the Platonic idea of the divine mind as the measure, the origin, and the end of all phenomenal reality. This revision, in accord with Kant's critical project, must represent the Platonic idea as a regulative ideal or fiction: Shelley's "void that forever craves fresh food." The goal of the critical quest is to approximate in one's life of writing the ideal of this divine mind. Textual production creates what Wallace Stevens calls the image of "the impossible possible philosophers' man," "the man of glass."

Nietzsche and Bloom, in their own critical projects, wrestle with this Kantian dragon. Nietzsche attempts to use it by creatively revising it and by substituting for it the ideal of the transfiguration of the human species according to his vision of the *Übermensch*, a transfiguration which would make us all capable of the demonic laughter he envisions. Bloom, in his turn, would parody and reductively invert Nietzsche's own revision: "Nietzsche, until he went mad, did not confuse himself with his own Zarathustra" (*PRR*, 242). But the irony of revisionism which stems from Kant and his critical-recuperative, his aesthetic project, is an irony that cannot be avoided no matter how self-conscious the critic of Kant or how intentionally repressive and sublime the would-be critic of such critics. The oppositional critics of our culture would critique the last vestiges of the ascetic ideal as it makes its appearance both in the work of art of our culture and in the latest models of the revisionary ideal by ironically mating or identifying with their own self-created phantasmagoria "found" in the "voids" of past texts. The aim is to reproduce themselves as the divine child of yet another potentially liberating vision that deserves, ultimately, to be parodied, too. The ultimate word on this irony of revisionism which plagues the critic's romance of interpretation is, perhaps, not Nietzsche's or Bloom's, or Kant's, but Joyce's from the Ithaca Chapter of *Ulysses*.

As Leopold Bloom settles into bed, he examines the reasons why apparently he no longer can feel anger at his wife's repeated infidelities, but instead feels only a superior kind of amusement:

If he had smiled why would he have smiled? To reflect that each one who enters [the bed] imagines himself to be the first to enter whereas he is always the last term of a preceding series even if the first term of a succeeding one, each imagining himself to be first, last, only and alone, whereas he is neither first nor last, nor only nor alone in a series originating in and repeated to infinity.[31]

Could it be that this bed is the text, that Molly, the unfaithful wife, is the void that forever craves fresh food, and her lovers are the line of oppositional critics that stems from Kant? And that Bloom, Leopold Bloom that is, is? And Joyce is? Perhaps my title can suggest answers to these questions?

In summary, then, one could say that the irony of revisionism inevitably entails a guilty rebellion against the present decadence (however defined), in the name of a more creative future which is fearfully envisioned according to the most archaic of phantasms from the past. But for Nietzsche and Joyce, unlike for Bloom (Harold Bloom that is), one can master this irony of revisionism by masterfully parodying it—by sublimely representing it as the eternal recurrence of the perverse romance of interpretation of the would-be uroboric critic. But can one imagine it really: how the eternal moment of paralysis that so afflicts the one who would act must be repeatedly bitten off with a bloody smile?

NOTES

1. James Joyce, *Dubliners: Text, Criticism, and Notes*, ed. Robert Scholes and A. Walton Litz (New York: Penguin, 1976), p. 40.

2. Don Gifford, *Notes for Joyce* (New York: E. P. Dutton, 1967), p. 37.

3. Joyce, p. 41.

4. The allusions in the story to St. Margaret Mary Alacoque suggest that Eveline sees Frank largely in terms of a redeemer figure. See Joyce, *Dubliners*, p. 470.

5. Joyce, p. 38.

6. Joyce, p. 37.

7. Joyce, p. 9.

8. Friedrich Nietzsche, *On the Genealogy of Morals*, trans. Walter Kaufmann and R. J. Hollingdale (New York: Vintage, 1967), pp. 77-78.

9. Nietzsche, p. 89.

10. Nietzsche, pp. 162-63.

11. Friedrich Nietzsche, *Ecce Homo*, trans. Walter Kaufmann (New York: Vintage, 1967), p. 335.

12. My point is perhaps most succinctly put by Oscar Wilde in his brilliant dialogue "The Decay of Lying" in *The Artist as Critic*, ed. Richard Ellmann (New York: Vintage, 1969), p. 307: "Paradox though it may seem—and paradoxes are always dangerous things—it is none the less true that Life imitates art far more than Art imitates life." For Nietzsche's only attitude on this Quixote Syndrome, see Walter Kaufmann, *Nietzsche: Philospher, Psychologist, Anti-Christ* (Princeton: Princeton University Press, 1967), p. 72.

13. Percy Bysshe Shelley, "A Defence of Poetry," *The Norton Anthology of English Literature*, Vol. II, ed. M. H. Abrams, et al. (New York: Norton, 1979), p. 787. See, also p. 785: "All the great historians . . . make copious and ample amends for their subjection to facts, by filling the interstices of their subjects with living images."

14. Longinus, *On the Sublime: The Greek Text Edited After the Paris Manuscript*, ed. W. Rhys Roberts (Cambridge at the University Press, 1935), p. 67.

15. Friedrich Nietzsche, *The Gay Science*, trans., Walter Kaufmann (New York: Vintage, 1974), p. 110.

16. Nietzsche, *The Gay Science*, p. 254.

17. Nietzsche, *Ecce Homo*, pp. 308-9.

18. For a discussion of the Nietzsche phenomenon in America earlier in the century, see Patrich Bridgewater, *Nietzsche in Anglo-Saxony* (Leicester, England: Leicester University Press, 1972), pp. 149-62.

19. See David P. Allison, "Destruktion/Deconstruction in the Text of Nietzsche," *boundary 2*, Vol. VIII, No. 1 (Fall 1979), 197-222; and David Couzens Hoy, "Forgetting the Text: Derrida's Critique of Heidegger," *boundary 2*, Vol. VIII, No. 1 (Fall 1979), 223-36.

20. Jacques Derrida, *Spurs*, p. 139.

21. Harold Bloom, *Yeats*, p. 81; and *AI*, p. 85.

22. Harold Bloom, *The Flight to Lucifer: A Gnostic Fantasy* (New York: Farrar, Straus, Giroux, 1979), p. 193.

23. Bloom, *Yeats*, p. 405.

24. Friedrich Nietzsche, *Thus Spoke Zarathustra*, trans. R. J. Hollingdale (New York: Penguin), p. 179.

25. Nietzsche, *Zarathustra*, p. 44.

26. Nietzsche, *Zarathustra*, p. 178.

27. Nietzsche, *Zarathustra*, pp. 179-80.

28. Nietzsche, *Zarathustra*, p. 180.

29. Northrop Frye, *Anatomy of Criticism* (Princeton: Princeton University Press, 1957), 186.

30. Immanuel Kant, *Critique of Pure Reason*, trans. F. Max Muller (Garden City, N.Y.: Doubleday & Co. Inc., 1966), pp. 385-86.

31. James Joyce, *Ulysses*, p. 731.

Part III

History, Theory, and Influence:
Yale Critics as Readers
of Maurice Blanchot
Donald G. Marshall

One difficulty even for sympathetic readers of the Yale critics is simply a difference of bibliography. The main reference point for American academics is New Criticism, which long ago triumphed both over historical scholarship and over doctrinally based political and social commentary. Protest over the war in Vietnam stirred recollections of these earlier debates about the historical context and social function of both literature and criticism, but masked the simultaneous and more enduring infusion of European theory into American criticism. While Paul de Man contributed a quite orthodox essay to Reuben Brower and Richard Poirier's New Critical collection *In Defense of Reading* (1962)[1] and also reprinted an essay on formalism in *Blindness and Insight*, his book was largely concerned with writers who were hardly more than names to many American academics in 1971: Husserl, Binswanger, Blanchot, Derrida. By the time a certain political numbness allowed these imported theories to emerge to full prominence, ordinary Americans found themselves in a room crowded with faces sometimes strange, sometimes strangely altered: Hegel, Nietzsche, Saussure, Freud in oddly stylish French garb, Heidegger. The contemporary critics who were joined in lively talk with them apparently took for granted not only their ideas, but a particular understanding of their ideas, which they took no time to expound for the uninformed bystander. Instead, their commentaries always began on the other side of those occasionally tedious, but courteously helpful explanations American academics customarily provide their readers. As a result, one got the effect of a conversation among close friends about some absent person who is treated with tactful obliquity, though not otherwise spared rigorous examination.

The difficulty here is not simply one of "reading up" background figures, even granting that titles multiply alarmingly as one tracks the sources of sources. The problem is to understand critics who do not so much expound and argue a view as conduct toward some conclusion polemical oppositions to and alliances with established premises. The risk is equal whether one decides in exasperation that these premises are unwarranted generalizations and unexamined assumptions or whether one begins to pick up the jargon, mouthing it instead of genuinely joining a conversation one understands. And the risk increases where a figure is well-known to the critics in question, but not to their audience. A useful illustration is the case of Maurice Blanchot, born in 1906, the author of a score of books, about equally divided between narratives and collections of critical essays. His advantage for me is that the conversation about him among Geoffrey Hartman, Paul de Man, and Jacques Derrida is relatively short and explicit, though by no means over. Evidence of his importance may be found in a remark from "Pas," one of the essays in which Derrida responds to Blanchot:

S'il y avait, ce que je ne crois pas, quelque pertinence à lui en faire l'éloge, s'il n'y avait là grossière attribution de maîtrise et si *Le pas au-delà* ne périmait d'avance telle métaphore, je dirais que jamais, autant qu'aujourd'hui, je ne l'ai imaginé si loin devant nous. Nous attendant, encore à venir, à lire, à relire par ceux-là même qui le font depuis qu'il savent lire et *grâce* à lui.[2]

[If there were—and I don't believe there is—any pertinence in singing his praises, if doing so were not a crude imputation of mastery and if his book *A Step or Not Beyond* had not wiped out in advance any such metaphor, I would say that never as much as today have I pictured him so far ahead of us. He waits for us, still to come, to be read and re-read even by those who have been doing it since they knew how to read and *thanks* to him.]

Paul de Man begins his essay on Blanchot with a rapid survey of fashions in French writing since the war. He singles out for praise those writers who have ignored trendiness and kept in touch with the deeper currents of French writing, and in particular, Blanchot. Were Blanchot not almost legendarily reclusive, he would doubtless already have been offered a post at Yale. Nevertheless, I would stress that my aim here is not to do even minimal justice to Blanchot's considerable body of writing, though I hope his thought may be reflected, even darkly, in the glass Hartman, de Man, and Derrida hold up to it. My concern here is, rather, with what their responses to Blanchot may tell us about these critics.

First in the field is Geoffrey Hartman's "The Fulness and Nothingness of Literature," an energetic, though somewhat sprawling essay he has not chosen to reprint. In a headnote, he modestly calls it "a preliminary essay to serve as an introduction to the work of Maurice Blanchot." It appeared in a 1956 issue of *Yale French Studies* entitled "Foray Through Existentialism." Blanchot's explicit debt in critical theory to Hegel, Nietzsche, and Heidegger, coupled with his early novels' obvious affinities with Kafka and a laudatory essay by Sartre on his second novel, *Aminadab* (1942), doubtless determined this somewhat misleading attempt to locate Blanchot within a literary and philosophical tradition. Yet in the same issue René Girard's "Existentialism and Criticism" concludes by distinguishing Blanchot sharply from Sartre and adding that with Blanchot and a few other recent critics "the approach to the work of art is so original, the future is still so rich with promise that any attempt to cling to doctrinal labels seems futile" (p. 52). Nevertheless, Hartman tries to build his own context for interpreting Blanchot's narrative work. Drawing on Mallarmé, Valéry, Gide, Sartre, and Camus, he formulates a set of problems concerning the relation between the novel and "life." The opening sentence of the essay states this problem succinctly: "The doubting of literature began with the doubting of fiction, which began with a knowledge internal to the writer concerning his inevitable abuse of the immediate and life-giving power of words." The tension here between a historical rhetoric of beginnings and the writer's immediate consciousness of the essence of his art will frame Hartman's interpretation of Blanchot. Hartman opposes Valéry's claim that the novel's task is to give "the impression of life intensely lived" against Gide's view that if the novel establishes such an impression, it must promptly undermine it. This dilemma presents itself to the novelist as a problem of language: the novel's openness to commonplace language permits it to present or represent quotidian life, but at the same time, conceals the fact that the artist's imagination is what has established the scene within which this impression of reality transpires. The locus of concern here is the artist's self-conscious knowledge of the paradoxes inherent in the experience of creating, and this is Blanchot's chosen problem: "the psychological origin and the psychological effect of art." Although he acknowledges Blanchot's familiarity with romantic literature, Hartman distinguishes Blanchot's from the romantic theory of "creativity," because Blanchot rejects mystical or religious analogues. Blanchot's remains "a vitally human concern," which can be supported by the evidence of artists' "life-work" and the "researches of psychology in the last hundred and fifty years." Hartman praises Blanchot's admirably acute and detailed sensitivity to "the way many artists consider word and imagination inextricably necessity and danger." But what remains decisive is that Hartman is reading Blanchot essentially psychologically, as an analyst of the way a literary work presents itself to its creator's consciousness.

The second section of the essay pursues the same "vital human concern": the artist's consciousness is exemplary of all consciousness, and the artist's temptation with respect to words is specifically analogous to the mind's temptations "with respect to time and world." This temptation is to "see immediate life where immediate life is not, and to produce by the power of words the phantom of immediacy." This problem, "the passion of the artist," is presented by Blanchot, according to Hartman, through the myth of Orpheus and Eurydice. Picking up Blanchot's citations of Hegel and Heidegger, Hartman recognizes in words themselves the "most evident example" of the mind's power of abstraction from immediacy. Yet the figure of Eurydice represents the artist's counterbalancing desire for "the *face* of the truth, the phantom of immediacy." In his narratives, Blanchot analyzes this general dilemma of mind by concentrating on the writer's relation to language, his word-consciousness. His narratives proceed not by following a plot, but by posing a verbal commonplace or some simple, yet disturbing question, such as, "Are you writing *at this very moment?*" and then drawing out the seeming immmediacy these words create in a "long internal modification, question and answer of great discretion and subtlety," which dispels immediacy, entangling the reader in "a gordian knot which no desire for abridgement may undo." The result is to deny ordinary immediacy and yet glimpse "a new and original immediacy." This is accomplished paradoxically, not by overcoming the writer's failure to achieve immediacy, but by making immediate the phantom of immediacy, that is, making the immediate work out of the failure of the artist's quest for immediacy. By this reflexive twist, Blanchot solves the problem of the mind's lack of immediacy without leaving the domain of consciousness. The paradoxes of consciousness are a fire "through which most writers pass, but in which Blanchot has managed to persist with the unscathedness of the legendary salamander." Again, for Hartman this persistence distinguishes Blanchot from the authors of the romantic tradition.

The final section of the essay turns to Blanchot's narratives and interprets them in the light of the problems of consciousness previously defined. In the relations between characters and between characters and their world these narratives exhibit a ceaseless interchange of "intimacy and estrangement," of immediacy and the failure of every effort to achieve immediacy. "Here is a consciousness," Hartman remarks, "which appears to have lost its first term and its last, and this loss constitutes its sufferance as its vagrancy." Thus, in Blanchot we find a language classic in its simplicity, yet evasive of "punctual meaning," so that the narratives ceaselessly demonstrate that words do not genuinely mean or communicate. Blanchot's scenes are reduced to a few places and objects, paralleling "the reduction of consciousness to a few apparently commonplace sets of question and reply." Yet, Hartman argues, "Every one of his récits has at its center (but this 'center' is often dissembled) an incident where an empty space suddenly reveals its secret plenitude." This reversal is the "dominant theme" of all Blanchot's writings. It incarnates his view that the reduction of consciousness is not an "escape" from the world, but opens a prior and impersonal origin of both world and man. In the case of the work of art, which is exemplary, by suffering the loss of his ordinary world and ordinary personality, the artist opens a void which paradoxically reverses itself into a presence that is the work's origin. Where Sartre attacks the modern writer's "commitment to failure," Blanchot accepts this failure and denies any stigma attaches to it. While Blanchot holds a muted conviction that the dilemmas of art occupy a prophetic place in our historical moment, he believes, as Hartman argues, that the artist achieves this "truth" only by refusing the immediacy of being and expression, and instead committing himself to the errant "realm of the apparently insignificant."

I will defer for the moment any remarks on the adequacy of this interpretation. Hartman suggests the importance Blanchot holds for him when he insists that Blanchot's account of the perilous twists of artistic consciousness in the presence of its creative work is "a vital human concern." The reduction of consciousness together with and in narrative to a minimal essence produces a "simple decor" within which "is revealed a mystery analogous to that contained in the great myths of antiquity." Hartman even commits a modest contradiction, for he had earlier said Blanchot rejected the mystical or religious analogues invoked by the romantic theory of "creativity." What Hartman wishes is to connect his interpretation of Blanchot with the main thesis of *The Unmediated Vision* (1954), which found in Wordsworth, Hopkins, Rilke, and Valéry a "common striving for pure representation," where "the poet represents the mind as knowing without a cause from perception, and so in and from itself; or he will represent the mind as no less real than the objects of its perceiving" (p. 128). In the concluding sentence of this summation, Hartman contrasts the modern writer to the traditional writer as one who knows no mediation on his orphic journey through experience, but finds in nature, the body, and human consciousness the only text (p. 155). Romanticism did not abandon religious categories of thought, but penetrated to experiences which may be considered as underlying religious thought. Modern writing preserves its continuity with this romantic project, but decisively abandons any intention of reinstituting transcendence. The question is whether literature can survive without the experience of wonder, magic, or transcendence which is disclosed in imagination and which flowers in religious thinking. This is not only a broadly cultural, but a specifically artistic problem, particularly as it manifests itself in the writer's "word-consciousness."[3] The philosophical co-ordinates Hartman establishes for Blanchot in Hegel and Heidegger do not make philosophy a primary category, but represent an effort to think through the relation of literature to transcendence and to ask whether art has been superseded by "enlightenment." This is also, of course, a critical problem, for criticism's divided loyalties have always drawn it both to abstract thought and to participation in wonder, a tension that can be felt in criticism's own language. In strictly personal terms, it must be remarked that Hartman's greatest strength as a critic has always been an uncanny power of participation in the poet's consciousness of his own work. It is precisely an understanding and an incarnation of this intuitive sympathy which Hartman senses in Blanchot.

A second essay, "Maurice Blanchot: Philospher-Novelist," published in 1962 and collected in *Beyond Formalism* (1970), focuses the issues more sharply and brings Blanchot into line with Hartman's understanding of romanticism, particularly "Romanticism and Anti-Self-Consciousness," also first published in 1962 and included in the same collection. As we shall see, this alignment of Blanchot with a romantic tradition challenges both his distinctness and his merit. The romantics, Hartman argues, sought "remedies for the corrosive power of analysis and the fixated self-consciousness," but sought them outside the traditional controls religion imposed on intellect. Art was a remedy that did not check mind, but drew "the antidote to self-consciousness from consciousness itself." Similarly, the central dilemma of Blanchot's work is "art and its relation to consciousness," and the artist's dilemma specifically is "that of a mind that seeks to overcome itself from within, to pass into reality rather than into more and more consciousness," but to do so through art. "Art," Hartman says at the end of the essay, "is not consciousness per se, but rather its antidote, evolved from within consciousness itself."

What complicates the artist's "quest to make the mind real rather than more conscious" is the parallel "quest for and impossibility of realizing the self via symbols." Blanchot's narratives simultaneously posit and question the very word-notions which are their precondition: I, he, here, now, us, end, the notions of time, way, directedness. Narrative thus moves forward by the force of its own self-questioning rather than by plot, relations between characters, the analysis of thoughts or feelings, or acquiescence in any other illusory "beyond," whether "nature, supernature, or symbolic existence." One model, for example, is a narrative showing a consciousness which wishes to be, precisely, a writer. The self-estrangement in which the writer seeks his own identity in the very act which ought to confer it parallels the shift a writer desires from speaking only out of his own consciousness as an "I" to speaking out of another consciousness, a "he," whether narrator or character. Yet this very shift to what is "other" than the writer's consciousness deprives it of reality, making it depend on the consciousness which seeks it, even while it directs that seeking consciousness back to its own reality as what it, as "other," lacks. The point is that both in the artist's relation to language and in his consciousness, something in the very project of art prevents its "making the mind real rather than more conscious." Blanchot's narratives labor continually to keep open the space in which this effort of consciousness takes place and in which a narrator endures its failure or perdures through a spiral of attempt and failure. This space is not quite real, not quite irreal, a realm improbable rather than frankly fantastic, where consciousness, to be sure, is real, but never substance, hovering in some ghostly ontological between. Blanchot's novels are thus all middle, strange dialectics of intimacy and estrangement between two characters or protagonist and world, where existence is an irresolvable erring, consciousness' ceaseless quest for concreteness coupled with the peculiar increase of consciousness at each successive failure, a movement impelled by a constantly renewed forgetfulness.

This interpretation of Blanchot's narratives represents a considerable gain in subtlety and power, but remains continuous with the earlier essay. What is instructive is the change in the way Hartman treats the philosophical context he invokes for Blanchot, a change which supports his aligning Blanchot with romanticism. Thus, the formula of an existence made up of erring and forgetfulness precisely duplicates Heidegger's for man's relation to Being. But Hartman stresses we must not conclude that Blanchot's novels are "a kind of allegory, which they are not." Rather, Blanchot's understanding of Heidegger has already been mediated by a knowledge of Heidegger's own sources in German romanticism. Moreover, according to Hartman, Heidegger's "forgetfulness of Being" has subtly transformed Plato's "mythically expressed theory of reminiscence," a myth "revived in all its potency in the Romantic period." The key term here is "myth," which transforms philosophy or mediates between philosophy and literature. The line from the romantic revival of Plato to Heidegger to Blanchot (or the complicated intermediations among them called "recovery" and "understanding") represents a "quest for an adequate theory of unconscious or creative self-oblivion." We are thus led back to the romantic problem of consciousness (as well as to the tension between its linear development and its eternal recurrence).

Similarly, the mind's inability to make itself real through symbols recalls for Hartman Hegel's prediction that the consciousness exhibited by and through art would be superseded by the state consciousness achieved in religion and ultimately in philosophy. In *L'Espace littéraire*, Blanchot concedes that the dilemma of artistic consciousness exposes most acutely that of all consciousness desiring yet alienated from reality. But he argues against Hegel that this project of self-alienation cannot be overcome. Hartman says that in this critique of Hegel Blanchot "enlists" Kierkegaard, and Hartman quotes *The Sickness Unto Death*: despair cannot "consume the eternal thing, the self, which is the ground of despair, whose worm dieth not, and whose fire is not quenched." Blanchot certainly knows Kierkegaard, but does not, so far as I can see, use him in this context. The same quotation does appear, however, in "Romanticism and Anti-Self-Consciousness," amid a list of those Solitaires—Cain, Ancient Mariner, Faust, Wandering Jew, culminating in the *poète maudit*—who quest in a realm of "between-ness" (*BF*, 303-304). Hartman lists the same figures, calling them types "of the alienated mind," as the ancestors of Blanchot's characters, and more fully describes the "between" which is also the space of Blanchot's narratives: "This is a new and hard concept of mediation, which defines man purely by the quality of the void in him, and the artist by a resistance to symbols, human or divine, that would fill this void" (*BF*, 108). "Bringing to bear on Blanchot a particular philosophic tradition" thus leads to the view that Blanchot's is an "anti-self-consciousness theory," approached in adequacy by Yeats's "mask," Pound's "persona," Eliot's "impersonality," and American formalism's "ironic structure," though no other theory "has been quite as influential or provided a better foundation for understanding art generically."

In his second encounter with Blanchot, Hartman thus manages to coordinate three of his chief concerns: the problem of consciousness, the history of romanticism, and the relations between philosophy and literature. Blanchot's *récits* exemplify a new form of writing, rooted in romanticism, and one Hartman himself continues to have ambitions to practice in criticism: "neither philosophy nor straight fiction but an autonomous middle form," they constitute "a new genre, or even type of literature, in the making." They can be approached through "a distinctive branch of inquiry—call it problematics," which would "consider each work as standing in a dialectical relation to consciousness and a critical relation to the whole activity of art." Hartman elaborates this conception in the essay "Toward Literary History" (*BF*, 356-386), and yet his text shows a prophetic uneasiness with his own argument. He concedes that "of course" the dialectic between consciousness and anti-self-consciousness "is found in every age and not restricted to the Romantic" (*BF*, 304). Hartman saves his phenomena by distinguishing religious means of easing the burden of history and consciousness from the romantic "aggrandizement" of art as a means to the same end. This distinction between religion and art, he argues,

can take a purely historical form. There clearly comes a time when art frees itself from its subordination to religion or religiously inspired myth and continues or even replaces them. This time seems to coincide with what is generally called the Romantic period: the latter, at least, is a good *terminus a quo*. Though every age may find its own means to convert self-consciousness into the larger energy of imagination, in the Romantic period it is primarily art on which this crucial function devolves.

The nagging hesitation here between an unrestrictedly general conception and a historical scheme overflows into a footnote, where Hartman concedes he has "omitted here the important role played by the French Revolution." This omission exposes not only the problem of relating an artistic "problematics" with a history thus in principle placed "outside" it, but also the difficulty that Hartman has offered no explanation of why this historical moment should be situated at this particular time. Yet his deepest instincts compel Hartman to project the "problematics of consciousness" he finds in Blanchot into a "history of consciousness" that begins with and conforms to a romantic, Hegelian model. This ambivalence emerges in an evaluation that closes the essay on Blanchot, almost like a seal on a letter: "Sometimes," Hartman confesses, "I have a sinking feeling that a few verses from Rilke or Valéry express all he has to say." Yet he concedes this feeling may arise simply from the fact that Blanchot "has taught me to read more strongly and relevantly" those same key lines of Rilke and Valéry. On the one hand, having placed Blanchot in his "tradition," we discover he is a weak latecomer, living out the artistic achievements of the masters; on the other hand, it is perhaps reading Blanchot which enables us to "invent" the very works and tradition in whose light he appears secondary and even occasionally tedious. Hartman's capacity to interpret a work as it presents itself to the writer's historically situated consciousness is the very substance of historical participation and thus of literary history. But given his ambivalence, it is not surprising that Hartman's labors in the history of romanticism have been sidetracked by defensive measures against the uncompromising anti-historicism of deconstruction (the very possibility of any genre, including one whose law was a new literary history as "problematics," is challenged by Derrida's "The Law of Genre," which I will consider a little later).

It will consequently be all the more illuminating to turn to Paul de Man's "Impersonality in the Criticism of Maurice Blanchot" (published in French in 1966, collected in *Blindness and Insight* in 1971), especially since he focuses on the same issues as Hartman, namely, the intricate evasions of the self and the relation of critical or philosophical to imaginative or narrative writing. De Man begins with Blanchot's practice and theory of reading. Blanchot's criticism "never intended to perform a task of exegesis that would combine earlier acquired knowledge with new elucidations." Nor is it any form of self-confession, such as would be conveyed by acts of judgment or sympathetic insight into an author. By locating the reading process "au delà ou en deçà de la compréhension" ("beyond or this side of understanding"), Blanchot's interpretations escape both the subject-object polarities which govern the objective description of texts as things and the intersubjective approach to an author, "in which two subjects engage in a self-clarifying dialogue." It will not be pertinent to rehearse de Man's objections to both objective and subjective modes of criticism, which include, for him, virtually all contemporary criticism, but the central issue is whether Blanchot may have found a way of evading the circularities of blindness and insight which are de Man's theme.

The demonstration that he has not leads through the concept of impersonality. The author, according to Blanchot, is so definitively detached from his own work that he is unable to read it. "For the author," de Man says, "the possiblity of being read transforms his language from a mere project into a work (and thus forever detaches it from him)." In Blanchot's paranomastic language, the work of writing ("l'oeuvre") withdraws behind the written work ("livre") as authorship yields to readership. This incapacity, this asymmetry between author and reader, is connected for Blanchot (as de Man asserts, but without citing specific texts) to the issue of beginnings. The writer can only begin his work by forgetting "that this presumed beginning is, in fact, the repetition of a previous failure, resulting precisely from an inability to begin anew." The reader, whose act is not a new beginning, but simply an acceptance of the work as it exists, can ignore what a work's author would be obliged, in reading, to remember: "that the work asserted in fact the impossibility of its own existence." Yet Blanchot writes both criticism and narrative: how can he at once remember and forget? De Man replies, "the impossibility of self-reading has itself become the main theme, demanding in its turn to be read and interpreted." Blanchot's criticism prefigures the act of self-interpretation, of self-reading accomplished in the narratives: the critical work serves as "the preparatory version"of the narrative. "The movement of Blanchot's critical mind," de Man concludes, "reflects the circular pattern that can be found in all acts of literary invention."

De Man's exposition of Blanchot is condensed and virtually unsubstantiated. It contains a number of puzzling statements and expository leaps which we may defer considering. He goes on to demonstrate the "circular pattern" he describes in Blanchot's criticism of Mallarmé. Again, to pursue the details of this demonstration would carry us far afield. It leads in any case toward a divergence between Blanchot's criticism and a full reading of Mallarmé. Blanchot omits, de Man argues, Mallarmé's concept of a "dialectical growth by means of which the particular death of the protagonist [of *Igitur*] becomes a universal movement, corresponding to the historical development of human consciousness in time." Blanchot asserts rather that such "dialectical growth toward a universal consciousness was a delusion and that the notion of a progressive temporality is a reassuring but misleading myth." It is one of the "stratagems, ruses of language and thought," by which we try "to protect ourselves" against "a persistent negative movement that resides in being."It is worth noting that as de Man reads him, Blanchot firmly rejects the very model of history Hartman used to interpret him. By implication, Hartman has missed the full force of Blanchot's thought. As de Man summarizes it, what Blanchot asserts in his reading of Mallarmé, but as it were against Mallarmé, is that "knowledge of the impossiblity of knowing precedes the act of consciousness that tries to reach it. This structure is a circular one." Yet the remembrance of this forgetting does not destroy Blanchot's impulse to produce literature; for though its circularity leads to repetition, Blanchot writes that "the development of what remains the same has infinite richness in its very repetition."

De Man suggests that "Blanchot is very close here to a philosophical trend which tries to rethink the notion of growth and development no longer in organic but in hermeneutic terms by reflecting on the temporality of the act of understanding." De Man refers here to Gadamer and especially to Heidegger, for whom Being is a self-concealment disclosed to man's consciousness precisely by his forgetting of Being. Criticism shows "how poetic language always reproduces this negative movement, though it is often not aware of it." The later Heidegger, de Man says, seems to believe that we could "assert our ontological insight in a positive way"; but for Blanchot, consciousness' movement of remembering and forgetting circles endlessly around an inaccessible center: "We are separated from it by the very substance of time, and we never cease to know that this is the case." Blanchot makes clear that it takes great effort to construct and hold oneself on this circle of lucid nothingness. The self which

begins in self-alienation returns to reflect on its own impossible, but inevitable situation. Blanchot thus turns "his conscious attention toward
himself, and not toward a forever unreachable form of being." And this
turn is a movement of self-interpretation, of self-reading. Thus the impossibility of an author's reading himself reverses itself into the peremp-
tory necessity for an author to read himself. The "askesis of depersonaliza-
tion" is an "extreme purification" which exposes "the truly temporal
dimensions of the text" in which there returns "a subject that, in fact,
never ceased to be present."

Within their shared emphasis on the "hermeneutic of the self," de
Man's Blanchot is clearly a more powerful and disturbing figure than
Hartman's. It is certainly unnerving to face the knowledge of the impossibility of knowledge without the self-protective ruses of progressive
temporality, whether of consciousness or of history. Yet a different Blanchot, perhaps even more subversive, might be drawn out of his writings
and occasionally intrudes even into the texts of Hartman and de Man.
Such an alternative interpretation can only be suggested here, but it would
begin with the claim that Blanchot's chief debt to Heidegger may be
methodological. When Heidegger undertook to raise the question of Being, he observed that the difficulty was just the commonness of Being.
Since everything simply "is," where should our inquiry begin? His answer
is neatly logical: begin with that being for which its Being is a question,
namely, human being, Dasein. Similarly, Blanchot inquires into
"writing," or more accurately, into the work of writing ("l'oeuvre").
But the nature of writing always conceals itself behind our concern with
whatever appears "in" writing. Blanchot therefore begins his inquiry with
those for whom writing is a question, namely, writers, whose very being
derives from their relation to writing. But a writer will be in quest of
this relation only when he is unable to write, not when he writes with
fluent mastery. Thus a writing which arises by a preserving reversal of
this inability will declare the nature of writing, a nature already glimpsed
in writing's concealment of its nature behind what appears "in" it. That
nature is withdrawal.[4]

Blanchot reaches the same conclusion in a parodic Hegelian narrative,
a "crude scheme" ("un schéma grossier") he turns against Hegel himself.
The work of verbal and written art appears first as the speech of the gods.
But as it becomes what precedes and is the condition of their manifestation, it comes to be the speech of their absence and becomes instead the
precise, balanced speech of Man. In the religious and cultural diversity
of late antiquity, the speech of "Man" becomes in turn the speech of
"Man's" absence, the speech of men in all their diversity, the speech
of what does not speak in "Man," but speaks man's dispossession from

his own essence and self-presence. In this history of withdrawal, writing ends with nothing left to say, so that the work ultimately becomes the speech of itself: "In the work which has disappeared, the work itself wishes to speak, and this experience becomes the quest for the essence of the work, becomes the affirmation of art, the concern for its origin" (*EL*, 314). Deprived of their traditional ends, suspicious of the connections, whether natural, rational, or conventional, established between their means and those ends, all the modern arts become ends and means at once in an attempt to establish themselves within a circular and contradictory movement.

In this conception of writing as withdrawal, the writer, whether a consciousness or a self, is of curiously little importance. The writer becomes a writer insofar as writing becomes its own source through him. A narrative or poetic image emerges not out of an exercise of the writer's will or possibilities, but as what is impossible for the writer's ordinary self. The necessity which compels the work of writing must arise from writing itself, from a conversion of the anonymity, the indeterminacy, the void opened by the withdrawal of writing into a necessity which compels writing. It would be possible to expand this rigorously "sublime" account of writing into something clearer and perhaps more persuasive. But my point is that Blanchot's interest is in writing, and writing emerges in relation only to itself, not to an artist, a consciousness, or a self. Years after *Being and Time* appeared, Heidegger came to regret his ingenious methodology, which had misled some readers into supposing his focus was on Dasein. He reasserted his interest purely in Being and repudiated any "humanism." Blanchot's focus on writing seems to me similarly ontological; even de Man's "self" in all its lucid evasions is relatively comforting compared to this austerity.

We can find traces of such an understanding of Blanchot in Hartman, for instance, in his earlier essay, when he says Blanchot's question concerns "the psychological origin and the psychological effect of art," but adds that this is a concern for what in the writer responds "to the immediacies of literature." The emphasis here ought to have fallen on "the immediacies of literature." In the same essay, he recognizes Blanchot's contention that in our post-Hegelian era, "art appears for the first time free of all personal, psychological, social, and similar 'immediate' values, being involved in a self-concentrated investigation of its own essence." But I think Hartman draws back from the full force of "its own" in order to focus on the situation of the artist. Similarly, de Man recognizes that "Blanchot expects us to understand the act of reading in terms of the work and not in terms of the constitutive subject, although he carefully avoids giving the work an objective status." But his conclusion brings us "back to the question of the subject." Though Blanchot asserts very plainly that writing withdraws the writer from his "being-in-the-world" and from the self correlated with world, de Man asserts that the writer "remains a self that must reflect on its own situation." He must, de Man says, turn "his conscious attention toward himself, and not toward a forever unreachable form of being." That the work of writing ("l'oeuvre") is an unreachable, impossible form of being Blanchot certainly agrees; but not, I think, that the writer must therefore "return toward a subject that, in fact, never ceased to be present." Against the sharp distinction de Man asserts between reader and author, one can set Blanchot's explicit statement, "Author and reader are on an equal footing in front of the work and in it" (*EL*, 307). What is essential here is Blanchot's version of the ontological difference: again, the work of writing ("l'oeuvre") withdraws behind the written work ("livre"), but this difference and this withdrawing are inscribed within writing from the beginning, in the "torn intimacy" ("intimité dechirée") which is the work's very being. The author cannot reread his work *as author*, for this would mean re-opening the space of writing, revising, adding to, or subtracting from the work (as Blanchot himself did with the second version of *Thomas l'Obscur*). In such a case, the work becomes something else. The exclusion of the author from his work means that the work has completed itself. This completion appears as the "torn intimacy" between the necessity of writing and the necessity of reading. The written work ("livre") "needs the reader in order to affirm itself a thing without author and also without reader" (*EL*, 257). "Literary reading" ("lecture littéraire") is not the exegesis which builds on acquired, in this case, historical knowledge, as Hartman does; nor is it a turning toward a self which was there all along, as de Man claims. For Blanchot, it is "au-delà ou en deçà de la compréhension," in the reader's entrance into the ontological difference which raises up the written work ("livre") to the work of writing ("l'oeuvre"), and thereby raises up the work of writing to being (*EL*, 261).

There is, however, an important truth in de Man's insight that Blanchot's criticism is a "preparatory version" of his narrative, though this somewhat misleading phrase undermines de Man's central thesis. Blanchot's double status as writer and reader is affirmed in every one of his books, without distinction. In his "critical" books, a "creative" writer submits himself to the impersonality, the self-effacement, demanded by criticism, a form of writing which seeks its necessity outside the critic. This submission echoes precisely that anonymity in which the writer seeks not what he "can" write by an exercise of his own powers, willful however masterful, but rather what he is compelled to write by a necessity arising from writing's own reversal of its withdrawal into a power. It is misleading to say that we here encounter "the general structure of all literary consciousness" or "the circular pattern that can be found in all acts of literary invention." Blanchot warns against the reader's "will to remain himself in front of what he reads, the will to be a man who knows how to read in general" (EL, 265).[5] The authority of Blanchot's writings does not rest on a claim either to provide or incarnate a general theory of literature, of reading and of writing; nor does it rest on an artist's "inside knowledge" of creative psychology. It rests simply on the existence of the whole body of his writings. It is this body as a body that de Man neglects.

If we take Blanchot seriously (and whether or how seriously we should take him remains an open question), we shall have to respond not to a historical tradition, nor to the situation of an artistic self, but to a corpus of texts. On his own terms, we should not try to understand these texts, but to possess them by dispossessing them of their language, restoring it to its inherent anonymity. This is the formula of what Harold Bloom calls "influence," and—to continue in Bloom's terms—only a writer as strong as Blanchot could open himself to Blanchot's influence. Because Jacques Derrida has accepted this risk, he has produced at once the least and the most evasive of the responses to Blanchot we will consider. At the invitation of Frédéric Nef, he contributed "Pas," part of which was published in an issue of the review *Gramma* devoted to Blanchot (1975). Overlapping with "Pas" at several points is "Living On· Border Lines," published in *Deconstruction and Criticism* (1979), and "The Law of Genre," published both in *Critical Inquiry* and *Glyph 7* in 1980. "Pas" is the most interesting and least accessible of these texts, and I shall concentrate on it.

Derrida describes it as fragmentary, indirect, unfinished, and as far as possible fictive, the "preamble" to a reply to Nef's invitation; in all these respects, it seems to draw near to Blanchot's text as a mimesis or simulacrum. The text begins with the word "Viens," "Come," an order to become present, an intimate, second-person singular imperative— and, it soon appears, a quotation from Blanchot's *L'Arrêt de mort*. If every word is a citation (a word that had never been and could never be repeated would arrest the exchange of language), if every word has invisible quotation marks around it, then what is the nature of this "speech event"? It is a speech event without speaker, addressee, or message, an event which names only itself, calls itself ("s'appeler") to be present. The arrival of this event, which does not occur, but re-curs, is re-cited in all of Blanchot's "ré-cits" (a uniquely French literary term I will leave untranslated). In citing and re-citing it here, Derrida enters into the movement of Blanchot's writing while remaining at a distance from it. The command immediately invokes an interlocutor, a woman whose sex is marked only by a few silent grammatical endings. Derrida's relation to Blanchot thus enters into the intimate distance of his relation to an "other," to speech itself ("la parole"). "There is 'language of the other' whenever there is a speech-event," Derrida writes. "This is what I mean by 'trace' " (*DC*, 149).[6]

What makes it possible to enter into such a relationship is the strange, supplementary logic of words—of "pas," for example. When Derrida wrote this text, Blanchot's latest book was *Le Pas au-delà* (1973). Is this "a step beyond," or does it assert there is "no beyond"? Or do invisible quotation marks surround the "pas" ("le 'pas' au-delà"), so that the word "pas" lies beyond—itself? By a "heterological inclusion" the word already comprises mutually cancelling meanings, and the invisible quotation marks erase the border between signifier and signified, making the word both at once (the word "word"). Titles establish no context sufficiently to produce the illusion of determinacy, so that Derrida can track "pas" through all of Blanchot's titles, from *Celui qui ne m'accompagnait pas* even to the word's phonic trace in *La Part du feu* and *L'Espace littéraire*. The doubling of irreconcilable, indeterminable, undecidable meanings in "pas" makes it a step not a step ("pas pas"), a doubling of negation ("ne . . . pas") as unsettling as the doubling of affirmation ("oui, oui"), which undermines the singularity, the uniqueness of truth. This is a step without a step ("pas sans pas"), a stepless step. Every word overflows itself unreservedly in just this way, erasing the boundaries between meanings, words, parts of speech, texts.

I do not intend to follow the whole course of Derrida's analysis. Suffice it to say that he is also concerned with the nature of narrative as a speech "event" which never "arrives." He proceeds in the by now orthodox manner of deconstruction to expose in a cluster of related words the untranslatable, undecidable, irresolvable linguistic transgression which occurs without metalanguage and undermines every fixed distinction, overflows every semantic or textual border, cancels all those logical and commonsensical principles by which our era pretends to limit the dissemination of "effects of meaning" (P, 146-47). The obvious question is what all this has to do with Blanchot: in what sense is this a "reading" of Blanchot's text? "If reading means making accessible a meaning that can be transmitted as such," Derrida observes, then everything in Blanchot is "unreadable" (*DC*, 116). "But this unreadability," he goes on, "does not arrest reading, does not leave it paralyzed in the face of an opaque surface: rather, it starts reading and writing and translation moving again." "Reading" here traces the open dissemination of language which traverses the "immense" corpus of Blanchot's writing (or that of any writer). The anonymous interlocutor of "Pas" objects to this procedure of citation, which extracts passages from a unique text, in order to lend them to new linkages, to shadows ("simulacres") of demonstration, to other shapes ("configurations"). But she then reverses this view with the realization that the texts lend themselves to these re-figurations, and indeed that doing so is what makes them readable in the very uniqueness of their place. If I may venture my own speculative fiction, I would say that Nef invited Derrida to "read" Blanchot, and to read himself in relation to Blanchot. At the time Derrida replied, *Le Pas au-delà* was Blanchot's most recent book. Derrida obligingly proceeds, in all bland innocence, backward, beginning with "pas," the first word of the latest book. But the reading itself, the "lecture," never arrives, remains distant from the text to which it is closest. He never arrives ("aborder"), because "pas" overflows ("deborder") into the whole corpus of Blanchot's writings. The reading of "pas" (reading of *Pas*, "lecture de pas") is therefore no reading ("pas de lecture"), a reading without reading ("lecture sans lecture"), which defines the rigorous logic of Derrida's evasion. "The part is always greater than the whole," he remarks (*DC*, 96; and see LG, 70-72). Every work contains "an internal pocket larger than the whole" (*DC*, 59).

Nor is the relation between Derrida's text and Blanchot's as simple even as this. For insofar as Derrida does not arrive at his reading of Blanchot and yet ceaselessly tries courteously to meet Nef's request, his situation mimes that of the narrator of Blanchot's récit *Celui qui ne m'accompagnait pas*. Hartman translates its opening line, "I tried, this time, to approach him directly" ("je cherchai, cette fois, à l'aborder"; translated somewhat differently, *DC*, 83), and observes that every word is subjected to a subversive questioning which moves the récit forward: who is the narrator? who is his companion? when does the récit take place? We can only conclude that "the narrator is the one who narrates, his companion someone inseparable from the act of narration, time and space simply that of narration itself." This is precisely the form of Derrida's text "Pas." Hartman observes of Blanchot that, though the end of this questioning leaves us "with as little as we started with, it does make the *void* of thought visible as the *space* of art," which appears as "an effort of distance, as if the writer were constantly in danger of being tricked by the nature of words or crushed by some endless automatic process of mind murmur, of mental conjunction." In Derrida's own words, "Each 'text' is a machine with multiple reading heads for other texts" (*DC*, 107). "Reading" means that Derrida's relation to Blanchot emerges into the space opened by his relation to his own text, a relation opened in turn (from the initial quoted "viens") by Blanchot (Derrida learned to read "grâce à lui"). Where "Pas" opens into a strange internal dialogue, "Living On · Border Lines" doubles Shelley's *Triumph of Life* with two récits by Blanchot and then redoubles with a marginal text beneath.

The undecidable interplay of intimacy and distance in reading is nowhere more acute than in the issue of quotation. I have already quoted one objection by Derrida's interlocutor to quotation's power to disrupt the uniqueness of the quoted text. Here is another: "Nothing more vulgar and slavish, indiscreet, unnamable than the gams in which to quote, extract, teach, one generalizes the diverting, one thinks one appropriates to oneself the unique."[7] Derrida replies that Blanchot has refused this "non-secret," having striven instead for an anonymity which renounces the property rights held by a signature, and at the same time renounces lecturing, teaching, generality. Derrida rejects "the entire conventional system of legalities that organizes, in literature, the framed unity of the corpus," sealed by the author's signature (*DC* 142; cf. *DC*, 101-2 and LG, 66). Derrida quotes from Blanchot, then asks,

> Shall we leave this text on its own power?
> We should neither comment, nor underscore a single word, nor extract anything, nor draw a lesson from it. One should not, one should refrain from— such would be the law of the text that gives itself, gives itself up, to be read [qui se donne à lire]. Yet it also calls for a violence that matches it in intensity, a violence different in intention, perhaps, but one that exerts itself against the first law only in order to attempt a commitment, an involvement, with that law. To move, yieldingly, towards it, to draw close to it fictively. The violent truth of "reading." (*DC*, 152)

In "Pas," the interlocutor accuses Derrida of bringing out with heavy-handed explicitness what is discretely left to chance in Blanchot's text. And Derrida admits his prepossession for rubbing out by indiscretion, for a withdrawing ("retrait") that steals away from coming again on the traces of the other ("se dérobant à repasser sur le trait de l' autre," P, 147-148). One might translate more periphrastically here, and suggest that Derrida by his very indiscretion is trying not merely to follow in Blanchot's footsteps. Derrida is challenging the law which governs all schools of reading. And yet, though Blanchot's renunciation of private claims on his discourse authorizes a commentary which "uses" him without reserve, the profoundest expropriation would be mere quotation. The very borders which put Blanchot's text "beyond" Derrida's are thus undermined: "Rather than accompany such a text with a commentary it passes by, like every other, as surely as it requires it, I will read it slowly, underlining here and there" (P, 171). The words quoted may be Blanchot's, but in his quest for impersonality Blanchot has uncompromisingly withdrawn himself from his own signature and withdrawn himself equally from the confusion of the writer with that person whose possession of writing is established by the legal system. And even in a quotation which does not underline, which changes nothing, which cites an author "totally," the "total" would be missing, for this total includes the text's limitless potential for re-citation. Both "Living On · Border Lines" and "Pas" end by transcribing large portions of texts by Blanchot. "Pas" is doubly interesting because it uses *Thomas l'Obscur*, Blanchot's first novel and the only one he revised, shortening it into a récit and thus implicitly revealing what was before the novel actually published earlier. This reversal of earlier and later permits Blanchot, as it were, to begin his career again already at a later stage. I would concede we are told we have only part of the text Derrida actually wrote (assuming we know what a "part" is), but the whole of "Pas" may be seen as positioning the reader now to read this quotation from Blanchot so completely through Derrida's eyes that it becomes Derrida's own writing (just as Blanchot himself re-wrote *Thomas l'Obscur* as though he had written the later version earlier). Even more extreme than pure quotation, if that is possible, are those bare imperatives in "Pas," addressed perhaps to the reader, perhaps to Derrida's nameless interlocutor, and thus to his own text, "read," "lis . . ." (P, 209, 212, etc.)

The name which emerges in "Pas" for this interplay of possession and dispossession, of intimacy and distance is friendship. When Derrida says "tu" (or quotes it), his interlocutor asks, "do you dare tutoyer Blanchot?" (P, 119) She is equally shocked when he quotes from *L'Amitié*, a work which should be "sealed by the absolute uniqueness of a lonely friendship, that of Maurice Blanchot and Georges Bataille" (P, 157). Derrida recognizes his presumption, the blunder of making intimacy seem possible, even though he adds that all of Blanchot could be read "as a patient and endless meditation on saying 'tu' " (P, 119).[8] He admits that his "reading" indiscreetly makes visible what is disseminated or left to chance in Blanchot. But he defends himself with the observation that Blanchot's text

unchains the law of absolute discretion, pushes it ahead with the most intractable rigor and on its own turf ravishes it with an obscenity beyond measure. But to surprise his indiscretion with just that indiscretion which would remain impossible for him, this would be to dwell still, within friendship, beneath the law of the other, the sole sign of friendship, but as if effaced in advance. (P, 143)

Late in the text, the interlocutor remarks, "I always have the feeling that you speak to me in his name, since his name, within his name" (P, 208). "A language can never be appropriated," Derrida writes; "it is mine only as the language of the other, and vice versa" (*DC*, 154-55).

It is not clear whether Derrida's "friendship" can be assimilated to Harold Bloom's "influence," but I believe it can. I have no intention of applying to Derrida Bloom's "map of misreading," partly because that sequence of defenses, tropes, images, or revisionary ratios was developed in the specific context of post-Enlightenment English lyric, partly because this tentative connection should be left supple, rather than prematurely hardened. What will count here is how Bloom can help us see that Derrida's response to Blanchot precisely in its evasiveness may be more faithful than either Hartman's or de Man's. Even more than with Hartman or de Man, Derrida leaves a reader undecided whether he should read with an eye to Blanchot or to Derrida. Instead of an authoritative exposition, we have an idiosyncratic re-figuration. But the intricacy and depth of Derrida's response reopens with an energy that will not easily be damped the question of Blanchot himself: what is the significance and the continuing power of his writing?

NOTES

1. "Symbolic Landscape in Wordsworth and Yeats."

2. My translations throughout from "Pas" (P).

3. For Hartman's studies of "word-consciousness," see "The Voice of the Shuttle: Language from the Point of View of Literature," *BF*, 337-55; as the issue relates to critical language, *CW*, *passim*; and "Words and Wounds," in *ST*, pp. 118-57.

4. Blanchot presents his theory repeatedly throughout his works, but my remarks here focus chiefly on *L'Espace littéraire* (1955), which I cite in the "Collections Idées" edition (Paris: Gallimard NRF, 1968). Further citations in the text will give *EL* and page number.

5. In *LG* Derrida analyzes a text by Blanchot in the course of discussing "genre." But though he thus limits himself, he claims to exclude nothing, "the relationships here no longer being those of extension, from exemplary individual to species, from species to genre as genus or from the genre of genre to genre in general; rather, as we shall see, these relationships are a whole order apart. What is at stake, in effect, is exemplarity and its whole *enigma*—in other words, as the word 'enigma' indicates, exemplarity and the *récit*—which works through the logic of the example" (LG, 59). At the end of the same essay, he denies that Blanchot's narrative is "exemplary" of any general trait or any general or generic whole. It is "wholly counter-exemplary," undermining all the orders of thought which have been based on genre (LG, 81). Although Derrida here "uses" Blanchot as an example in a more restricted way than in his other two essays on Blanchot, his awareness of the issue of exemplarity makes me doubt his issue is subject to the strictures I here raise against de Man's.

6. "The Law of Genre" allows us to elaborate this feminine interlocutor. Reading Blanchot's *La Folie du jour*, Derrida remarks "the first and surely most impossible word" of the narrative, "I." Opposed to the marked and colored "narrational voice" with which, for example, "point of view" analysis is concerned, is what Blanchot calls the "narrative voice," peculiarly neutral (cf. *DC*, 104); or as Derrida says, "the 'I'-less 'I' of the narrative voice, the I 'stripped' of itself, the one that does not take place" (LG, 77). In *La Folie du jour*, the "I" "does not take place" in the sense that it is unable and refuses to recite its "story," to situate itself in relation to and as possessor of its narrated experience, and thus "says 'I' " but "does not manage to say 'I' " (LG, 68). Throughout Blanchot's narrative work, this "I" which does not accompany itself, achieves "a

neutral genre/gender," whose neutrality is not "*negative* (neither . . . nor), nor dialectical, but affirmative, and doubly affirmative (or . . . or)" (LG, 74). The "I" doubles into "a 'female element,' which does not signify a female person" (LG, 78). This "female element" comprises a series of terms: speech ("la parole"), thought ("la pensée"), truth ("la vérité"), voice ("la voix," especially narrative voice), law ("la loi"). This double of the "I" is an "effect of his desire, child of his affirmation, of the genre 'I' clasped in a specular couple with 'me' " (LG, 78), the figure of the law of genre/gender "who, throughout an account [un récit], forms a couple with me, with the 'I' of the narrative voice" (LG, 77). We therefore have "an I/we couple" (LG, 78). This line of thought may clarify not only the "I/Thou" relationship within Derrida's text, but the "I/Thou" relationship between Derrida and Blanchot, or more accurately, between Derrida's text and Blanchot's, which is the precondition of the genre "commentary" or "interpretation." Needless to say, Derrida would regard this textual relation as a structure of double invagination (effected through quotation or re-citation) reduplicating the one he finds in Blanchot's narrative *La Folie du jour* (see LG, 70-71 on double invagination; or *DC*, 94-103, which repeats LG in miniature form).

7. Derrida's diction and word plays complicate the translator's task, of course. "Gam" comes from *Moby-Dick* and names the exchange of letters and news by ships meeting at sea; Derrida's word is "arraisonement," a nautical term for hailing a ship or inspecting its papers.

8. Later, Derrida says it is possible "tutoyer sans dire toi" and "dire toi sans tutoyer," a distinction perhaps not entirely convincing.

Joining the Text:
From Heidegger to Derrida
Rodolphe Gasché

But because the word is shown in a different, higher rule, the relation to the word must also undergo a transformation. Saying attains to a different articulation, a different melos, *a different tone.*

Heidegger

In an article entitled "The *Retrait* of Metaphor," Jacques Derrida argues that within a certain context (but only in the limits of this context), the French word *retrait* is "the most proper to capture the greatest quantity of energy and information in the Heideggerian text." *Retrait*, having a variety of meanings in French like retrace, withdrawal, recess, retraction, retreat, etc., translates (without translating) Heidegger's notion of a withdrawal of Being (*Entziehung, Entzug*).[1] If this word became indispensable to Derrida when trying to account for Martin Heidegger's statements on metaphor, it becomes indispensable to me as well when trying to assess, in as economic a way as possible, the nature of the relation between Heidegger and Derrida. Considering that the very nature of this relation is far from obvious, and that even the discursive levels of such a comparison of these two philosophers have still to be determined, the Heideggerian notions of trait (*Zug*) and retrait (*Entzug*) promise perhaps the most effective treatment of this relation. Let us then attempt to understand how the word *retrait* (*Zug-Entzug*) structures Heidegger's text, as well as the text of Derrida's exchange with Heidegger.

In the first place, what is a trait or a *retrait*? The trait is *retrait*, the trait is withdrawn, writes Derrida: It signifies an "essential and in itself double, equivocal movement" (RM, 22). But what are the different moments that characterize this essentially plural word? Let us try to account for these moments in a stepwise fashion so that the reasoning will be quite clear.

First of all, the word trait (*Zug*) refers to the tracing of a way or a rift (*Riss*) which, as an in-between (*Zwischen*), opens a first relation (*Bezug*). The trait accomplishes the differential mark that allows language to name and to put into relation what it names. Yet, the trait is nothing before the tracing it achieves or before what it subsequently brings into relation. The trait is not independent of what it permits to come into its own.

Second, the trait withdraws, retreats, in the very act of its tracing an in-between for a relation. However, being nothing except what it gives rise to, the trait is not to be mistaken for the results of what it brings forth. Indeed, "the trait is, *a priori, retrait*, i.e., unappearance, and effacement of its mark in its incision." The trait comes forth only by being blotted out. It "*succeeds only in being effaced (n'arrive qu'à s'effacer).*" "The *re-* of *retrait* is not an accident occuring to the trait" (RM, 29). On the contrary, this self-eclipsing of the forthcoming trait characterizes its double and equivocal movement.

Third, the trait cannot simply be identified with this seemingly alternating movement of forthcoming and subsequent extinction, because the retreat of the trait is also what allows the trait to come forward from under its obliteration as *retrait*. Without a retreat of the *retrait*, without a *retrait* of the *retrait*, the trait would not be capable of tracing its self-eclipsing way or opening in the first place. Derrida writes:

"The trait of the incision is . . . veiled, withdrawn, but it is also the trait that brings together and separates (*écarte*) at once the veiling *and* the unveiling, the *withdrawal* and the *withdrawal of the withdrawal*" (RM, 31).

The trait is always *retrait*, withdrawal. But this withdrawal of the trait operates not according to a simple structure of ambiguity in a well equilibrated exchange of opposing meanings, it takes place in an essentially dissymmetric manner. The *re-* of the *retrait* is double as it accounts for both the veiling and the unveiling of the trait. Because the *re-* of the trait as *retrait* dominates its structure, its movements are fundamentally dissymmetric. Derrida emphasizes this dissymmetry when ascertaining that the trait "withdraws *itself* (*se retire*) but the ipseity of the pronominal *se* (itself) by which it would be related to itself with a trait or line does not precede it and already supposes a supplementary trait in order to be traced, signed, withdrawn, retraced in its turn" (RM, 33). The trait does not affect or reflect itself into an identity. Because such a reflection presupposes the supplementary trait which is being brought forth by the trait's withdrawal, the trait is barred forever from itself.

Yet, to what does the word "trait" (and the movements that characterize it) refer in Heidegger's work? As I have tried to argue elsewhere,[2] the word trait gathers Heidegger's most radical developments on Being *as* Being. The question of Being is a question which concerns Being *as such*, the meaning or the truth of Being as never explicitly reflected upon in the history of Western metaphysics. Indeed, Western philosophy, as onto-theo-logy, has always determined Being in terms of what is (*Seiendes*), i.e., as just another, although higher being in the chain of beings. It has thus eluded the question of the ontico-ontological difference, the difference of Being and beings, of Being *as* Being. Contrary to what one may be inclined to think, the question of Being is not just one more philosophical question in a process of escalating abstraction. As a question concerning the ontico-ontological difference itself, it is, rather in a strange way, the last possible *question*.[3] With the insight that metaphysics presupposes the difference of Being and beings without, however, being able to think Being other than just another, although higher, being (as God, the Spirit, etc.), the ontico-ontological difference becomes thematized as such. As the question of the meaning of Being, of Being as Being, this thematization of the difference of Being and beings becomes an interrogation of the very opposition and hierarchy of what constitutes the traditional dyad. Thus the effort to think the meaning of Being as the ontico-ontological difference itself is to think on an altogether different level than the onto-theo-logical determination of Being as an infinite being reigning over all finite beings. With the question of Being as a question of difference as such, notions like opposition and hierarchy cease to be leading categories. The same is true of such dyads as the abstract and the concrete, the universal and the particular, infinity and finitude. As an inquiry into the difference of Being and beings, the question of Being demonstrates the essential finitude of infinity (God as always another, only higher, being) and thus questions its hierarchical status as well as the nature of its difference from finite beings. The question of Being is thus the question of finitude *par excellence*, precisely because it is an investigation into the ontico-ontological difference. Heidegger's subsequent determination of Being in terms of temporality and historicity (*Geschichtlichkeit*), i.e., in terms of finitude, is only a consequence of this inquiry into the difference itself.[4] As difference, as *Unter-Schied* (as Heidegger will later spell this word), the meaning of Being or Being *as such* is, then, radically different from a romantic chiasm as an endlessly engendering and procreating gap, as well as from any constituting transcendental in both a Kantian or Husserlian fashion. The rift of Being (*Fuge des Seins*), instead of *engendering*, finitizes everything that is to be referred to it as to the locus of its coming forth.[5]

This being established, it becomes possible to indicate in which way Heidegger's most penetrating meditations on Being *as* Being culminate in the idea of the trait. Instead of representing a mere weakness of Western thought, says Heidegger, the obliteration of the question of Being is inscribed in the original event (*Ereignis*), at the dawn of Western metaphysics itself. This event is characterized by the fact that Being originally revealed itself only to instantly withdraw again. The forgetting of Being is, consequently, the very destiny of Being (*Geschick des Seins*). However, this forgetting of Being characteristic of Western man, brings about the danger of a growing alienation from that destiny itself. Hence the necessity of a *step back* in a gesture comparable to Nietzsche's *active forgetfulness*, so that this withdrawal may lift again the original retreat of Being at the moment of its revelation. Such a stepping back, such a withdrawal of withdrawal, is no reflection, as if the original event was something that could be objectified by a subject. It is what Heidegger calls a *Besinnung* or an *Andenken* which allows for the return of the forgotten. Consequently, the question of Being yields to the "double, equivocal movement," or, more precisely, to the threefold movement that distinguishes the "logic" of the trait.

But as the forgetting of Being is decreed by Being itself, and as the step back coincides with a listening to Being (*hören auf*), to think the history of the forgetting of Being, as well as to inaugurate a *destruction* of the tradition of this forgetting by Western philosophy, is to think Being as such. And Being as such appears to be "nothing" but this essentially double movement of its dissimulating disclosure and of its return through a step back.

After this all too succinct presentation of Heidegger's question of Being as the question of the trait, let us linger, nevertheless, for a moment upon "The Anaximanderfragment." In this text, which commonly has been misunderstood as a return to a very traditional notion of beginning (since this fragment is considered to be the oldest of Western thinking), Heidegger, with an increasing acuteness of vision, risks the statement that Being revealed itself at the origin of Western thought as, precisely, this trait of Being.[6] If Being disclosed itself in a gesture of simultaneous dissimulation, it is only because Being is the same as the trait as *retrait*. Indeed, in its greatest simplicity, Being coincides with the trait of *A-letheia* (truth) wherein the movement of *retrait* is greatest in the very disclosure of Being. But since Being is "nothing" but this trait itself, Being is, then, the trait folded back in the very moment of its coming forth, a folding back which simultaneously lifts again the veil of the initial concealment. Being-*as*-trait—Being-*as*-*retrait*. For being, what lifts concealment by concealment and what is simultaneously revealed in concealment, Being-*as*-trait is a trait dissimilar to itself, in which the thrust to disclosure never equals the pulling back into retreat.

Because of this fundamental dissymmetry one may want to call the trait non-reflexive. Indeed, it will never coincide with itself, for the *re-* of the trait as *retrait* is always in excess over any possible identity. But to talk here of reflexivity is short-sighted insofar as reflexivity is a function of a subject-object relation constitutive of self-consciousness.[7] The "logic" of the trait, however, precedes and governs all reduction of Being to objectivity and its subjection to a non-mundane subject of cognition. The trait is in excess over all self-affection which itself is the condition of possiblity for self-reflection. For reasons of strategy, however, and within the limits of this context, I will call non-reflexive this lack of self-coincidence of the trait.

By determining the meaning of truth as Being as the trait of Being, Heidegger's question concerning Being *as* Being (*ens tanquam verum*) appears to be an inquiry into the very structure of thinking and understanding. In his lectures on "Logic. The Question of Truth," given during the Winter semester 1925/26 in Freiburg, and which represent an attempt to approach the essence of language, Heidegger determined the primary structure of understanding as the as-structure (*Als-Struktur*).[8] Yet, the question of Being, as a question concerning Being *as such*—the *tanquam* of the *ens tanquam verum*—is "nothing else" but an inquiry into the structure of the *as* as such. In other words, the structure of Being as trait is the *same* as the structure of primary understanding. Thus, the question of Being as the question of the trait coinciding with the structure of thinking leads to a determination of the as-structure as the differential and non-reflexive instance of language. The question of Being and the question of analogy are the same.[9]

However, with the question of Being turning into a question of the *tanquam*, into a question of the smallest philosophical operator, it becomes possible to ascertain that Heidegger's notion of Being and Derrida's notion of text are akin. If the structure of Being is understood according to the "logic" of the trait, Being and text appear to be words that can be exchanged and substituted for one another. The Derridean word *text* is a translation (without translation) of the Heideggerian word *Being*.[10]

By affirming the similarity of Heidegger's notion of Being and Derrida's notion of text, one immediately excludes a variety of definitions of textuality. No doubt, Derrida's notion of text does not refer to the colloquial understanding of the text as a sensible and palpable corpus to be encountered in empirical experience. It also leaves little doubt that Derrida's notion of text cannot be equated with either an intelligible or ideal definition (the text as the entire sum of all the connections between the differential features of the linguistic signs that form a text) or with a dialectical concept according to which the text as "form" would sublate both its sensible and intelligible components. On the contrary, like the notion of Being, the notion of the text, as it is employed by Derrida, is *rather* the result of a transcendental experience following the systematic bracketing of all the regions of natural (and even eidetic) experience. Not having been obtained through a factual or regional experience, and, thus, having little in common with the object of linguistic or literary studies, the notion of text in Derrida is a *sort of* transcendental concept. Vincent Descombes rightly remarks that Derrida "refers to a *general* experience," "the experience of the *universal* text," i.e., not to a particular and, thus, empirical experience.[11] Yet precisely because this general experience is the experience of a non-philosophical (because non-present) thought, the thinking of this experience does escape not only empiricism, but "philosophical empiricism" as well, as Descombes notes. But then it becomes, strictly speaking, impossible to call such an experience a general, universal, or transcendental experience. And, as a corollary, the object of such an experience cannot claim to any universality either. The transcendental experience of the text is, indeed, neither the experience of a universal and eidetic *object* nor simply a repetition of a *transcendental experience* in either a Kantian or Husserlian sense. The transcendental gesture in Derrida simultaneously serves to escape the danger of naive objectivism and the value of transcendentality itself. In *Of Grammatology*, Derrida has clearly stated that the thought of the trace, and consequently of the text, can no more "break with a transcendental phenomenology than be reduced to it" (*G*, 62). The notion of text, as already in the Heideggerian notion of Being, literally "occupies" the locus of the transcendental concept, which is to say that the former is not identical with the latter. The text, like the trace, is to be understood as a pathway (*parcours*) through that locality. Thus, the notion of the text corresponds to a transformation of the transcendental concept and of the very locus that it represents. The text is certainly no eidetic object. It has no constitutive function. It is not an *a priori* condition of possibility for, let us say, signification and meaning. (Nor is it, let us add, a chiasm of engenderment and destruction, precisely because of its structure as a chiasmatic *invagination*).[12] Thus, it needs to be emphasized that the notion of text in Derrida can be understood only if one is aware of its function and effects with regard to the transcendental.[13]

Only on this background will it be possible to proceed to outlining the concrete resemblances of Being and text, and to evaluating the specific philosophical problems both notions are addressing. One will certainly not be surprised to learn that this demonstration hinges on Derrida's reading of Mallarmé's textual practice. But before unfolding Derrida's notion of text and textuality, let us briefly question the reasons that make it possible to introduce Mallarmé and his writings in this particular context. The point I will try to make is—and this may come as a surprise to both the philosopher and the literary critic—that the notion of text developed by Mallarmé is a non-empirical concept and operates in the realm of what one calls the transcendental. Moreover, Mallarmé anticipated some of Heidegger's major insights. Instead of a detailed demonstration, let us consider only the last paragraphs of Mallarmé's "Notes sur le théatre." Toward the end of this essay, Mallarmé ascertains that for him who has mediated about men and about himself, there is nothing else in the mind but "un compte rendu de purs motifs rythmiques de l'être, qui en sont les reconnaissables signes."[14] For Mallarmé then, as for Heidegger, Being is neither substance nor form. It is rhythm. Mallarmé evokes the purely rhythmical motives of Being; Heidegger speaks of "the domain pulsating in itself (*in sich schwingender Bereich*)," of "the moving wave (*bewegende Woge*), of language as "the all-containing undulation (*alles verhaltende Schwingung*)," etc.[15] Both mean by rhythm an ordered and recurrent alternation. Both evoke what was considered, until Emile Benvéniste's essay "La notion de 'rythme' dans son expression linguistique," its etymological root: *rein* (the regular flow of waves). But both Mallarmé and Heidegger also refer to the genuinely Greek meaning of rhythm as the well-proportioned arrangements of parts in a whole. Heidegger writes:

"Rhythm, *rhusmos*, does not mean flux and flowing, but rather form (*Fügung*). Rhythm is what is at rest, what forms (*fügt*) the movement of dance and song, and thus lets it rest within itself. Rhythm bestows rest."[16]

This meaning of *rhuthmos* or *rhusmos*, which, as Benvéniste has argued, dates back to the inventors of atomism, to Democritus and Leucippus, is equivalent to *schema*, and approximately signifies something like "form," configuration, disposition. In the same way as Mallarmé claims to have discovered purely rhythmical motives of Being by meditating on himself and others, the Greeks employed *rhuthmos* to designate the individually distinctive "form" of the human character.[17] As Heidegger has stressed in his seminar on Heraclitus (1966), this meaning of rhythm as "form" implies a determination of "form" as imprint, seal and character.[18] Yet, precisely this meaning of rhythm is to be found in what Mallarmé calls *sceau, moule, coupe*, etc. Let us quote one example of Being as a mold, drawn from "Solennité."

Signe! au gouffre central d'une spirituelle impossibilité que rien soit exclusivement à tout, le numérateur divin de notre apothéose, quelque suprême moule qui n'ayant pas lieu en tant que d'aucun objet qui existe: mais il emprunte, pour y aviver un sceau tous gisements épars, ignorés et flottants selon quelque richesse, et les forger.[19]

Because the supreme mold to which Mallarmé refers does not take place insofar as that of any existing object—because this mold, consequently, does not exist in the same way as the existing objects (because it does *not take place* altogether)—it is then, like the essence, the truth or meaning of Being, no longer of the order of what is present, i.e., just another being. Like Being, the supreme mold withholds itself in what springs forth from it.

Mallarmé likes to decipher the visible signs of Being as rhythm (*il me plaît de les partout déchiffrer*). These signs of Being as rhythm are to be discovered in what Mallarmé designates as "great traits." At the end of "Notes sur le théâtre", we read:

Tenez que hors du récit fait à l'imitation de la vie confuse et vaste, il n'y pas de moyen de poser scéniquement une action, sauf à retrouver d'instinct et par élimination un de ces grands traits, ici non le moins pathétique, c'est l'éternel retour de l'exilé, coeur gonflé d'espoir, au sol par lui quitté mais changé ingrat, maintenant quelconque au point qu'il en doive partir cette fois volontairement, où! en enveloppant d'un coup d'oeil les illusions suggérés à sa jeunesse par le salut du lieu natal.[20]

What then is a "great trait," which as a sign of Being as rhythm, makes it possible to stage an action that does not coincide with any mimetic representation of the turmoils of life? As the quoted passage suggests, Mallarmé detects such a non- or pre-mimetic trait in the (rhythmical) motive of the eternal return of the exiled to a homeland that has become so unaccommodating that he will, this time, leave it voluntarily. The return to the homeland, following an exile and preceding another, characterizes this sequence of events as yielding to the double or threefold "logic" of the trait as *retrait*. As a sign of Being, Mallarmé's great trait corresponds to Heidegger's notion of Being as *Zug* and *Entzug*.

In short, then, both Mallarmé and Heidegger understand Being as no longer to be predicated in terms of being (and beings).[21] Both make an attempt at determining the nature of Being as *don* or *Gabe*, as gift, as an allowing to come forth of what, according to the repetitive and temporal structure of the *rhuthmos*, is folded back in the very moment of its coming forth into presence. With this information at hand, it is possible to infer the concrete similarities between Heidegger's question of Being and Derrida's notion of text. To demonstrate what may already appear as an identity, I will limit myself to a most concise analysis of Derrida's "La double Séance."

In this essay, Derrida establishes that a text like Mallarmé's "Mimique" deconstructs the platonic values of truth and reference of mimesis as subject to these values. If "Mimique" does not simply invert the platonic hierarchy between the original and the copy, mimetic art and the discourse of truth, but undertakes a genuine deconstruction of these values as well as of the very idea of hierarchy, it is not because "Mimique" would be characterized by what is called literariness since the Russian Formalists, but because it is a text in a very particular way. In what follows, I will try to determine in as precise a manner as possible this particular notion of textuality—what I will from now on call the textual instance. According to Derrida, the subjection of mimesis to a horizon of truth is radically displaced at the moment when writing marks and doubles in a certain syntactical operation the marks of the text by means of an undecidable trait. "This double mark escapes the pertinence or authority of truth: it does not overturn it but rather inscribes it within its play as one of its functions or parts" (220).[22] In the context of "La double Séance," the textual mark is determined as a double mark or *re-mark*. But what is a re-mark?

Because "Mimique" does not abolish the differential structure of mimesis in spite of its deconstruction of the platonic distinctions, it is a simulacrum of platonism. "Mimique" achieves such a simulacrum not only by means of an extraordinary formal and syntactical *tour de force*, but on the thematic level as well. The event narrated by the mime of "Mimique" is a hymen, the marriage of Pierrot and Columbine. This marriage culminates in Pierrot's subsequent assassination of his wife by tickling her to death (that is to say, by means of a perfect crime which leaves no traces), and on Pierrot's final death in front of the laughing portrait of his victim (a death which will not show any traces either). The two deaths, resulting from an orgastic spasm, represent Pierrot's and Columbine's consummation of their marriage. The miming of this event in which nothing has taken place exhibits the textual structure of Mallarmé's "Mimique." "It is a dramatization which illustrates nothing, which illustrates the *nothing*, lights up a space, re-marks a spacing as nothing, a blank: white as a yet unwritten page, blank as a difference between two lines" (236-237). Yet, this dramatization is nothing but a staging of the theatrical space itself. What remains when the stage comes to double the stage, when the mimed hymen is nothing but an illustration of the theatrical space itself, i.e., a miming of miming, without referent, a miming that mimes only reference, is what Mallarmé calls "the pure milieu, of fiction," a "perpetual allusion without breaking the mirror."

A hymen, at first, names the fusion of two during the consummation of marriage. It signifies the abolition of difference between desire and satisfaction. Moreover, it leads to the suppression of the difference between image and thing, empty signifier and the signified, imitation and the imitated. It leads to a complete confusion of exteriority and interiority. The hymen in Mallarmé's writing produces "the effect of a medium. . . . It is an operation that *both* sows confusion *between* opposites *and* stands *between* the opposites 'at once.' What counts here is the *between*, the in-between-ness of the hymen" (240).

But second, for Mallarmé, "the hymen, the consummation of differends, the continuity and confusion of the coitus, merges with what it seems to be derived from: the hymen as protective screen, the jewel-box of virginity, the vaginal partition, the fine, invisible veil which, in front of the hystera, stands *between* the inside and the outside of the woman, and consequently between desire and fulfillment" (241). Derrida can, thus, conclude that "with all the undecidability of its meaning, the hymen only takes place when it doesn't take place, when nothing *really* happens, when there is an all-consuming consummation without violence, or a violence without blows, or a blow without marks, a mark without a mark (a margin), etc., when the veil is, *without being*, torn, for example when one is made to die or come laughing" (241). The manner in which the double structure of the hymen relates to itself is that of a reflection without penetration: "The *entre* of the hymen is reflected in the screen without penetrating it" (244). This reflection without penetration, this doubling without overlaying or overlapping of the hymen, this is what constitutes, as the fictional milieu of Mallarmé's "Mimique," the textual mark as a remark.

If the mime of "Mimique" only imitates imitation, if he copies only copying, all he produces is a copy of a copy. In the same manner, the hymen that comes to illustrate the theatrical space reduplicates nothing but the miming of the mime. Miming only reference, but not a particular referent, Mallarmé keeps the platonic differential structure of mimesis intact while at once radically displacing it. Instead of imitating, of referring to a referent within the horizon of truth, the mime mimes only other signs and their referring function. Signs in the text of "Mimique" are made to refer to what according to metaphysics is only derived, unreal, unpresent, i.e., to other signs. Such a doubling of the sign, of a sign referring to another sign and to its function of referring, is what Derrida calls re-marking.

The copy of a copy, a simulacrum that simulates the Platonic simulacrum, the Platonic copy of a copy . . . , have all lost here the lure of the present referent and thus find themselves lost for dialectics and ontology, lost for absolute knowledge. (248)

This double sign, a sign referring to another sign, reflecting itself in it without penetrating it and without overlaying it, is *the* textual instance. The operation and re-marking that constitutes it is an operation by which what traditionally was conceived of as a mark for a present referent becomes duplicated and refers, not to itself, but to something similar to it, another mark. This re-marking of the platonic simulacrum—a scandal in the horizon of truth—gives rise to a *tertium quid*. "*Tertium datur*, without synthesis," writes Derrida (249). It is the textual instance, no longer to be conceived of as yielding to the platonic opposition of copy and original, but as a genuinely third entity.

The textual instance as illustrated by the hymen as a re-mark, as a reflection without penetration, as a duplication without identity, escapes and precedes all ontology of the text. All ontologies of the text, whether they determine text in terms of the sensible, the intelligible, or dialectically as form, remain within the horizon of metaphysics and its platonic notion of a mimesis subject to truth. The textual instance, on the contrary, as a mimesis of mimesis, as a hymen between mimesis and mimesis, appears as no longer contained in the process of truth. Instead, it is the horizon of truth that is inscribed in textual mimesis. Only an act of violence, either arbitrary or conventional, can make the textual mark signify a referent.

The reason why only violence can transform the textual instance into a platonic sign or simulacrum, into a sign signifying a referent, lies in the particular nature of the re-mark's undecidability. Note that what Derrida calls the undecidable is called so only "provisionally, analogically" (240). He writes:

"Undecidability" is not caused here by some enigmatic equivocality, some inexhaustible ambivalence of a word in a "natural" language, and still less by some "*Gegensinn der Urworte*" (Abel). In dealing here with *hymen*, it is not a matter of repeating what Hegel undertook to do with German words . . . marveling over that lucky accident that installs a natural language within the element of speculative dialectics. What counts here is not the lexical richness, the semantic infiniteness of a word or concept, its depth or breadth, the sedimentation that has produced inside it two contradictory layers of signification . . . What counts here is the formal or syntactical *praxis* that composes and decomposes it. . . . [A word like hymen] produces its effect first and foremost through the syntax, which disposes the "*entre*" in such a way that the suspense is due only to the placement and not to the content of the words. Through the "hymen" one can remark only what the place of the *entre* already marks and would mark even if the word "hymen" were not there. (249-250)

As Aristotle already demonstrated, semantic ambiguity can always be sublated or dissolved in a polysemic unity of meaning. Yet, the undecidability of the textual instance does not spring from any semantic richness, but from "the irreducible excess of the syntactic over the semantic." The syntactic in question can be either " 'internal,' articulating and combining under the same yoke . . . two incompatible meanings, or 'external,' dependent on the code in which the word is made to function. But the syntactical composition and decomposition of a sign renders this alternative between internal and external inoperative" (250). From everything seen up to this point, it is obvious that a word like "hymen" has a very specific relation to writing and the text. However, if it doubles the text in Mallarmé's "Mimique," if it re-marks its textuality, it is not because it would be a totalizing emblem which, like the romantic image, would assume the eschatological function of subduing a text to having its meaning in reflecting itself. If a word like "hymen" can have this specific relation to a text, it is, on the contrary, because it is a textual instance itself. It possesses a structure of re-marking and a syntactically determined undecidability. Thanks to this structure, the textual instance appears folded, as well as the text itself when re-marked by such words:

Insofar as the text depends on them, *bends* to them (*s'y plie*), it thus plays a *double scene* upon a double stage. It operates in two absolutely different places at once, even if these are only separated by a veil, which is both traversed and not traversed, *inter*-sected (*entr-ouvert*). (250-51)

To determine with greater precision the textual instance which now appears as a re-mark of syntactical undecidability, let us investigate the nature of the fold of the two heterogeneous marks (the simulacrum and the simulacrum of the simulacrum) which reflect each other without ever penetrating, without ever coinciding with each other.

The double mark that constitutes the textual instance does not only no longer refer to any referent, escaping in that manner the platonic determination of model and copy, but it also no longer belongs to the order of the sign, to the order of the signifier and the signified. "In folding it back upon itself, the text thus *parts* (with) reference," writes Derrida (270). In folding itself back upon itself, the textual mark discards at the same time all semiotic function. Yet this does not mean that the textual instance would refer to *itself* (reflexive pronoun). Precisely because the re-mark maintains the platonic differential structure of mimesis, it does not mark itself, but another mark. The re-mark, as well as the folding back of reference upon the text itself, undermines the text's reference to itself as to an ultimate referent. Indeed, if the text became its own referent, as is the case in romantic poetry, the text would remain within a simple inversion of Platonism. Such an inversion, by the way, would be as conventional, say, as the valorisation of empiricism. The doubly folded mark of the text is, as I said already, a *tertium quid*.

The textuality of a text is remarked in the fold and in the blank of a re-mark like the word "hymen" only under the condition that the angle and the intersection of the "re-mark that folds the text back upon itself, [does so] without any possibility of its fitting back over or into itself, without any reduction of its spacing" (282). Yet, if the re-mark represents a sort of doubling where the two sides of the fold do not coincide with each other although they mirror each other, the textual instance is not reflexive. It is precisely the excess of reflexivity, the supplement that exceeds what is reflected in the folded mark, which raises it to the status of a textual instance.

The fold is not a form of reflexivity. If by reflexivity one means the motion of consciousness or self-presence that plays such a determining role in Hegel's speculative logic and dialectic, in the movement of sublation (*Aufhebung*) and negativity (the essence is reflection says the greater *Logic*), the reflexivity is but an effect of the fold as text. (302)

The re-mark is a non-symmetrical instance. It is constituted by a supplement that exceeds any self-mirroring of the two sides of the fold. Dissemination, writes Derrida in *Hors Livre*, "is written on the reverse side—the tinfoil—of this mirror" of specular reflection (39).

To get a better understanding of the dissymmetrical and supplementary nature of the non-reflexive folding of the textual instance, it may be useful to circle back to the figure of the hymen, which may have appeared as nothing but a theme in Derrida's reading of Mallarmé. The hymen, as a theme, would then represent a sort of totalizing emblem by means of which it would be made to refer back upon itself in a gesture of closure. Indeed, as a supplementary mark the hymen comes to represent metaphorically and metonymically the whole series of double marks that constitute the text of "Mimique." But, at the same time, this mark is also only one among the many marks that form the text. The mark of the hymen, consequently, names the whole series of the double marks of the text by tropologically supplementing it while remaining inscribed in it. Yet, of the fan (éventail), another Mallarméan image, Derrida writes:

This surplus mark, this margin of meaning, is not one valence among others in the series, even though it is *inserted* in there, too. It has to be inserted there to the extent that it does not exist outside the text and has no transcendental privilege; this is why it is always *represented* by a metaphor and a metonymy (page, plume, pleat). But while belonging in the series of valences, it always occupies the position of a supplementary valence, or rather, it marks the structurally necessary position of a supplementary inscription that could always be added to or subtracted from the series.

The supplementary mark, instead of closing the text upon itself, in lieu of reflecting it into its own as a totalizing image is supposed to do, illustrates nothing but what Derrida calls "the general law of textual supplementarity" (286). The surplus mark re-marks the whole series of the double marks of the text by illustrating what always exceeds a possible closure of the text folded, reflected upon itself. In excess to the text *as a whole* is the text "itself."

Any double mark can, in this manner, represent the exceeding supplement of textuality. Any double mark can represent what makes the totality of all textual instances possible. In other words, any textual instance can assume the function of naming the whole series of the marks of a text insofar as it occupies the position of a supplement to that totality, a supplement which (as the text itself) is the locus of the "engendering" of the whole series. Suffice it to say that this "engenderment" of the whole series by its exceeding supplement is neither that of an emanation or creation of any sorts, nor a constitution by means of a transcendental instance.

The double mark is folded upon itself in such a manner, that that which exceeds its reflection becomes the locus of its coming forth; the double mark is abysmally dissymemetric. In the context of "La double Séance" this may be the most concise determination of a textual instance. Rigorously speaking, only when understanding text in this manner can the text be said to have any deconstructive properties. If one neglects that *text* is the dissymmetric excess of the folded mark, one will fall prey to textual fetishism and one will mistake its operation of deconstruction either for the romantic notion of a chiasmatic engendering (and destruction, or rather ironization) of the self-reflexive text, or for the dialectic sublation of opposite terms in the reflexive and speculative gesture of the philosophy of identity.

Because the textual instance is determined in terms of supplementarity, of an excess to itself, it will never be able to come into appearance as such. Because of what always exceeds the text as its supplementary scene of "engendering," the text as such necessarily remains concealed. When revealing itself as a whole, as a series of double marks, the text folds itself at once back into what, as a supplementary mark of comprehension, represents tropologically the whence of the whole series. For this very reason, there cannot be a phenomenology of the text. Especially not in the vulgar meaning of phenomenon. And as little according to the meaning of the Kantian formal concept of phenomenon. But can there be a phenomenology of the text in terms of the phenomenological concept of the phenomenon as "that which shows itself in itself (*das Sich-an-ihm-selbst-Zeigende*)?"[23] To decide upon this extremely delicate question one would first have to elaborate on what distinguishes the Heideggerian revelation of Being in beings from Derrida's determination of the relation of the supplement to the whole which it exceeds. As I cannot broach here an analysis of the specific similarities and differences that mark Heidegger's and Derrida's approach to the problem of transcendental derivation, I limit myself to the recognition that there cannot be a phenomenology of the text, as Derrida states (297), because as a supplement to itself, the text or the re-mark is in constant withdrawal, in constant retreat from itself. It does not exist, or more precisely, it is not. Yet if the text is not, it is precisely because *there is* text. *Il y a, es gibt* text. Derrida notes:

If there were no fold, or if the fold had a limit somewhere — a limit other than itself as a mark . . . — there would be no text. But if the text does not, to the letter, exist, then *there is* perhaps a text. A text one must make tracks with. (302)

The textual instance which is never present, but donates the text, "has no proper, literal meaning; it no longer originates in meaning as such, that is, as the meaning of Being" (259). "No present in truth presents itself there, not even in the form of self-concealment" (260). The textual instance by casting aside reference is *Being aside*, aside of Being (être à l'écart) (273). The textual instance occupies the margin of Being.

At the edge of being, the medium of the hymen never becomes a mere mediation of work of the negative; it outwits and undoes all ontologies, all philosophemes, all manner of dialectics. It outwits them and — as a cloth, a tissue, a medium again — it envelops them, turns them over, and inscribes them." (244)

At this point of our development of Derrida's notion of text, the continuity between the question of Being and the question of the text cannot be overlooked anymore. The question of the text repeats, in at least a formal manner, all the movements that characterize Heidegger's elaborations on Being. This similarity, however should not have made us blind to the (particularly in the last quotes) slight yet all the more persistent displacements which positively hint at the impossiblity of phenomenologizing the textual trace in even a Heideggerian fashion. Let us, indeed, not forget that, of all things, the phenomenon par excellence is Being. But before attempting to face what distinguishes the question of the text from the question of Being, the similarities of both questions are first to occupy us. In short, the logic of the trait as *retrait* to which the Heideggerian notion of Being develops, as well as the particular locus (*Ortschaft*) which Heidegger attributes to Being — its place at once inside and outside of all the conceptual dyads which it allows to come forth or as which it shows itself — represent the major formal similarities between the Heideggerian and the Derridean questioning. If these findings unmistakingly indicate on what level of philosophical reflection Derrida elaborates his notion of text, a level indeed which excludes all pragmatic, empirical, rationalistic, and dialectical approaches, and if they also already provide us with a hint at the nature of the problems that Derrida tries to solve by the question of the text, do they also allow us to conclude, as Granel does with regard to the Derridean notion of writing, that the question of Being and the question of the text are one and the same? Were they identical, why would Derrida shrink from admitting this identity? Granel suggests that Derrida may hesitate to confess the essential similarity of both questions because of a *"remaining kinship* [. . .] between the [Heideggerian] Difference which crosses out the origin, the ground, self-proximity, in short all the modalities of presence, *and* what it crosses out in this manner."[24] Although involved in the same philosophical enterprise of questioning Western metaphysics, Heidegger and Derrida would differ in their perception of the other of metaphysics. Granel adds: "Is the breeze of Danger that blows 'on the other side'—once one has climbed, followed and left the ridge of metaphysics—simply not the same, or is it not sustained and recognized by Heidegger and Derrida in the same way."[25] When in *Writing and Difference* Derrida agrees with Levinas upon the necessity of leaving the climate of Heidegger's philosophy, such a statement may serve to support Granel's argument. If one recalls that toward the end of "Violence and Metaphysics" Derrida wonders whether Heidegger's question of Being is not essentially a theological question and whether what Heidegger calls the historicity of being can be thought without invoking an eschatology, and if, on the other hand, in a lecture entitled "D'un ton apocalyptique en philosophie," Derrida raises the apocalypse to a sort of transcendental condition of all writing (and *a fortiori* of all thought), then the difference between the two philosophers may well be presented as one of tone, of accent, of style, etc.[26] Basically, this difference would then amount to the not unimportant one between the comforting tone of the Black Forest philosopher who, dwelling near the origins, calls upon Hölderlin to assure us that where there is danger there grows also what saves, and what Derrida evokes as "the generalizing catastrophe" (RM, 24). No doubt, such a difference can easily be made out in the work of the two thinkers. Yet, to reduce their difference to a question of tone or style would imply that from Heidegger to Derrida little conceptual discovery has taken place, unless one were to demonstrate that the question of tone and style does not remain exterior to the effort of conceptualization. As seen, the questions of Being and of the text are indeed, conceptually speaking, the same. In terms of conceptual refinement there seems to be no great difference between the Heideggerian notion of trait and Derrida's notion of archetrace.

However, at this point, one can no longer avoid asking the question whether the relation of Heidegger and Derrida can still be examined in terms of concepts and of questions? It also becomes impossible to further shun the topic of the possible effects that a repetition of Heidegger by Derrida may have on the Heideggerian problematics itself. Does not the question of tone and style, then, point rather toward a radical rupture in regard to the philosophical problems with which Heidegger coped? And, finally, would one not have to acknowledge that though it formally repeats Heidegger's concept of Being, the text as a re-mark of Being may well be an entirely new concept?

Undoubtedly, Heidegger's repeated attempt to elaborate Being independently of being and beings, his inquiry into the ontological difference itself as that which donates all particular differences, is an approach to a meaning of Being which escapes all metaphysical determination hitherto. As Granel has emphasized, "meaning is understood here precisely as a *totally different* meaning compared to its understanding in the whole of Western metaphysics."[27] Yet, despite these insights into a meaning of Being that is no longer a meaning and does not refer to being anymore—insights which constitute that "other language" which already haunts Heidegger's admittedly still metaphysical discourse— Heidegger's philosophy remains within the horizon and the themes of Western philosophy. One of these themes, the major one, has always concerned being. The question of Being in all its *radicality*, and perhaps precisely because of it, continues this problematic. Despite his extraordinary use of language, Heidegger's philosophy remains subjected to the traditional ways in which these problems were expected to be solved. Moreover, in conceiving of the quest for the meaning of Being in terms of a history of the fates of Being, Heidegger bends to the traditional canon of problems that constitutes philosophy, saving, in addition, the pretension of classical philosophy to universality. If these all too hasty remarks contain a grain of truth, then the question of the difference between Heidegger and Derrida cannot be reduced simply to one of climate or tone.

Derrida has made it clear that the word text can be substituted for the word Being. Text is a translation for Being. It is a word, the use of which became indispensable to him in a very specific historical situation. For this very reason its importance is only strategic, and there is no intrinsic value to it. Thus while naming Being, the text is also something very different, if not without any relation at all to Being.[28]

To conclude, let us try to assess as succinctly as possible the difference at issue. To begin with, one has to realize that Derrida's determination of metaphysics in terms of *ethico-theoretical decisions* opens up an entirely different level of debate than Heidegger's conception of metaphysics as a forgetting of Being. Consequently, with this passage to the order of discourse of philosophy, to its textual organization and rhetorics, the Heideggerian notions of trait, between, fissure, and so forth, become displaced in such a way as to form, together with the specifically Derridean notions of supplementarity, *différance*, re-mark, text, etc., "tools" which serve to account for the "deep structures" that organize the conceptual, reflexive, and speculative discourse of philosophy. In other words, though the notion of text in Derrida is formally the same as the notion of Being-as-trait in Heidegger, it assumes a very different function in Derrida's enterprise.

But the break between Heidegger's question of Being and Derrida's investigations of what is only provisionally termed text—an inquiry which, by the way, may no longer yield to the order of the question in Heidegger's sense—is even more thorough. It is almost indiscernible, but nonetheless all the more piercing.

Heidegger's turning away from Husserlian phenomenology was motivated by the need to more originally ground phenomenology. As an investigation into Being as Being, the question of Being crowns the attempt of the fundamental ontology to account for the coming into presence of the phenomena—Being being the phenomenon *par excellence*. Heidegger's philosophy, then, for continuing the problematics of being, but, in particular, for inquiring into the very meaning of Being, remains as such within the realm of metaphysics, as Derrida has argued.[29] But Derrida also locates, besides Heidegger's preoccupation with the meaning of Being which almost entirely constitutes his enterprise, another gesture in Heidegger's thinking.[30] This is a gesture which, contrary to the question of Being, risks as much as the very name, the very word of Being. By emphasizing this aspect of Heidegger's later philosophy, Derrida comes to drive the wedge into Heidegger's enterprise insofar as it still remains indebted to its initial orientation toward a fundamental ontology. The word text, the donation of the text, for re-marking the word Being, is precisely what is no longer answerable to the meaning of Being. With the word text, Derrida names an instance which, crossing out all the modalities of presence, at once *intersects* with that from whence the presencing of the presence comes to be, Being as the phenomenon *par excellence*. There is (*es gibt*) text, at the margin of Being. With the word text, with the elaboration of the law of supplementarity of the re-mark, Derrida unfolds a discourse which, although it repeats the question of Being, inscribes it, and thus remains altogether extraneous to this still philosophical question.

NOTES

1. RM, 19. See also the translator's note on the word *retrait* (p. 5); the translator, to preserve as much as possible the variety of meanings which this word has in French, decided to leave it untranslated.

2. "Du trait non adéquat: La notion de rapport chez Heidegger," in *Les Fins de l'homme. A partir du travail de Jacques Derrida"* (Paris: Editions Galilée, 1981), pp. 133-62.

3. "If we are inquiring about the meaning of Being, our investigation does not then become a 'deep' one (*tiefsinnig*), nor does it puzzle out what stands behind Being. It asks about Being itself insofar as it enters into the intelligibility of Dasein. The meaning of Being can never be contrasted with entities, or with Being as the 'ground' which gives entities support" (Martin Heidegger, *Being and Time*, New York: Harper and Row, 1962, pp. 193-94.) What remains is a deepening of this very *question*, a systematic exploration of what according to Heidegger is equiprimordial (*gleichursprünglich*) with this question.

4. If Heidegger, as H. Birault has demonstrated in "Heidegger et la pensée de la finitude," *Revue internationale de philosophie*, 1960, n. 52, progressively abandons the concept of finitude, it is to avert the theological implications of this concept. However, what Heidegger originally aimed at when using the concept of finitude, continued to preoccupy his thought in the form of the idea of a historicity (*Geschichtlichkeit*) and destiny (*Geschick*) of Being.

5. No doubt, this critique of the transcendental and of the romantic chiasm is far from being unequivocal. Yet, such Heideggerian notions as "coming forth," "setting forth," "belonging to," etc., and in particular the gift (*Gabe*) of Being or of the Word have to be understood as such an attempt to more originally think and to reinscribe the idea of constitution or of engenderment.

6. "The Anaximanderfragment," in Heidegger, *Early Greek Thinking* (New York: Harper and Row, 1975), p. 26.

7. Cf. Ernst Tugendhat, *Selbstbewusstsein und Selbstbestimmung*, (Frankfurt: Suhrkamp, 1979).

8. Heidegger, *Logik, Die Frage nach der Wahrheit, Gesamtausgabe*, Vol. 21, (Frankfurt: Klostermann, 1976) pp. 127ff.

9. Although the doctrine of an analogy of Being and its meanings, a doctrine which seems to go back to Thomas Aquinas's Aristotle exegeses, may be contrary to the spirit and the letter of Aristotle's text and represent a "Platonisation" of Aristotle, as Pierre Aubenque argues, *Le problème de l'être chez Aristotle* (Paris: PUF, 1966), pp. 198-206, it is important to realize that Heidegger's question of the meaning of Being originated in his reading in 1907 of Franz Brentano's dissertation entitled *"Von der mannigfachen Bedeutung des Seinden nach Aristoteles"* (1862) which pursued precisely the Aquinian exegesis of Aristotle.

10. In an excellent review of Derrida's *Of Grammatology*, a review which appeared in 1967 in *Critique* and which has remained one of the very few occasions on which pertinent questions were addressed to the work of Derrida, Gérard Granel already asked Derrida about the difference of the question of writing (écriture) and the question of Being. Indeed, the attentive reader of both Heidegger and Derrida will not be able to avoid realizing the striking structural similarities between writing and Being, as between text and Being. Gérard Granel, "Jacques Derrida et la rature de l'origine," reprinted in Gérard Granel, *Traditionis Traditio*, (Paris: Gallimard, 1972).

11. Vincent Descombes, *Le même et l'autre* (Paris: Minuit, 1979), pp. 175-76.

12. See, for instance, Jacques Derrida, "The Law of Genre," and "Living On," in *DC*.

13. Or as a radical empiricism, that is to say, as an empiricism that undoes its own philosophical foundations. Cf. *G*, 162.

14. "An exact account of purely rhythmical motives of being which are the signs by which it can be recognized." Stéphane Mallarmé, *Oeuvres Complètes* (Paris: Gallimard, 1945), p. 345.

15. These quotes stem from M. Heidegger, *Identity and Difference* and *On the Way to Language*.

16. Heidegger, *On the Way to Language* (New York: Harper and Row, 1971), p. 149.

17. Emile Benveniste, *Problèmes de linguistique générale*, Vol. 1 (Paris: Gallimard, 1966), pp. 327-335).

18. Cf. also the remarkable text by Philippe Lacoue-Labarthe, "L'écho du sujet," in *Le sujet de la philosophie, Typographies I* (Paris: Aubier-Flammarion, 1979), in particular from p. 285 on.

19. Mallarmé, *ibid.*, p. 333: "Sign! at the central abyss of a spiritual impossibility that nothing is exclusively to all, the divine numerator of our apotheosis, some supreme mould which does not take place insofar as that of any existing object: but, in order to animate a seal in it, it borrows all the scattered, unknown and richly floating veins, then to forge them."

20. *Ibid.*, p. 345: "Note that beyond the narration created to imitate life in its confusion and vastness, there are no means by which to theatrically reproduce an action; except to rediscover by instinct and through elimination one of these great traits, here not the least pathetic; it is the eternal return of the exile, his heart filled with hope, to the earth which was forsaken by him but changed into an ungrateful one, now someone at the point where he must leave it voluntarily this time, where! with a glance he surveys the illusions suggested to his youth by the beckoning of the native land." (I thank Maria Assad for translating these Mallarmé passages for me.)

21. "Which does not take place in as far as that of any existing object," writes Mallarmé; "What is peculiar to Being is not anything having the character of being," (*Das Eigentümliche des Seins ist nichts Seinsartiges*), writes Heidegger in *On Time and Being* (New York: Harper and Row, 1972), p. 10.

22. I am very grateful to Barbara Johnson for providing me with an advance copy of her excellent translation of Derrida's *La Dissémination* (Chicago: University of Chicago Press, 1981). The page indications in the text refer to the original.

23. Heidegger, *Being and Time*, p. 51.

24. Granel, p. 168.

25. *Ibid.*, p. 156.

26. Derrida, *Writing and Difference*, (Chicago: University of Chicago Press, 1978), p. 148. The lecture "D'un ton apocalyptique en philosophie" is in *Les Fins de l'homme*. As to the problem of eschatology in Heidegger, see for instance: "As something fateful (*geschickliches*), Being itself is inherently eschatological," in "The Anaximander Fragment," *Early Greek Thinking*, p. 18.

27. Granel, pp. 126-127.

28. See discussions in *Les Fins de l'homme*.

29. See "Ousia et Gramme," *Marges*, pp. 59 and 73.

30. Toward the end of "Ousia et Gramme." See also *Spurs*.

Afterword
Jonathan Arac

I

"Few facts about the life of our culture are more striking than the recent growth of literary criticism in both extent and prestige." It is now "fiercely professional, an 'institution' as well as a discipline, a self-contained world as well as a secondary branch of humane letters." When Irving Howe wrote this in 1958, the end seemed near to what Randall Jarrell had called "The Age of Criticism." M. D. Zabel noted in 1962 "the effect of self-cancellation which a large part of contemporary critical writing conveys." Yet to mark this effect, Zabel reached back to Mencken's mockery of "criticism of criticism of criticism."[1] This triplication defines an uneasy, self-enclosed vitality. Criticism is literary writing that begins from previous literary writing, and it thus questions that literature is limited by canons of "imitation" of the world or "expression" of an author, by the exigencies of conventional form or the growth of organic form. In the isolation of such freedom, writing and readers proliferate but are restricted to an ever more marginal coterie. This is how Swift and Pope portrayed Grub Street. Since then, the publics for literature have grown, but other technical skills have proved far more socially powerful than the mastery of words as codified in rhetoric. Proliferation inseparable from marginality remains the paradox of literature in consumer democracy, only more visibly exacerbated in the case of criticism. May a margin function as a leading edge? Those who came to intellectual maturity in the shadow of Modernism, in "The Age of Criticism," recall excitedly running to their little-magazine shop to get the new issue with its Blackmur essay. But those joys are past: "The most intense moment in the history of modern criticism, the moment of its greatest hold upon the imagination of serious young people, has probably just come to an end," declared Howe in 1958 (p. 8). To an older generation nostalgic for the great days of *Partisan* and the old *Kenyon*, the current scene is debased parody, a frivolous reenactment, because it is not grounded in the "overwhelming power" of "the *avant-garde* experience."[2] The contributors to this collection think otherwise.

I shall return to other relations of criticism and an avant-garde, but I do not think the very particular circumstances of sixty years ago should establish a dogma. In Valéry, Eliot, Benjamin, Jakobson there exists a close link between literary innovation and what we judge the best criticism, theoretical as well as practical. Wellek's *History of Modern Criticism* has institutionalized this perspective in its judgments of critics from 1750 to 1900. Nonetheless, in the history of criticism in English, it is not clear that this model prevails. Sidney wrote his *Apology* before the great literature of the Elizabethan age; Ben Jonson devoted little of his *Timber* to his own time, and his most generous estimate of Shakespeare came only after his rival's death; Dryden's intense poetic engagement with Milton has little place in his best critical prose; and Samuel Johnson's greatest critical performances treat Shakespeare and Pope (dead over thirty years when Johnson wrote his life). The dogma of the necessary subordination of criticism to the advanced literature of its time has distorted our understanding of Coleridge's *Biographia Literaria*, causing neglect of its first half. Even more damagingly, this dogma has encouraged an easy superiority to Matthew Arnold that hides the extent to which our critical institutions remain Arnoldian.

The one possible "avant-garde" writer crucial for all the Yale Critics is Jacques Derrida—or is he rather himself one of them? In this collection, between the introduction and this afterword fall eight essays, the central four on the "Yale Critics proper," surrounded by two on each side. Derrida appears in all the framing essays but very little in the central essays. This status of Derrida as parergon, a supplementary frame, evokes a problematic that he has explored in detail (in *La Vérité en peinture*) and solicits further questions. He is the French philosopher most widely influential in translation in America at this date, and matched in the twentieth century only by Bergson and Sartre. But what is this "influence"? Can anything be gained by "translation," or is there only loss? What occurs in the metaphorization of terms and practices as Derrida's work is transported from French to English, from Europe to America, from philosophy to criticism?

One striking difficulty in translation occurs at the most fundamental level of disciplinary practice. Derrida began writing as a professional philospher within a culture where philosophy—the study of a canonized body of texts in the last year of *lycée*—held a crucial place in the system of humanistic education. American philosophy is preoccupied not with the names of philosophers and the bodies of their texts, but with ''problems'' and ''arguments.'' So in crossing over to America, Derrida made his impact more immediately upon literary studies, which is organized by name and corpus. As a new practice of reading, his work was innovative both in French philosophy and American criticism. In France, where philosophers still figure largely in public life and consciousness—Sartre, Aron, Althusser—Derrida's intervention could arouse radical political hopes. In the American academy, however, it has also a conservative effect, like that of Leo Strauss upon American ''political science.'' After American academic culture had largely given up reading philosophical classics (the History-of-Ideas emphasis on the ''unit'' idea in this respect reinforced analytic philosophy), it became once again necessary to read at large in Plato, Aristotle, Descartes, Kant, Hegel.[3]

Such translation, which can make a radical gesture conservative, helps account for the ambivalence the Yale Critics arouse in the contributors to this volume. None of us is a disciple, yet we have all felt our own work inflected by the force of their practice. But the Yale Critics also awaken our ambivalence toward the institution of literary study itself. They have seized the middle ground between the ''literarily conservative'' and the ''politically radical'' (Johnson, ''Nothing Fails like Success,'' p. 7). Just as Carlyle in ''Signs of the Times'' (1829)—a founding essay of modern critical consciousness—preempted the middle ground between the religious ''Millenarians . . . on the right'' and the utilitarian ''Millites on the left,'' so have Yale Critics centralized their extremity. They are attacked both by those who wish to preserve the institutions of literary study unchanged and by those who want change but deny that the Yale Critics are producing any. We may now survey the contributors' concerns with these issues.

II

In the detailed establishment of context, Wallace Martin's introduction travels a route from the fifties to the seventies like that Frank Lentricchia charts in *After the New Criticism*. Yet Martin's much briefer survey travels

closer to the ground; it prefers dealing precisely with the discursive practices of criticism rather than pursuing large theoretical issues of Kantian
aestheticism.

Three key points of Martin's merit special attention. First is the question of whether the Yale Critics are "iconoclasts" or "wily conservatives."
This volume as a whole suggests "conservatives." Martin himself shows
that while the Yale Critics have helped change the terms and practices
of criticism, they have not smashed criticism into ruins. To adjudicate
the distinction between conservative and iconoclast depends upon what
frame you place the actions within. The second point also concerns frames.
In addressing the relation of literary study to philosophy Martin suggests
that American criticism has taken from Derrida's philosophy a new
vocabulary and rhetoric; a set of terms and ways of deploying them. Traditional philosophy would judge such a change no change, for vocabulary
and rhetoric are inessential.[4] Richard Rorty, in contrast, has found such
changes crucial in the impact of Wittgenstein, Dewey, and Heidegger.[5]
Not only do the studies of Thomas Kuhn and Michel Foucault in their
different ways support Rorty, but in literary studies *The Mirror and the
Lamp* by M. H. Abrams demonstrates that the largest transformation in
English criticism was a shift in rhetoric. Finally, Martin touches upon the
social and political implications of thinking about literary study. Like all
of us he has some difficulty. Both the practice and theory of criticism
are separate from the sociology of literature or any other of the "different
fields of study" that our disciplines have defined. On the other hand,
he finds that the "traditional compartmentalization of disciplines" blocks
valuable work in the human sciences, and he finds too that Derrida's
work challenges these disciplinary frames—and thus the autonomy of
criticism.

These concerns of Martin's move into the forefront in Paul Bové's
"Variations on Authority: Some Deconstructive Transformations of the
New Criticism." For Bové adopts a stance toward critical institutions like
that which Foucault takes toward the disciplines in *Surveiller et punir*.
This makes differences that were extremely important in Martin's analysis
become much less so, just as Foucault in *Les Mots et les choses* argued
that within political economy Marx had done nothing more innovative
than inverting a possibility already present in Ricardo. Thus in fine detail,
Bové shows that key moments in de Man, Miller, and Derrida effect a
mirror-reversal of certain new-critical positions. Unlike Miller or de Man,
Derrida was not thinking of New Criticism when he wrote. This difference,
however, is not important for Bové's attention to the reception of Derrida within a critical community defined by New Criticism.

De Man's essay on New Criticism, Bové argues, both seized authority and worked to hold in place the institution from which that authority derived. That essay also demonstrates the force of Bové's observation that what differentiated deconstructive criticism from New Criticism was not even any technical gain in exegetical power, but a new critical *style*. For de Man's interpretation of the New Critics has never been accepted, even by his sympathetic readers, as accurate (see Culler, "The Frontiers of Criticism"). In Bové's terms, it is a clear case of "challenge" as "calumny." Yet it sets going a new vocabulary and new paths of reading that have been greatly effective, even while the Yale Critics have not allowed us to forget the terms of their predecessors, but have preserved those terms as the necessary counterpoint to their new terms.

To complement Bové's choice of New Criticism as frame for deconstruction, Wlad Godzich in "The Domestication of Derrida" starts from speech-act philosophy. For New Criticism and speech-act philosophy together represent the Anglo-American environment of empiricism and ingenuity in which we felt at home before strange guests began to arrive. Godzich focuses upon a discursive event that introduced "deconstruction in America": Paul de Man's reading of Jacques Derrida's reading of Rousseau. The topic of "domesticating Derrida" in America could be addressed in much broader terms that would draw in Joseph Riddel's *The Inverted Bell* (1974), Geoffrey Hartman's review-essays on *Glas* (now in *ST*), Gayatri Spivak's introduction to *Of Grammatology*, Edward Said's "The Problem of Textuality," Richard Rorty's "Philosophy as a Kind of Writing," and Barbara Johnson's "The Frame of Reference." But Godzich has focused the problem of translation and application on one instance, which allows us to observe in precise detail the transaction that has led to charges that the Yale Critics adulterate Derrida. Moving from the problems of the quasi-translation of the Queen's pronouncement at the Olympics, to the implications of de Man's publishing his essay first in French and then in English, to the significance of Gayatri Spivak's translation of "*araisonner*," Godzich forces us to ask, what is the "same" and how does it "work"? He investigates the term "*arraisonner*" (on which Donald Marshall also fastens), which allows us to see de Man's relation to Derrida as one that both "brings to reason" and "smuggles in contraband." Godzich shows how the key term of Derrida's passage, "production," disappears from de Man's representation of Derrida and is replaced by the term "reading." This terminological shift elides both the Marxist-materialist and the philosophical-transcendental implications of "production" and leaves instead a term firmly placed within literary studies. Godzich then suggests through a speculative philosophic narrative that the "story of reading" frustrates any attempt to get "beyond" deconstruction. Thus he and Bové differ in judging the applicability of

Derrida's term "production" in American deconstructive criticism, yet both agree that an impasse has been reached.

Michael Sprinker turns from the ever-closer textual examinations by which Martin, Bové, Godzich stage their critical histories, and in the first essay devoted to a single figure he places Geoffrey Hartman in the large history of "Aesthetic Criticism" since the time of Schiller. This turn differentiates Sprinker from both Yale and New Critics and joins him to Fredric Jameson, whose reflections upon historicist thinking inform his meditations upon Hartman. Sprinker's essay specifies crucial issues Martin touched upon: the interrelations of Romanticism and literary history, to which I shall return. Bové suggested the importance of style in thinking about the Yale Critics, and style is Sprinker's focus. He shows that the debate between Hartman and Harold Bloom over Wordsworth, and thus over Romanticism, and consequently our whole modern literature, hinges on critical style.[6] Bloom is more boldly assertive and perhaps therefore the more "influential," while Sprinker, echoing T. S. Eliot on Henry James, finds in Hartman a critical appreciation of poetic structures so fine that no systematic idea (such as Bloom's revisionary schemata) can violate them. Yet this very finesse carries penalties. People said of Macaulay's assertive, highly pointed history-writing that it was impossible to tell the truth in such a style. Does Hartman's concern for gentle subtility, both in what he reads and in what he writes, produce a style in which it is impossible to write history?

Donald Pease places the career of J. Hillis Miller, "The Other Victorian at Yale," in relation to the aftermath of political turmoil during the 1960s, a context more local than Sprinker's, yet broader than those of the first essays. Pease joins the individual and institutional through his attention to a series of encounters in which Miller defined his own critical "conversion" and elaborated the significance of this turn for American criticism: Miller's reviews in *Diacritics* (in which all the Yale Critics early appeared) of books by M. H. Abrams, Joseph Riddel, and Edward Said; and Miller's debate with Abrams at an MLA panel, with its later consequences. In terms that Bové and Godzich have highlighted, we see a series of "challenges" and "arrests." Pease is less immediately concerned with the techniques of literary study as such and like Kenneth Burke is more attentive to the symbolic values that emerge from (or are attached to) particular techniques. He finds in both politically "relevant" criticism and in "reader" theories a democratizing push that in the sixties threatened to make literature banal, purely sociological. This thrust the Yale Critics have effectively resisted by re-emphasizing the mystery and power of literature—and thus of criticism also.

In analyzing how the institution of criticism has held itself together through Miller's provocation of crises, Pease approaches Victor Turner's anthropological investigations of "liminal" and "liminoid" experiences in societies at moments that threaten—or promise—change. Sacvan Bercovitch's use of Turner in studying *The American Jeremiad* is relevant here, if we take seriously the displacement of sermons by critical essays as the major change in the last century of American humanistic discourse. Bercovitch finds in the history of the Jeremiad the same pattern that Pease discerns in Miller's interventions: the provoking of a crisis that leads to a renewed consensus, an enclosure against a threat now safely held on the outside. New-critical "paradox" and "irony" as reconciliation extend what Bercovitch defines as the power of the Jeremiad, its capacity to contain contradictions, to join what were in earlier traditions separate and contradictory positions or perspectives.

Stanley Corngold's attention to "Error in Paul de Man" highlights a matter mentioned by Bové and Godzich that is important for several reasons. It accounts for some of de Man's strangeness. In an American critical tradition that, like the Jeremiad, depends upon blurring distinctions inside itself while sharply distinguishing what is outside itself, concern with "error" seems alien, even "unamerican." Thus New Critics enforced a strong distinction between literary and scientific uses of language, but within literary language emphasized plurisignification. Both de Man and E. D. Hirsch (in *Validity in Interpretation*) challenged this stance from the European hermeneutic tradition, but Hirsch offered a stability like that of science, thus creating an even larger unification. De Man, in contrast, argued both for the necessity of recognizing error— that is, for holding to a standard of correctness in interpretation—and for the inevitability of committing error. It is both necessary to choose between right and wrong and impossible to remain correct in one's choice. Corngold finds little import in de Man's shifting the grounds for this necessary error from Heideggerian temporality to Derridean textuality, for it was never the "vulgar" history of power and politics that concerned de Man.

The problem of error raises again the relation of criticism to philosophy. For Richard Rorty, de Man clings to a no longer useful conception of philosophy: "Epistemology still looks classy to weak textualists" ("Nineteenth Century Idealism and Twentieth-Century Textualism," p. 171). De Man's epistemological concerns have nonetheless infiltrated our critical discourse and require the clarification Corngold provides. His emphasis on error operates within the anti-aesthetic strategy that moves de Man's essayistic style, yet modern epistemology and aesthetics alike are part of the history that proceeds from Kant, and it is not clear why there is any liberation in preferring one to the other. Liberation, however, may be itself too aesthetic a goal; de Man claims for the epistemological standard a greater *rigor*. Such a claim has warranted his tremendous authority, and Corngold opens that claim to genealogical investigation. De Man has emphasized the Nietzsche who explored figurative language as the subversive ground of knowledge. Corngold recalls as well Nietzsche's concern with the practice of devout observances, with the power of figures as well as their unreliability—a Nietzsche closer to Foucault than to Derrida.

Both these Nietzsches play their turns in Daniel O'Hara's "The Genius of Irony: Nietzsche in Bloom." This essay offers a large context that complements the detailed study Harold Bloom's works and career have already received both in reviews of his nine recent books and in synoptic essays. Bloom differs from his Yale colleagues in another way that this essay only obliquely addresses: his close involvement with the contemporary practice of poetry. Hartman reviewed for *Kenyon* and *Partisan* over twenty years ago; de Man gave early attention to Borges, but only Bloom's continuing essays on Geoffrey Hill, John Ashbery, and others resemble the modernist model of advanced critic in dialogue with advanced literature (and thus make Bloom easier to admire for those who still uphold this model).

Modernism as well as Nietzsche is at stake in O'Hara's essay. He freshly reappropriates modernism by an unexpected use of Joyce. The cluster Yeats-Nietzsche-Bloom is familiar, but Joyce displaces this series and even makes possible links between Hugh Kenner's modernism and Bloom's. Joyce's crucial disorienting force is generic. To replace the lyric Yeats by the narrative Joyce opens the place of the narrator as a possible escape from the dizzying regression that the "romance of interpretation" otherwise entails. In defining this self-destructive entailment, a Nietzschean "sacrifice to the ancestors," as the basis for critics' "romance of interpretation," O'Hara joins Bloom and Hartman in exploring the archaic ground of killing ideals on which criticism as well as literature moves. The interplay between the interpretive quest (like Bloom's "internalization of quest romance") and the "irony of revisionism" that frustrates it resembles also another critical model for narrative, Edward Said's "molestation and authority" (in *Beginnings*). The authority is like that of a god building a self-contained aesthetic world, and thus O'Hara shares Michael Sprinker's concern with critical style and the history of aestheticism since Kant. In beginning by reading from *Dubliners* and ending with a passage from *Ulysses*, O'Hara has left the intermediate space of his essay for a portrait of the (critic as) artist: doomed to embody less the object of his hopes than of his fears.

Bloom re-emerges in Donald Marshall's "History, Theory, and Influence: Yale Critics as Readers of Maurice Blanchot." Bloom provides Marshall with a way of thinking about why Derrida's "idiosyncratic refiguration" of Blanchot seems more compelling than the "authoritative expositions" of Hartman and de Man. Yet in using Bloom, Marshall revises him and risks idealization in transposing Bloom's concern with "possession" into the key of "friendship." Marshall's essay makes clear the importance of Blanchot's fascinating work. Since a swerve from Sartre to Blanchot marks the trajectory of many important figures in current French culture, crucial features of Foucault, Derrida, the Yale Critics, will pass us by so long as Blanchot remains unfamiliar in America. Marshall locates in Hartman's early essay on Blanchot a motif that remains fundamental. Hartman found there the writer's dream of "the *face* of truth, the phantom of immediacy," and in his current work Hartman still meditates on the "unimaginable face" of Yeats's Leda (*CW*, 35). Blanchot's obsession with the problematic of writing provides intermediate ground between Heidegger and Derrida. Through Blanchot, Marshall poses again the question of Romanticism and Hartman's "sidetracking" from his major literary-historical project. I shall return to the gain or loss in the detour Hartman has followed and the possibility of a "new literary history" still to come.

The problems of Heidegger's philosophy link Marshall's essay to Rodolphe Gasché's "Joining the Text: From Heidegger to Derrida." Gasché's dense and provocative argument draws the traits of Derrida's remarkable originality, yet it also reminds us that when we speak of Derrida's "French" influence on America, we elide a vast German connection. This volume attends to Nietzsche and Heidegger but still neglects Freud, Husserl, Hegel. Three further points raised by Gasché demand attention. First, he implies that "deconstructive criticism" in America rests upon a misinterpretation of Derrida. ("Deconstruction as Criticism" argues this fully.) It treats "text" as a phenomenal entity—writing on paper—rather than recognizing in Derrida's use of it something closer to a transcendental concept. Yet Gasché's rigorous distinction between philosophical and critical practices jars somewhat against Marshall's argument that Blanchot understands writing as "withdrawal." For if Derrida's "textualization" of Heidegger's "Being" as "*retrait*" (withdrawal) has already been mediated through Blanchot's literary criticism, may not criticism take back (*retirer*) what Derrida has withdrawn from it? Second, Gasché specifies the "textual instance" as something very special and rare, in no way so common as "literary language." That is, "textuality," in its technical sense, does not characterize everything we loosely call "texts." Finally, Gasché finds in Derrida's work a deep critique of

Romantic notions of the reflexive totality of a work or image, but he finds in American deconstructive criticism a reinforcement of these notions. Thus for Gasché, American deconstructive criticism is the history of a mistake. Yet this mistake happened, and this volume explores some of its consequences. By calling attention to de Man's mistaken translation of Nietzsche on error, Corngold has put most literally the problem of translation that Gasché poses most broadly: what happens between European philosophy and American criticism?

III

The contributors recurrently return to the institution of literary study. Certain dangers attend upon attempts to analyze the institutions one works within. There is moralistic complacency—if only everyone *else* would straighten themselves out, everything would be all right. There is also a danger in a more subtle self-satisfaction. If we have not broken the frames of discipline, if the Yale Critics have only ensured its survival— well then, so much the better. At least we have survived! This hidden message of comfort threatens to disarm any self-questioning. Yet the actual condition of academic literary studies has been severely eroded in the last decade by inflation for those employed, and all of us are faced by budget cuts, enrollment drops, hiring freezes, and unemployment—a cycle that threatens established literary study far more than do the Yale Critics.

We must not only confront our economic conditions, we must also specify our intellectual system. In the 1940s English studies in America took on a new shape of which New Criticism was only a part. After several decades of challenge both by humanism and by a socially oriented liberalism, the old symbiosis of belletrism and philology finally yielded to a four-fold disciplinary apparatus, two parts historical—American Studies and Comparative Literature—two parts linguistic—New Criticism and Composition.[7] With the appearance of *College English* (1939, superseding *English Journal*), the publication of *Understanding Poetry* (1938), and founding of The *Explicator* (1942), New Criticism and Composition were already making their places before the newly world-dominant position of the United States after the war gave impetus for Comparative Literature and American Studies: to specify and glorify the national essence, and to set in order the world of literary knowledge, using the intellectual resources newly transferred from Europe. *Comparative Literature* began in 1948; *American Quarterly* in 1949. Both historical fields preserved, while neutralizing, residues of thirties Marxism. American Studies rectified the anglophile scorn for American culture, while it mystified American history by "occidentalism": positing a national essence that overlooked social conflict and enforcing a dualism between America and the rest of the world. Comparative Literature rectified American isolationism, while it mystified the literatures of the world by producing the "tradition" of Irving Babbitt's "all-seeing, all-hearing gentleman."[8] New Criticism (to separate itself from Agrarianism) and Composition (to separate itself from ruling-class traditions of rhetorical training) both developed technical emphases that removed them from concern with the specific life-contexts of reading and writing, while increasing their generalized pedagogic power. Yale Criticism arises at the intersection of Comparative Literature and New Criticism. Several opponents of the Yale Critics—such as Frederick Crews and E. D. Hirsch—are linked with Composition. Thus far the Americanists remain aloof from serious intellectual engagement.

Beyond this sort of detail stand further levels of study. In *Toward Freedom and Dignity*, O. B. Hardison has done an "archaeology" of English catalogue listings: Over a century of stratification accounts for the various types of courses, for courses have almost never been dropped, only displaced by the addition of others. Richard Ohmann's *English in America* analyzes the service literary study performs for the larger world; it is complemented by David Noble's *America by Design*, which by focusing on Engineering delineates the marginal function of English studies in the transformation of universities around the first world war. Taken together, the two works suggest the paradox of higher literary studies. We share a prestige largely derived from the technical prowess of natural and social scientists—Nobel Prize winners and government advisors— while our own work is taken as disciplinary in the most chillingly reduced sense ("You teach English? I'd better watch my grammar!"). For the United States no works like Raymond Williams's *Culture and Society* and John Gross's *Rise and Fall of the Man of Letters* describe the place of the non-academic critic in the larger national life. Given Mencken, Lewis Mumford, Edmund Wilson, this lack signals more a failure in scholarship than a real difference between the national cultures of England and America. Finally, the large-scale ideological studies of specialized discourses in Edward Said's *Orientalism* and Sacvan Bercovitch's *American Jeremiad* have made clear the social power exercised through the organizing tropes of a discipline.

I shall touch some points in this sequence with regard to the Yale Critics. Their early work challenged the prevailing new-critical practices of the 1950s and 1960s, by bringing them closer to Comparative Literature. Thus Harold Bloom popularized the work of Northrop Frye and its conviction that a work of literature could not be understood by itself, but only in relation to other works of literature. Bloom's later "revisionism" maintains this fundamental premise of Frye's theory of archetypes. If through Frye he challenged the autonomy of the individual poem, Bloom's own gift of critical quotation made Frye more available, for Frye's distance from the specific words of poems was most alien to New Criticism. Hillis Miller helped to popularize the work of Georges Poulet and its conviction that a work of literature was most valuably understood not in itself but as part of its author's spiritual project. Thus in *Poets of Reality*, the individual poems of Yeats, Eliot, Stevens—prooftexts for New Criticism—are dissolved into readings of careers. Yet Miller's first book effected a compromise between Poulet and New Criticism by reading individual works of Dickens at much greater length than Poulet read any single works. Miller at once challenged American practices and accommodated foreign ways to America, helping New Criticism overcome its early emphasis on lyric. Geoffrey Hartman popularized the practice of aesthetic philology. The philologist's synecdochal wager, that in reading a single work as closely as possible you were en route to the largest matters of cultural concern, distinguished Hartman. *The Unmediated Vision* is still untimely, but it was much more so in 1954, only seven years after *The Well-Wrought Urn*, the year after Earl Wasserman's *The Finer Tone*—which for all its philosophic energy did not seek to go beyond Keats's poems themselves. Reading four lyrics printed in full, Hartman's book physically appears new-critical, but its close readings do not close. De Man heightened such refusal of closure by insisting upon contradiction or error.

Now after a decade of the Yale Critics as a group, what difference have they made in the canon, the practice of reading, the object of literary study, the profession at large? Among the greatest changes in the postwar system of literary research and teaching have been the rise of feminist criticism and the growing importance of women in the profession. For reasons that need further study, women have made notable use of the Yale Critics in effecting both these changes. Not only are the important books of younger critics associated with the Yale Critics largely by women: Frances Ferguson, *Wordsworth: Language as Counter-Spirit*; Patricia Parker, *Inescapable Romance*; Margaret Homans, *Women Writers and Poetic Identity*; Barbara Johnson, *The Critical Difference*; Margaret Ferguson, *Trials of Desire: Renaissance Defenses of Poetry*.[9] But also in *The Madwoman in the Attic*, which culminates a decade's work of feminist critical revisionism that many have shared, Sandra Gilbert and Susan Gubar assert that they "based" their method upon Bloom's influence-studies.[10]

Despite their usefulness to Gilbert and Gubar's feminist transformation of the canon, the relation of the Yale Critics themselves to the canon is less innovative. Here they differ as well from New Criticism and structural narratology, each of which has brought large new areas into the classroom: the masterpieces of modernism and popular, formulaic genres. The triumphs of the Yale Critics have been largely restorative. They appear "wily conservatives" rather than "iconoclasts," yet there is iconoclasm in a "revival." To make the statue come to life destroys its fixed form as surely as would shattering it with a hammer. Thus, both New Critics and Yale Critics canonize Yeats and Stevens, but New Critics read them through an Eliotic-Coleridgean poetics, while Yale Critics find in them principles of poetics that not only give them a strange new life but also transform other poets. In the relation of literature and philosophy, likewise, it makes a difference whether one fixes a poem as a display in the "history of ideas" or instead mobilizes it in relation to writers who live vividly for us at this moment. Hegel, Heidegger, Nietzsche, and Freud are obvious examples.

In their virtuoso prowess of reading, the Yale Critics have done most to reinforce the basic standard of our criticism. Among other "advanced" critics only Stanley Fish matches them in brilliance of reading, and they thereby maintain authority among what Barbara Johnson calls the "literarily conservative."[11] In the intimate relation between their larger claims and their particular readings, the Yale Critics differ from such opponents as E. D. Hirsch, M. H. Abrams, Gerald Graff, and Frederick Crews. Paradoxically, in this respect the Yale Critics support old-fashioned American aversion to theory.[12] For after Heidegger and Derrida, the philosophical tradition of "theory," as the systematic enclosure of being within the gaze of knowledge, has lost its authority for them. To the extent, however, that they produce a troubled practice which moves between the earth of exegesis and the air of speculation, which sets aside the split of "reading" and "theory," they become truly radical. For this practice would undo the disciplinary subdivisions of New Criticism and Comparative Literature and would threaten the division between literature and philosophy.

The "object" of literary study has been displaced by the Yale Critics. Like Conrad's Marlow in *Heart of Darkness* they care less for the kernel of certain meaning than for the moonshiny halo that surrounds a "work" and gives it a place in a history, even if a history of moonshine, misprision, error, wanderings like those of romance. This has consequences for the classroom. A new-critical textbook like *Understanding Poetry* isolates the poems it contains. In reaction, "historical" anthologies offer poems grouped by author and in chronological sequence, but teachers still commonly teach each poem individually. Bloom gives the teacher reason to turn back to earlier pages when reading a poem, for, he would claim, the very definition of the later poem depends upon its relation to the earlier. De Man likewise encourages the study of reception by defining a text through its capacity to engender misreadings. The Yale Critics' refusal to enclose the single aesthetic object carries a forceful appeal, but what lies "Beyond Formalism"? Is it language, (inter)textuality, history? Does a denial of closure bring with it a denial of difference?

IV

The most fundamental challenge of the Yale Critics to our ways of literary study falls within the interlinked topics of Romanticism, narrative, and the question of writing in criticism, history, philosophy. Bloom has written a history of Romanticism as a falling from Milton and what follows as a falling from Romanticism; Miller has written such essays as "Tradition and Difference," "Narrative and History"; but more ominous than either of these are the unwritten histories of Romanticism by de Man and Hartman. Their rigor of renunciation may count for more than endlessly successful deconstructive readings.[13]

Against the new-critical, modernist devaluation of Romanticism, there seemed an easy historical response: to join Northrop Frye, Frank Kermode, Raymond Williams, Robert Langbaum in establishing the significant continuities that link modernism to Romanticism. This move, however, is vulnerable to Gerald Graff, who revives Irving Babbitt's and Yvor Winters' condemnations of modernism itself as merely Romantic. Such a double condemnation is well established in Germany, as de Man observes in "Literary History and Literary Modernity" (*BI*, 144). But the continuity between Romanticism, modernism, even "postmodernism" that Graff defines—the fetishism of the "symbol" and the "self-sufficient" artwork leading both "formalist" and "visionary" critics to unite in adoring the "fusion of dancer and dance," relativistically denying "error," in defiance of reason or logic—all these de Man had already castigated as misreadings of Romanticism.[14] To understand that allegory projects as narrative the contradiction that ironically rends any moment; to understand that allegory represents an unreachable, barren, painful anteriority; and to find such allegory in Rousseau, Wordsworth, Hölderlin, is to protect Romanticism against any attack it has yet faced in America. But it also discredits the "false historicism" and utopian formalism that have made possible any narrative Romantic history (ICF, 496). At moments de Man idealized this condition as perfect lucidity and thus fell into a Romantic myth of reflexivity. But his recent work avoids this temptation.

This real but imperfect self-consciousness of Romanticism Hartman associates with experimental prose forms that mingle literary theory and practice with the writing of philosophy, and Richard Rorty's literary understanding of Hegel supports this ("Nineteenth-Century Idealism and Twentieth-Century Textualism," pp. 162-64). Hartman takes Arnold's charge against the Romantics that they did not know enough as meaning that they failed to agree with Arnold that self-consciousness is paralyzing. The "Arnoldian Concordat" thus preserved criticism by subordinating it to literature and separating both from philosophy. For Arnold, to recognize philosophy as writing would diminish its conceptual force, while to recognize criticism as writing would compromise the aesthetic form of literature.[15] Arnold could then narrate a history of the development from Romantic ignorance of these imperatives to a later and more perfect understanding. Romanticism is the name in our culture for the entanglement Godzich has described that joins the philosophy of history with the history of philosophy with the theory of narrative.[16]

The fullest engagement with these matters comes in Hartman's recent books, which proclaim the revaluation of Romanticism and consequent "rethinking of literary history" (*CW*, 44). Such large issues have local consequences, for Hartman finds that the same fallacy which confused the relation of Romanticism to modernism threatens our thinking about the critical career of Walter Benjamin. Its "development" is "apparently progressive yet radically unprogressive," and, therefore, the "very notion of progress has become problematic" (*CW*, 72). Hartman turns to de Man for aid in his "effort to overcome falsely progressive (Hegelian and dialectical) theories of art" (*CW*, 107). Theories of loss and gain, or even of transformation, are all suspect, even when used in defense of Romanticism, for "at its most radical" the project of contemporary criticism—what Hartman calls "Revisionism"—"challenges all historic explanation" insofar as it is based on "concepts of fall, secularization, restoration, etc." that forge a drama in which the "natural supernaturalism of art" regains "something 'divine' that is lost" (*CW*, 180).[17] Such myths of progress and loss comprise a "historicism" that is "monumentalizing" (*CW*, 110) and therefore deadening and oppressive. Hartman parallels Nietzsche's critique of monumental history and of critical history: there is danger to life in overvaluing the past, no less than present.

The same "hygiene" (cf. *BF*, 256) that should sanitize our dealings with history or a career guides the "hermeneutics of indeterminacy" that Hartman proposes for reading a poem. We must avoid the masterful temptations of "technocratic, predictive, and authoritarian formulas" (*CW*, 41). Rather than judgment, true criticism instead is "suspensive discourse," less cognition than commemoration. Engaged with a poem, we should feel responsible to "hold it in mind" rather than to "resolve it into available meanings" (*CW*, 274). Heidegger's critique of technology and insistence on "letting be" echo here, as in Hartman's resolve not to "coerce the future" by prediction (*CW*, 162).

Even more than Heidegger, however, Hartman echoes the Wordsworth he has so long and lovingly held in mind. The critic who resists the theory of progress finds his emblem in the "halted traveller" of *Wordsworth's Poetry*. (As Wordsworth confronts his imagination in Book VI of the *Prelude*, he is "lost/Halted without an effort to break through.") The theorist of "suspensive discourse" echoes the poet who made a signature of the word "hang."[18] Hartman's fear of preemptive closure shares Wordsworth's aspiration toward "something evermore about to be" (*Prelude*, VI). Thus, Romanticism properly read saves us from all that the misunderstanding of Romanticism has cost. The critic should "accept" rather than "subvert or overlook" the "language of great writers" (*ST*, xv).

In the language of a great writer, unprecedented "national events" in politics, the "increasing accumulation of men in cities," and in work a new "uniformity of their occupations," while the growth of mass media facilitated "rapid communication"—all together threatened to "blunt the discriminating powers of the mind," making the humanities marginal or degraded. Wordsworth's Preface to *Lyrical Ballads* proclaims the need for sober and serious opposition to what Pope and Swift could dismiss with satiric scorn. Arnold, Eliot, and Leavis subsequently accepted this call. In going behind Arnold to Wordsworth, therefore, Hartman has preserved deep concerns, and he has also challenged our current institution of literary study by questioning Arnold's modest critical prose-pose. For Hartman knows that such modesty is politically significant (*CW*, 50), and he knows also that Wordsworth never renounced the immodest energy of "Hannibal among the Alps,"[19] yet Hartman does not want to cause trouble.

Hartman defuses the political implications of his institutional challenge by removing the threat of avant-garde coerciveness, refusing to join Wordsworth in sometimes traveling "before." Arnold had seen critics as avant-garde, perishing in the wilderness while pointing the way to a promised land for poetry; but Hartman insists, "This wilderness is all we have" (*CW*, 15). Hartman likewise revises Georg Lukács's definition of the essayist as a John the Baptist preaching "in the wilderness," the "pure type of the precursor," a road needing its end to be complete.[20] He suggests rather that as critics "we are forerunners to ourselves" (*CW*, 15). This comforting persistence of critical identity ("where they are, there I shall be") may cover the line Carlyle-Ruskin-Pater, yet in the relations Carlyle-Dickens, Ruskin-Proust, Pater-Joyce I find distinctions between precursor and after-runner larger than Hartman's formula would suggest. His denial of closure threatens a coercive denial of difference.

Let us, therefore, think again through Hartman's argument. He wants a history that does not become "monumental and preemptive." Critics must "avoid historicism," that is the "staging of history as a drama in which epiphanic raptures are replaced by epistemic ruptures [a witty parody of secularization models], *coupures* as decisive as Hellene and Hebrew, or Hegel and Marx" (*ST*, xx). The pointedly contrasted parallels in Hartman's prose foreground stylistics. "History-writing as Answerable Style" (cf. *FR*, 101-113) should resemble what Hartman finds in Wordsworth: unpointed yet finely nuanced, a medium that preserves the archaic while gently purifying it and allowing it to mingle with a popular, everyday influx. "Perhaps the only true literary history we have" is Auerbach's *Mimesis* (*CW*, 235), devoted to the stylistic mingling that overcame—at certain moments—the classical separation of levels. Yet even as I thus summarize Auerbach, a "drama" begins—one that caused Auerbach uncertainty and aroused criticism. For he expressed second thoughts about his fundamental contrast between Homer and the Bible, while E. R. Curtius argued that more flexibility existed among stylistic levels than allowed for by Auerbach's story.[21] Nonetheless, he went on in his final book toward the goal of disclosing a whole which "takes on the character of a dialectical unity, of a drama, or as Vico once said, of a serious poem."[22]

Consider Hartman's own story in *Criticism in the Wilderness*. It runs from the Arnoldian Concordat through the New Critical Reduction to the Revisionist Reversal. This is so bald a version of loss and gain that it signals parodic self-deprecation, yet it is meant to work also. And when Hartman fears "the Critic become the Commissar" (*CW*, 162), we feel the alliterative point dotted full seriously. Perhaps matters of practical concern—the freedom to write, one's own place among critics—enforce the need for historical differentiation.

Consider another invocation of history as a matter of real interest, part of "Saving the Text" by bringing the philosophic vocabulary of Derrida's deconstruction over into literary studies. Since "dissemination" is what "does not return to the father," Hartman links Derrida's term to the interplay in the Middle Ages and Renaissance between the authoritatively learned, classical, patriarchal language (*sermo patrius*) and the naturally imbibed, vernacular, mother tongue (*lingua materna*) (see *CW*, 88; *ST*, 154). In using deconstructive semantic play to enrich Auerbach's analysis of tensions between classical and Christian, Hartman *combines* the two tendencies in current criticism—Auerbachian spiritualizing and Derridean mechanizing—which Bloom had hoped to stay *between* (*MM*, 79).[23] By this means, Hartman hopes to save literary "deconstructive" practice from being what Gasché calls "a mechanical exercise similar to academic thematism or formalism" ("Deconstruction as Criticism," p. 178). He will avoid the "abstract and monotonous vigor of its application to this or that slice of text" (*ST*, 49). To prevent this deathly repetition requires placing "dissemination" in a "differentiated series" of stylistic practices including "imitation, translation, contamination, secularization, and (sacred) parody."[24] In his own need for differentiation, Hartman refers to the "evolution" of language and charges that Derrida "fails to provide a history that charts the path from 'imitation' to 'dissemination' " (*ST*, 49). Hartman's language rejoins Arnold and Lukács; rather than resting in the wilderness with Derrida, he follows the road to a new end.

Hartman wants history-writing to shun "historicism" while preserving the truly "historical," which pertains to our "mortal" being and "threatens lasting monuments or totalizing mind" (*CW*, 110). This evokes the project of a Heideggerian literary history, a project made arduous because there may be "no indication that Heidegger thinks that poetry has a history."[25] The conjunction of history with mortality again links history to our interests. Yet I find a monumentalizing that deadens Hartman's historical prose. He writes that "the political and economic unrest" of the 1930s "made it important to protect art from imperious demands of an ideological nature, emanating from politics" (*CW*, 284). Perhaps historical sentences need not have human agents, but to avoid the monumental they must at least have interested parties. To whom was it important?

Hartman's theoretical unease with history damages his practice when he, inevitably yet as if inadvertently, writes historically. His sentences become indistinguishable from those of Gerald Graff, for whom history is in theory no problem: "As the growth of class-consciousness threatened the stability of the established order, reason was associated with a blind fanaticism" (*Literature Against Itself*, p. 41). Again, to whom was this association significant? Graff shares with Hartman a fear of coercing reality. He insists on our knowing the object as in itself it really is "before leaping in with our value judgments" (*Literature Against Itself*, p. 86). Here too a hermeneutics of indeterminacy operates. We must be responsible to the whole being, rather than focusing only on what touches us, for "the existing order . . . has to be understood as it is before it can be altered" (*Literature Against Itself*, p. 27).[26] This statement is false: we have yet to understand the southern slave system or the Third Reich, yet those existing orders were altered. If Graff means an order *should* be understood before altered, I wonder who will define the object. The debate on the standard of living in nineteenth-century England still persists among historians. Should a worker unemployed by the new industrial "order" have waited for our results before breaking frames?

Even if the overall standard rose, there were moments, places, persons, for whom it did not. Human interests differ, and only in a radically different society from ours would a community of interest make possible consensually shared knowledge in the most urgent matters.

We are limited beings, yet a hermeneutics of indeterminacy refuses to accept our determinations, actively resists our ends, and thus contradicts the necessary "historical" concern with our mortality. A valuable openness may become a fearful refusal. Hartman's sense of reading in "How to Reap a Page" (in *ST*) could take as emblem Cleopatra's dream of Antony:

> For his bounty
> There was no winter in't; an autumn 'twas
> That grew the more by reaping.
> (V. 2. 86-88)

The dream defies the reality of Antony's death, even as the accepted emendation of the Folio reading "an Antony it was" into "an autumn 'twas" displaces the mortal human name by the natural force of the season. In refusing to look ahead with Arnold or Lukács to the end of the road, the promised land, Hartman undertakes instead to make the wilderness blossom:

> Roses are planted where thorns grow,
> And on the barren heath
> Sing the honey bees.
> (Blake, *The Marriage of Heaven
> and Hell*, plate 2)

He exchanges the future-orientation of Shelley's "Ode to the West Wind"—which sees autumnal destruction but looks ahead to the promise of spring—for the presentness of Keats's "To Autumn." The difference between seasons yields to the dilation of a moment. Yet as William Empson has objected, Hartman's own brilliant reading of Keats's ode elides any consciousness that Keats wrote it while knowing he would soon die. To move from Yeats's "Byzantium" to Keats's "Autumn" makes gentler the wish to be invulnerable to time, yet "suspensive" criticism resembles the hovering of ironic disinterest. Hartman's endless "hesitation" repeats I. A. Richards on the tragic "attitude" (in *Principles of Literary Criticism*), a frozen readiness that never commits itself, a monument of "patience" (*FR*, 109).[27]

When Keats glories in the "energies" of a "quarrel in the streets" (letter of 14 February—3 May 1819), it would be priggish to demand that he abandon his spectatorship and join in, or try to stop it. Yet in writing history, such Burckhardtian aestheticism joins with cynical pessimism about the future, as Hayden White has argued in *Metahistory*. Fredric Jameson has tried, however, to integrate an aesthetic moment with a more positive orientation to the future. To complement the necessary cynicism of ideological analysis, he urges a utopian, "anticipatory" analysis that finds figures for what will be fully realized only when all human beings can act and speak freely together as equals.[28] Social conflicts bring together even those most committed to atomic individualism and unite them in larger, common purposes. Ideological analysis criticizes the purpose; anticipatory criticism appreciates the union. Thus the solidarity of millowners conspiring to blacklist dissident workers prefigures what we may enjoy in a "finer tone" (Keats, letter of 22 November 1817) in an imagined end to history. Our judgments of present interest are suspended, but only for a moment, as part of moving toward a new goal. In its isolating an energy, in breaking the frame of value, overturning our moral conceptions, such a moment is Nietzschean, as is Derrida when he sets in play the deconstructive energies within the monuments of logocentrism.

Yet Hartman fears the "abstract and monotonous vigor," the deadly repetition-compulsion in Derrida, and he fears also utopian avant-gardism like Jameson's. The history of terms meaning "avant-garde" is not encouraging. When Keats's Coelus assures Hyperion that his "ethereal presence" will allow him to be "in the van of circumstance" (I, 34-44), Hyperion launches himself only into his own fall. In the first figurative adaptation to culture of the military term "vanguard," Carlyle writes that "at length Germany and Weisnichtwo were . . . in the vanguard of the world" (*Sartor Resartus*, I, iii), but this mocks the establishment of a "Professorship of Things in General" (*Allerley-Wissenschaft*) that lacks both teaching responsibilities and pay. This commitment to "Affirmation and Reconstruction" was in "Name merely." The Yale Critics prefer not to "travel before" but to walk alongside of received opinion, a paradoxical sidling that supports what it somehow also stands apart from. By the logic of the American Jeremiad, the very crisis provoked by the Yale Critics—their "unamericanness"—sets to work a process that reaffirms the solidarity of what it encloses. In shunning the purposiveness of "ideological criticism" and preferring a "deliberately relaxed style" in essays that are "digressive yet powerfully recursive," Hartman follows Lionel Trilling and bids to succeed him as "Man in the Middle" (*FR*, 294-297). We remain suspended always on the threshold of a change that never occurs.

The Yale Critics manifest a timidity that threatens to make literary studies "merely the name . . . for an academic department where memories of youthful hope are cherished, and wistful yearnings for recapturing past glories" (Rorty, "Nineteenth-Century Idealism and Twentieth-Century Textualism," p. 163). As readers we need less of Hartman's hesitant "patience" for ourselves and need more confidence in what Frank Kermode calls the "patience"of great literature. We must not fear that if we make interpretive decisions rather than indeterminations—and thus try to make literature part of our future as well as our present—we will somehow destroy or violate the works we care for. Despite Hartman's critique of the historicism of gain and loss, he fears losing the object. *Saving the Text* has at least this meaning.

Such loss is possible. Hazlitt's prose Immortality Ode "On Reading Old Books" laments the vanishing of privileged early moments of literary experience. Hazlitt's long love for Wordsworth diminished his response to Keats: "The sharp luscious flavor, the fine *aroma* is fled. . . . But it was not always so. There was a time when . . . every word was a flower."[29] Emerson's "Experience" of reading charts a series of lost objects: "Once I took such delight in Montaigne that I thought I should not need any other book; before that in Shakespeare; then in Plutarch; at one time in Bacon; afterward in Goethe; even in Bettine, but now I turn the pages . . . languidly." Of painting, "How strongly I have felt . . . that when you have seen one well, you must take your leave of it, you shall never see it again." Such loss is possible, but it is not the end. The object remains, but no longer ours. We go on.

Emerson and Foucault define a relation to history different from any which has supported the institutions of reading Hartman and Derrida function within. I mean more than the term "power" Hazlitt and Emerson share with Foucault. This distrust of the ingenuities needed to startle familiar texts into life makes attractive Foucault's archival research that finds fresh material bearing on our interests. Even Emerson's notorious disappointment that Shakespeare used his genius only as "master of revels to mankind" (*Representative Men*) joins an analysis of literature as an agency of social power: "Where Montaigne withdrew to his study, Shakespeare became the presiding genius of a popular, urban art form with the capacity to foster psychic mobility in the service of Elizabethan power."[30] Such a view emphasizes less the antithesis of Shakespeare to the mass media that culture critics from Wordsworth to Leavis have maintained than the similarities.

I do not think such revisions are violations or that they will lose utterly Shakespeare or anything else we value. I have yet to see any demonstration that to reduce the hierarchical power of canonical literary texts will destroy them as surely as the bombing of Monte Cassino. I agree that artworks are not there for us to use in any way we want. The world of nature, however, is even less there for us to use, yet our lives depend on taking the chance that we may find a proper use. I have resisted the rhetoric of Nietzschean activism and must also resist the rhetoric of tactful purism such as Wordsworth addresses to the "dearest maiden" at the end of "Nutting." As she moves through the groves, she must only "with gentle hand/ Touch—for there is a spirit in the woods." How does the speaker know? Because after long lingering in a state of suspension, hesitation, indeterminacy ("A little while I stood . . . or beneath the trees I sate. . . . Perhaps it was a bower . . ."), he rose into action that brought "pain" but also the knowledge of the "quiet being" he now wishes to protect. What the grove "patiently gave up" to him, is still there for the maiden. As teachers we must not try to deny our students the experiences that have brought us our deepest conviction. The voice of criticism need not be the voice of caution.

If the history of the Yale Critics has been the history of a misunderstanding, it has nonetheless occurred. The daring imputed to them may help to move a new enterprise: "The really subversive form of criticism begins when people ask whether a specific social function needs to be performed at all."[31] If historical experience teaches us anything, we may expect that whatever promised land lies beyond the answers to such questions, powers and institutions will still be part of it, again to be remade; texts again to be read, critics criticized.

NOTES

1. Irving Howe, "Modern Criticism: Privileges and Perils," in *Modern Literary Criticism*, ed. Howe (Boston: Beacon, 1958), p. 1; Morton Dauwen Zabel, *Literary Opinion in America* (1937; 3d ed., revised, New York: Harper, 1962), p. xix.

2. Howe, p. 4; and A. Walton Litz, "Literary Criticism," in Daniel Hoffmann, ed., *Harvard Guide to Contemporary American Writing* (Cambridge: Harvard Univ. Press, 1979), p. 74.

3. For further contrasts between the French and American academics, see Emmanuel Le Roy Ladurie, *Guide Rouge*, trans. David Bellos (review of Régis Debray, *Teachers, Writers, Celebrities: The Intellectuals of Modern France*) *New York Review of Books*, 21 January 1982, e.g., p. 60: In contrast to the centralized enclosure of France, "An academic in the US lives in the enormous ghetto of the English-speaking University world, so vast that its walls are not visible from the inside."

4. Jane P. Tompkins shares this position, holding that since the decline of New Criticism, "Professors and students alike practice criticism as usual; only the vocabulary in which they perform their analyses has altered." See "The Reader in History," in *Reader-Response Criticism*, ed. Tompkins (Baltimore: Johns Hopkins Univ. Press, 1980), p. 225.

5. Richard Rorty, "Overcoming the Tradition: Heidegger and Dewey," in Michael Murray, ed., *Heidegger and Modern Philosophy* (New Haven: Yale Univ. Press, 1978), pp. 242-244.

6. Hartman explicitly reflects on this matter in "The Poetics of Prophecy," p. 36.

7. See Lionel Trilling, "Reflections on a Lost Cause: English Literature and American Education" (1958), in *Speaking of Literature and Society*, ed. Diana Trilling (New York: Harcourt, Brace, Jovanovich, 1980); and John Higham, "The Cult of the 'American Consensus': Homogenizing Our History," *Commentary* 27 (February, 1959).

8. Irving Babbitt, quoting Emerson, in *Literature and the American College* (Boston: Houghton Mifflin, 1908), p. 244.

9. This younger generation has not yet received much comment. See, however, Wallace Martin, "Playing Around" (response to Johnson, "Nothing Fails like Success"), in *SCE Reports*, no. 9 (Summer 1981), pp. 3-10.

10. Sandra M. Gilbert and Susan Gubar, *The Madwoman in the Attic* (New Haven: Yale Univ. Press, 1979), pp. xii-xiii.

11. See also Jonathan Culler, *The Pursuit of Signs* (Ithaca: Cornell Univ. Press, 1981), esp. pp. 14-16.

12. Richard Rorty recognizes and elaborates this paradox in "Criticism without Theory," presented at the 1981 MLA convention.

13. I treat Bloom at greater length in "The Criticism of Harold Bloom: Judgment and History," and de Man in "To Regress from the Rigor of Shelley: Figures of History in American Deconstructive Criticism," and "Aesthetics, Rhetoric, History."

14. Graff, *Literature Against Itself*, pp. 48, 13, 136, 62; de Man especially in RT, ICF, "A New Vitalism," and *AR*, pp. 3-19.

15. I summarize Hartman's views, which I contest in "The Arnoldian Prophecy: Making Critical History," forthcoming. For aid in thinking about Hartman, I am grateful to unpublished work by Daniel O'Hara.

16. For a valuable analysis of the Hegelian "end of history" as the fundamental problematic of Foucault, Derrida, Deleuze, and others, see Descombes, *Modern French Philosophy*, passim.

17. Hartman's allusive attack on the defense of Romanticism by M. H. Abrams, *Natural Supernaturalism* (1971), recalls a significant fact: At Cornell, Abrams was Bloom's teacher, and a senior colleague to de Man and Hartman, before the attacks on his positions began in RT and Miller's "Tradition and Difference."

18. See, for example, 1850 *Prelude* I, 330; V, 381 and 392; and the discussion of the Imagination in Wordsworth's 1815 Preface.

19. On this figure from Wordsworth's Essay, Supplementary to the Preface of 1815, see my "Romanticism, the Self, and the City," *boundary 2* 9:1 (1980).

20. George Lukács, "On the Nature and Form of the Essay," (1910), in *Soul and Form*, trans. Anna Bostock (Cambridge: MIT Press, 1974), pp. 16-17. Hartman thus also opposes the reading of M. H. Abrams in *Natural Supernaturalism*, which finds a completed pattern of journeying characteristic of Romanticism, and of Wordsworth above all. See on this topic my "Bounding Lines: *The Prelude* and Critical Revision," *boundary 2*, 7:3 (1979), which sides with Hartman. Yet even if "the artist is surely the liminal or threshold person par excellence" (*FR*, 109), one need not require the critic to be so.

21. See E. R. Curtius, "Die Lehre von den drei Stilen in Altertum und Mittelalter" and Auerbach's reply "Epilegomena zu *Mimesis*," in *Romanische Forschungen* 64 (1952) and 65 (1953).

22. Erich Auerbach, *Literary Language and Its Public in Late Latin Antiquity and in the Middle Ages* (1958), trans. Ralph Manheim (New York: Random House, 1965), p. 7. See again p. 21: the book is "a kind of drama which advances no theory but only sketches a certain pattern of human destiny. The subject of this drama is Europe."

23. Within the practice of philology, Derrida's psychoanalytic attention to the word resembles Leo Spitzer's stylistic analysis and contrasts with Auerbach's syntactic emphasis. See Lowry Nelson, Jr., "Erich Auerbach: Memoir of a Scholar," *Yale Review* 69 (1980): 314 (who does not mention Derrida). For a radically different constellation of "vernacular," "mother tongue," and *sermo patrius*, see Ivan Illich, "The War against Subsistence," *democracy* 1:3 (1981), esp. pp. 72-76.

24. See M. M. Bakhtin, "From the Prehistory of Novelistic Discourse," in *The Dialogic Imagination*, ed. Michael Holquist, trans. Caryl Emerson and Michael Holquist (Austin: Univ. of Texas Press, 1981), esp. pp. 68-82 on medieval "polyglossia" and its relation to modern "heteroglossia."

25. Rorty, "Heidegger and Dewey," in Murray, ed., *Heidegger and Modern Philosophy*, p. 251. See in Murray also David Couzens Hoy, "History, Historicity, and Historiography in *Being and Time*"; and for an attempt at Heideggerian "new literary history," Bové, *Destructive Poetics*.

26. Jane Tompkins finds in all criticism since the Romantics this tendency "not so much [to] ignore the question of social relevance as postpone it, assuming that until the text is rightly understood it cannot be evaluated." See *Reader-Response Criticism*, p. 205.

27. Here I concur with Culler, *The Pursuit of Signs*, pp. 77-78: "One is always tempted by the synoptic view," but "to give the poem any force one must make choices," rather than attempt a reading that tries "to live happily with all possibilities."

28. Fredric Jameson, *The Political Unconscious: Narrative as a Socially Symbolic Act* (Ithaca: Cornell Univ. Press, 1981), p. 296, and, for context, pp. 289-291. For related arguments see Bruce Robbins, "Power and Pantheons," *Literature and History* 8:2 (1982).

29. The "flowers of language" and "language of flowers" recur crucially in *ST*.

30. Stephen Greenblatt, *Renaissance Self-Fashioning* (Chicago: Univ. of Chicago Press, 1980), p. 253.

31. Barrington Moore, *Injustice: The Social Bases of Obedience and Revolt* (White Plains, N.Y.: M. E. Sharpe, 1978), p. 510.

Bibliography

Bibliography

Under an author's name, publications are entered alphabetically to facilitate the location of titles mentioned in the text.

We have listed the books and articles of Bloom, Hartman, de Man, and Miller, but do not list articles subsequently collected in their books. If an uncollected article has been republished elsewhere, the later printings are not listed unless there has been a change of title or the earliest version is hard to obtain. Bloom and Hartman have contributed to *The New York Times Book Review* since 1969; Bloom has written reviews for *The New Republic* and (recently) *The Times Literary Supplement*. These have not been included, but we have included review articles by all four critics.

Only those of Derrida's publications mentioned in the text are listed. A complete bibliography of his writings up to 1977 can be found in *Edmund Husserl's "Origin of Geometry": An Introduction*, trans. John P. Leavey, Jr. (Stony Brook: Nicolas Hays, 1978). For Derrida's publications since 1977, and for information about essays that de Man later collected in his books, see Richard Barney's "Deconstructive Criticism: A Selected Bibliography," *SCE Reports*, no. 8 (1980), available from the Society for Critical Exchange.

Commentary on the Yale critics is fragmentary and uneven. The notoriety of a polemical article or review does not ensure its inclusion in this selective bibliography. For additional discussions of Hartman, see note 2 in Michael Sprinker's essay. The notes to Paul Bové's essay mention a number of works relevant to the Yale critics.

I am indebted to Jonathan Arac and Stanley Corngold for many of the following entries, and to the critics who are the subject of this collection for their help in tracking down their publications.

W. M.

Abrams, M. H. "The Deconstructive Angel." *Critical Inquiry*, 3 (1977), 425-38.
———. "How to Do Things with Texts." *Partisan Review*, 46 (1979), 566-88.
Adams, Robert Martin. "Extension and Intension." *Hudson Review*, 24 (1971-72), 687-96.
    Review of de Man, *Blindness and Insight*, and Abrams, *Natural Supernaturalism*.

Arac, Jonathan. "Aesthetics, Rhetoric, History: Reading Nietzsche with Henry James." *Boundary 2*, 9, no. 3 (1981), 437-54. Review of de Man, *Allegories of Reading*.

———. "The Criticism of Harold Bloom: Judgment and History." *Centrum*, 6, no. 1 (1978), 32-42.

———. "To Regress from the Rigor of Shelley: Figures of History in American Deconstructive Criticism." *Boundary 2*, 8, no. 3 (1980), 241-57.

Atkins, G. Douglas. "J. Hillis Miller, Deconstruction and the Recovery of Transcendence." *Notre Dame English Journal*, 13 (1980), 51-63.

Basset, Sharon. "Tristes Critiques: Harold Bloom and the Sorrows of Secular Art." *Literature and Psychology*, 27 (1977), 106-12.

HAROLD BLOOM

Agon: Towards a Theory of Revisionism. New York: Oxford Univ. Press, 1982.

The Anxiety of Influence: A Theory of Poetry. New York: Oxford Univ. Press, 1973.

Blake's Apocalypse: A Study in Poetic Argument. Garden City, NY: Doubleday, 1963.

"The Breaking of Form." In *Deconstruction and Criticism*. New York: Seabury, 1979, pp. 1-37.

The Breaking of the Vessels. Chicago: Univ. of Chicago Press, 1982.

"Commentary." In *The Poetry and Prose of William Blake*, ed. David V. Erdman. Garden City, NY: Doubleday, 1965, pp. 807-89.

Figures of Capable Imagination. New York: Seabury, 1976.

The Flight to Lucifer: A Gnostic Fantasy. New York: Farrar, Straus, Giroux, 1979.

"The Freshness of Transformation: Emerson's Dialectics of Influence." In *Emerson: Prophecy, Metamorphosis, Influence*, ed. David Levin. New York: Columbia Univ. Press, 1975, pp. 129-48.

"Introduction: Reading Browning." In *Robert Browning: A Collection of Critical Essays*, ed. Harold Bloom and Adrienne Munich. Englewood Cliffs, NJ: Prentice-Hall, 1979, p. 1-12.

Kabbalah and Criticism. New York: Seabury, 1975.

A Map of Misreading. New York: Oxford Univ. Press, 1975.

"A New Poetics." *Yale Review*, 47 (1957), 130-33. Review of Frye, *Anatomy of Criticism*.

Poetry and Repression: Revisionism from Blake to Stevens. New Haven: Yale Univ. Press, 1976.

"Recent Studies in the Nineteenth Century." *Studies in English Literature*, 10 (1970), 817-29.

The Ringers in the Tower: Studies in Romantic Tradition. Chicago: Univ. of Chicago Press, 1971.

Shelley's Mythmaking. New Haven: Yale Univ. Press, 1959.

"Viewpoint." *Times Literary Supplement*, 8 Feb. 1980, 137-38.

The Visionary Company: A Reading of English Romantic Poetry. Garden City, NY: Doubleday, 1961. Revised and enlarged ed., Cornell Univ. Press, 1971.

Wallace Stevens: The Poems of Our Climate. Ithaca, NY: Cornell Univ. Press, 1977.

Yeats. New York: Oxford Univ. Press, 1970.

Bové, Paul. *Destructive Poetics: Heidegger and Modern American Poetry*. New York: Columbia Univ. Press, 1980. Sections on de Man and Bloom.

Bruss, Elizabeth W. *Beautiful Theories: The Spectacle of Discourse in Contemporary Criticism*. Baltimore: Johns Hopkins Univ. Press, 1982. Chapter on Bloom, pp. 288-362.

Burke, Kenneth. "Father and Son." *New Republic*, 12 Apr. 1975, pp. 23-24. Review of Bloom, *A Map of Misreading*.

———. Review of Bloom, *Wallace Stevens. New Republic*, 11 June 1977, pp. 24-27.

Cain, William E. "Deconstruction in America: The Recent Literary Criticism of J. Hillis Miller." *College English*, 41 (1979), 367-82.

Christensen, Jerome C. "The Symbol's Errant Allegory: Coleridge and His Critics." *ELH*, 45 (1978), 640-59. Sections on de Man.

Culler, Jonathan. "Frontiers of Criticism." *Yale Review*, 61 (1971-72), 259-71. Review of de Man, *Blindness & Insight*.

——. *On Deconstruction: Theory and Criticism after Structuralism*. Ithaca: Cornell Univ. Press, 1982.

——. "Reading and Misreading." *Yale Review*, 65 (1975), 88-95. Review of Bloom, *A Map of Misreading*, and Hartman, *The Fate of Reading*.

Deconstruction and Criticism. New York: Seabury, 1979.

Derrida, Jacques. *La Dissémination*. Paris: Seuil, 1972.

——. "The Ends of Man." *Philosophy and Phenomenological Research*, 30 (1969), 31-57.

——. *Of Grammatology*, trans. Gayatri Spivak. Baltimore: Johns Hopkins Univ. Press, 1976. Translation of *De la grammatologie* (Paris: Minuit, 1967).

——. "The Law of Genre." *Critical Inquiry*, 7 (1980), 55-81. French text and English translation also published in *Glyph* 7 (1980), pp. 176-232.

——. "Living On   Border Lines." In *Deconstruction and Criticism*. New York: Seabury, 1979, pp. 75-176.

——. *Marges de la philosophie*. Paris: Minuit, 1972.

——. "Pas I." *Gramma*, nos. 3-4 (1976), pp. 111-215.

——. *Positions*. Paris: Minuit, 1972.

——. *Speech and Phenomena, and Other Essays on Husserl's Theory of Signs*, trans. David B. Allison. Evanston: Northwestern Univ. Press, 1973.

——. *Spurs: Nietzsche's Styles*, trans. Barbara Harlow. Chicago: Univ. of Chicago Press, 1979.

——. *Writing and Difference*, trans. Alan Bass. Chicago: Univ. of Chicago Press, 1978.

Descombes, Vincent. *Modern French Philosophy*, trans. L. Scott-Fox and J. M. Harding. Cambridge, England: Cambridge Univ. Press, 1980.

Donoghue, Denis. "Deconstructing Deconstruction." *New York Review of Books*, 12 June 1980, pp. 37-41. Review of *Deconstruction and Criticism* and de Man, *Allegories of Reading*.

——. *Ferocious Alphabets*. Boston: Little, Brown, 1981. Sections on Bloom and de Man.

——. "Reading about Writing." *New York Times Book Review*, 9 Nov. 1980, pp. 11, 32-33. Review of Hartman, *Criticism in the Wilderness*.

Ferguson, F. C. "Reading Heidegger." In *Martin Heidegger and the Question of Literature*, ed. William V. Spanos. Bloomington: Indiana Univ. Press, 1979, pp. 253-70. On Derrida and de Man.

Fletcher, Angus. "The Great Wordsworth." *Yale Review*, 54 (1965), 595-98. Review of Hartman, *Wordsworth's Poetry*.

——. "The Perpetual Error." *Diacritics*, 2, no. 4 (1972), pp. 14-20. Review of de Man, *Blindness & Insight*.

——. Review of Hartman, *Beyond Formalism*. *College English*, 34 (1972), 414-25.

Gans, Eric. "Anamorphose du cercle." *Critique*, 30 (1974), 927-40. On de Man.

Garber, Frederick. Review of Hartman, *The Fate of Reading*. *Comparative Literature*, 30 (1978), 172-78.

——. Review of de Man, *Blindness & Insight*. *Comparative Literature*, 26 (1974), 276-81.

Gasché, Rodolphe. "Deconstruction as Criticism." *Glyph* 6 (1979), pp. 177-215.

——. " 'Setzung' and 'Übersetzung': Notes on Paul de Man." *Diacritics*, 11, no. 4 (1981), 36-57.

Godzich, Wlad. "Harold Bloom as Rhetorician." *Centrum*, 6, no. 1 (1978), 43-49.

——. "Introduction: Caution! Reader at Work!" In *Blindness and Insight and Other Essays*, by Paul de Man. Minneapolis: University of Minnesota Press, 1983.

Graff, Gerald. *Literature Against Itself*. Chicago: Univ. of Chicago Press, 1979.

Handelman, Susan A. *The Slayers of Moses: The Emergence of Rabbinic Interpretation in Modern Literary Theory*. Albany: State Univ. of New York Press, 1982. Chapter on Bloom, pp. 179-223.

GEOFFREY H. HARTMAN

"The Aesthetics of Complicity." *Georgia Review*, 28 (1974), 384-88.
Akiba's Children. Emory, Va: Iron Mountain Press, 1978. Poems.
André Malraux. London: Bowes and Bowes, 1960.
"To Bedlam and Part Way Back." In *Anne Sexton: The Artist and Her Critics*, ed. J. D. McClatchy. Bloomington: Indiana Univ. Press, 1978, pp. 118-21. Originally appeared in *Kenyon Review*, 22 (1960), 691-700.
"Between the Acts: Jeanne Moreau's *Lumière.*" *Georgia Review*, 31 (1977), 237-42.
Beyond Formalism: Literary Essays 1958-1970. New Haven: Yale Univ. Press, 1970.
"Blessing the Torrent: On Wordsworth's Later Style." *PMLA*, 93 (1978), 196-204.
"Communication, Language and the Humanities." *ADE Bulletin*, no. 70 (1981), 10-16.
"The Concept of Character in Lawrence's First Play." *Bulletin of the Midwest Modern Language Association*, 10, no. 1 (1977), 38-43.
Criticism in the Wilderness: The Study of Literature Today. New Haven: Yale Univ. Press, 1980.
"Diction and Defense in Wordsworth." In *The Literary Freud: Mechanisms of Defense and the Poetic Will*, ed. Joseph H. Smith. New Haven: Yale Univ. Press, 1980, pp. 205-15.
The Fate of Reading and Other Essays. Chicago: Univ. of Chicago Press, 1975.
"Foreword." In *New Perspectives on Coleridge and Wordsworth*, ed. Geoffrey H. Hartman. New York: Columbia Univ. Press, 1972, pp. vii-xii.
"The Fullness and Nothingness of Literature." *Yale French Studies*, no. 16 (1955-56), pp. 63-78.
"Hermeneutic Hesitation: A Dialogue between Geoffrey Hartman and Julian Moynahan." *Novel*, 12 (1979), 101-12.
"How Creative Should Literary Criticism Be?" *New York Times Book Review*, 5 April 1981, pp. 11, 24-25.
"Humanistic Study and the Social Sciences." *College English*, 38 (1976), 219-23.
"Literature as a Profession II: The Creative Function of Criticism." *Humanities*, 2 (Dec. 1981), 8-9.
"The Malraux Mystery." *New Republic*, 29 Jan. 1977, pp. 27-30.
"Nerval's Peristyle." *Nineteenth-Century French Studies*, 5 (1976-77), 71-78.
"Plenty of Nothing: Alfred Hitchcock's *North by Northwest.*" *Yale Review*, 71 (1981), 13-27.
"The Poetics of Prophecy." In *High Romantic Argument: Essays for M. H. Abrams*, ed. Lawrence Lipking. Ithaca, NY: Cornell Univ. Press, 1981, pp. 15-40.
"Preface." *Deconstruction and Criticism*. New York: Seabury, 1979, pp. vii-ix.
"Preface." *The Gaze of Orpheus and Other Literary Essays*, by Maurice Blanchot. Barrytown, NY: Station Hill, 1981, pp. ix-xi.
"Preface." *Papers in Comparative Studies*, 1 (1981), 5-8.
"Preface." *Psychoanalysis and the Question of the Text*, ed. Geoffrey H. Hartman. Baltimore: Johns Hopkins Univ. Press, 1978, pp. vii-xix.
"Preface." *Romanticism: Vistas, Instances, Continuities*, ed. David Thorburn and Geoffrey H. Hartman. Ithaca: Cornell Univ. Press, 1973, pp. 7-9.
"Recent Studies in the Nineteenth Century." *Studies in English Literature*, 6 (1966), 753-82.
"Reflections on Romanticism in France." *Studies in Romanticism*, 9 (1970), 233-48.
Saving the Text: Literature / Derrida / Philosophy. Baltimore: Johns Hopkins Univ. Press, 1981.
"Signs and Symbols." *New York Times Book Review*, 4 Feb. 1979, pp. 12-13, 34-35. Review of Barthes, *Image—Music—Text* and *A Lover's Discourse*.
"The Taming of History." *Yale French Studies*, no. 18 (1957), pp. 114-28.
"A Touching Compulsion: Wordsworth and the Problem of Literary Representation." *Georgia Review*, 31 (1977), 345-61.
The Unmediated Vision: An Interpretation of Wordsworth, Hopkins, Rilke, and Valéry. New

Haven: Yale Univ. Press, 1954. New ed. (slightly revised, with a prefatory note), Harcourt, Brace, 1966.

"The Use and Abuse of Structural Analysis: Riffaterre's Interpretation of Wordsworth's 'Yew-Trees.' " *New Literary History*, 7 (1975), 165-80.

"Words, Wish, Worth: Wordsworth." In *Deconstruction and Criticism*. New York: Seabury, 1979, pp. 177-216.

"Wordsworth." *Yale Review*, 58 (1969), 507-25. Reprinted as the introduction to *Wordsworth: Selected Poetry and Prose*, ed. Geoffrey H. Hartman (New York: New American Library, 1970).

Wordsworth's Poetry, 1787-1814. New Haven: Yale Univ. Press, 1964. "Retrospect, 1971" added in the third edition (1971).

Hollander, John. Review of Bloom, *The Anxiety of Influence*. *New York Times Book Review*, 4 Mar. 1973, pp. 27-30.

Johnson, Barbara. "Nothing Fails Like Success." *SCE Reports*, no. 8 (1980), pp. 7-16.

———. *The Critical Difference: Essays in the Contemporary Rhetoric of Reading*. Baltimore: Johns Hopkins Univ. Press, 1981.

Kermode, Frank. "Notes Toward a Supreme Poetry." *New York Times Book Review*, 12 June 1977, pp. 9, 44. Review of Bloom, *Wallace Stevens*.

Kincaid, James R. "Antithetical Criticism, Harold Bloom, and Victorian Poetry." *Victorian Poetry*, 14 (1976), 365-82.

Klein, Richard. "The Blindness of Hyperboles: The Ellipses of Insight." *Diacritics*, 3, no. 2 (1973), 33-44. On de Man.

Langbaum, Robert. "Magnifying Wordsworth." *ELH*, 33 (1966), 271-78. Review of Hartman, *Wordsworth's Poetry*.

Lawall, Sarah. Review of *Criticism in the Wilderness*. *Comparative Literature*, 34 (1982), 177-81.

Leitch, Vincent B. "The Book of Deconstructive Criticism." *Studies in the Literary Imagination*, 12 (1979), 19-39.

———. "The Lateral Dance: The Deconstructive Criticism of J. Hillis Miller." *Critical Inquiry*, 6 (1980), 593-607.

———. *Deconstructive Criticism: An Advanced Introduction and Survey*. New York: Columbia Univ. Press, 1982.

Lentricchia, Frank. *After the New Criticism*. Chicago: Univ. of Chicago Press, 1980. Chapters on Bloom and de Man.

PAUL DE MAN

"Allegorie und Symbol in der europäischen Frühromantik." In *Typologia litterarum*, ed. Stefan Sonderegger et al. Zurich: Atlantis, 1969, pp. 403-35. Trans. as Part I of "The Rhetoric of Temporality," *infra*.

Allegories of Reading: Figural Language in Rousseau, Nietzsche, Rilke, and Proust. New Haven: Yale Univ. Press, 1979.

"Autobiography as De-facement." *MLN*, 94 (1979), 919-30.

Blindness & Insight: Essays in the Rhetoric of Contemporary Criticism. New York: Oxford Univ. Press, 1971. New ed., with other essays, Minneapolis: Univ. of Minnesota Press, 1983.

"The Crisis of Contemporary Criticism." *Arion*, 6 (1967), 38-57. Revised for publication in *Blindness and Insight*, pp. 3-19.

"La Critique thématique devant le thème de Faust." *Critique*, 13 (1957), 387-404.

"The Epistemology of Metaphor." *Critical Inquiry*, 5 (1978), 13-30.

"Les Exégèses de Hölderlin par Martin Heidegger." *Critique*, 11 (1955), 800-19.

"Foreword." *The Dissimulating Harmony*, by Carol Jacobs. Baltimore: Johns Hopkins Univ. Press, 1978, pp. vii-xiii.

"Giraudoux." *New York Review of Books*, 28 Nov. 1963, pp. 20-21. Review of Christopher Fry's translation, *Plays* (1963).

"Heidegger Reconsidered." *New York Review of Books*, 2 Apr. 1964, pp. 14-16. Review of William Barrett, *What is Existentialism?*

"Hypogram and Inscription: Michael Riffaterre's Poetics of Reading." *Diacritics*, 11, no. 4 (1981), 17-35.

"L'Image de Rousseau dans la Poésie de Hölderlin." *Deutsche Beiträge zur geistigen Überlieferung*, 5 (1965), 157-83. Trans. (revised) as "Hölderlins Rousseaubild," *Hölderlin-Jahrbuch, 1967-68* (Tübingen: Mohr, 1969), pp. 180-208.

"Impasse de la critique formaliste." *Critique*, 12 (1956), 483-500.

"Introduction." *Selected Poetry of Keats*, ed. Paul de Man. New York: New American Library, 1966, p. ix-xxxvi.

"Introduction." *Studies in Romanticism*, 18 (1979), 495-99.

"Introduction." *Toward an Aesthetics of Reception*, by Hans Robert Jauss. Minneapolis: Univ. of Minnesota Press, 1982, pp. vii-xxv.

"Keats and Hölderlin." *Comparative Literature*, 8 (1956), 28-45.

"A Letter from Paul de Man." *Critical Inquiry*, 8 (1982), 509-13. Concerns the essay by Stanley Corngold that appears in this collection.

"Literature and Language: A Commentary." *New Literary History*, 4 (1972), 181-92.

"The Literature of Nihilism." *New York Review of Books*, 23 June 1966, pp. 16-20. Review of Erich Heller, *The Artist's Journey into the Interior*, and Ronald Gray, *The German Tradition in Literature, 1871-1945*.

Ed. *Madame Bovary*. "Edited with a substantially new translation by Paul de Man." New York: Norton, 1965.

"Madame de Staël et Rousseau." *Preuves*, no. 190 (Dec. 1966), pp. 35-40.

"The Mask of Albert Camus." *New York Review of Books*, 23 Dec. 1965, pp. 10-13. Review of Camus, *Notebooks 1942-1951*.

"A Modern Master." *New York Review of Books*, 19 Nov. 1964, pp. 8-10. Review of Borges, *Dreamtigers* and *Labyrinths*.

"Modern Poetics: French and German." In *Princeton Encyclopedia of Poetry and Poetics*, ed. Alex Preminger et al. Princeton: Princeton Univ. Press, 1965, pp. 518-23.

"Montaigne et la transcendence." *Critique*, 9 (1953), 1011-22.

"Le Néant poétique: Commentaire d'un Sonnet hermétique de Mallarmé." *Monde nouveau*, no. 88 (1955), pp. 63-75.

"New criticism et nouvelle critique." *Preuves*, no. 188 (Oct. 1966), pp. 29-37. Revised for publication in *Blindness & Insight*, pp. 20-35.

"A New Vitalism." *Massachusets Review*, 3 (1962), 618-23. Review of Bloom, *The Visionary Company*.

"Pascal's Allegory of Persuasion." In *Allegory and Representation*, ed. Stephen J. Greenblatt. Baltimore: Johns Hopkins Univ. Press, 1981, pp. 1-25.

Ed. *The Portable Rousseau*. New York: Viking, forthcoming.

"The Resistance to Literary Theory." *Yale French Studies*, no. 63 (1982), pp. 3-20.

Review of *The Anxiety of Influence. Comparative Literature*, 26 (1974), 269-75.

Review of Derrida, *De la grammatologie. Annales de la Société J.-J. Rousseau*, 37 (1966-68), 284-88.

"The Rhetoric of Temporality." In *Interpretation: Theory and Practice*, ed. Charles S. Singleton. Baltimore: Johns Hopkins Univ. Press, 1969, pp. 173-209.

"The Riddle of Hölderlin." *New York Review of Books*, 19 Nov. 1970, pp. 47-52. Review of Michael Hamburger's translation, *Poems and Fragments*.

"Sartre's Confessions." *New York Review of Books*, 5 Nov. 1964, pp. 10-13. Review of Sartre, *The Words*.
"Shelley Disfigured." In *Deconstruction and Criticism* (New York: Seabury, 1979), pp. 39-74.
"Sign and Symbol in Hegel's *Aesthetics*." *Critical Inquiry*, 8 (1982), 761-75.
"Situation du roman." *Monde nouveau*, no. 11 (June 1956), pp. 57-60.
"Spacecritics." *Partisan Review*, 31 (1964), 640-50. Review of Miller, *The Disappearance of God*, and Frank, *The Widening Gyre*.
"Structure intentionelle de l'*image* romantique." *Revue internationale de philosophie*, 14 (1960), 68-84. Trans. in *Romanticism and Consciousness*, ed. Harold Bloom (New York: Norton, 1970), pp. 65-77.
"Symbolic Landscape in Wordsworth and Yeats." In *In Defense of Reading*, ed. Reuben A. Brower and Richard Poirier. New York: Dutton, 1962, pp. 22-37.
"Tentation de la permanence." *Monde nouveau*, no. 93 (1955), pp. 49-61.
"What is Modern?" *New York Review of Books*, 26 Aug. 1965, pp. 10-13. Review of Ellman and Feidelson, *The Modern Tradition*.
"Whatever Happened to André Gide?" *New York Review of Books*, 6 May 1965, pp. 15-17. Review of Wallace Fowlie, *André Gide*, and Gide, *Marshlands and Prometheus Misbound*.
"Wordsworth und Hölderlin." *Schweizer Monatshefte*, 45 (1966), 1141-55.

Marshall, Donald. "Criticism and Creativity." *Yale Review*, 71 (1981), 129-38. Review of *Criticism in the Wilderness* and *Saving the Text*.
McLelland, Jane. Review of de Man, *Allegories of Reading*. *MLN*, 96 (1981), 888-97.
Mellor, Anne K. "On Romantic Irony." *Criticism*, 21 (1979), 217-29. Treats de Man and Derrida.

J. HILLIS MILLER

"Afterword." *Our Mutual Friend*. New York: New American Library, 1964, pp. 901-11.
"The Anonymous Walkers." *Nation*, 190 (1960), 351-54.
"Antitheses of Criticism: Reflections on the Yale Colloquium." *MLN*, 81 (1966), 557-71.
"Ariachne's Broken Woof." *Georgia Review*, 31 (1977), 44-60.
"Ariadne's Thread: Repetition and the Narrative Line." *Critical Inquiry*, 3 (1976), 57-77.
"Beginning with a Text." *Diacritics*, 6, no. 3 (1976), 2-7. Review of Said, *Beginnings*.
"Béguin, Balzac, Trollope et la double analogic redoublée." In *Albert Béguin et Marcel Raymond*. Paris: Corti, 1979, pp. 135-54.
"A 'Buchstäbliches' Reading of *The Elective Affinities*." *Glyph* 6 (1979), pp. 1-23.
"Character in the Novel: A Real Illusion." In *From Smollet to James: Studies in the Novel and Other Essays Presented to Edgar Johnson*, ed. Samuel I. Mintz et al. Charlottesville: Univ. Press of Virginia, 1981, pp. 277-85.
"Charles Dickens." In *New Catholic Encyclopedia*. New York: McGraw-Hill, 1967, vol. 4, pp. 856-57.
Charles Dickens: The World of His Novels. Cambridge, Mass.: Harvard Univ. Press, 1958.
"The Creation of the Self in Gerard Manley Hopkins." *ELH*, 22 (1955), 293-319.
"The Critic as Host." *Critical Inquiry*, 3 (1977), 439-47.
"The Critic as Host." In *Deconstruction and Criticism*. New York: Seabury, 1979, pp. 217-53.
"Deconstructing the Deconstructers." *Diacritics*, 5, no. 2 (1975), 24-31. Review of Riddel, *The Inverted Bell*.
The Disappearance of God. Cambridge, Mass.: Harvard Univ. Press, 1963. Reissued, with a new preface, 1976.
"The Disarticulation of the Self in Nietzsche." *Monist*, 64 (1981), 247-61.

"Dismembering and Disremembering in Nietzsche's 'Truth and Lies in a Non-moral Sense.' " *Boundary 2*, 9, no. 3 (Spring, 1981), 41-54.

Fiction and Repetition: Seven English Novels. Cambridge, Mass.: Harvard Univ. Press, 1982.

"Fiction and Repetition: *Tess of the d'Urbervilles.*" In *Forms of Modern British Fiction*, ed. Alan Warren Friedman. Austin: Univ. of Texas Press, 1975, pp. 43-71. See also "A Panel Discussion," pp. 201-32.

"The Fiction of Realism: *Sketches by Boz, Oliver Twist*, and Cruikshank's Illustrations." In *Charles Dickens and George Cruikshank*, by J. Hillis Miller and David Borowitz. Los Angeles: W. A. Clark Memorial Library, 1971, pp. 1-69. Rpt. in *Dickens Centennial Essays*, ed. Ada Nisbet and Blake Nevius (Berkeley: Univ. of California Press, 1971), pp. 85-153.

"The Figure in the Carpet." *Poetics Today*, 1, no. 3 (1980), 107-18.

"Foreword." *Aspects of Narrative*, ed. J. Hillis Miller. New York: Columbia Univ. Press, 1971, pp. v-vii.

The Form of Victorian Fiction. Notre Dame, Ind.: Notre Dame Univ. Press, 1968. 2nd ed., with a new preface, Arete Press, 1980.

"Franz Kafka and the Metaphysics of Alienation." In *The Tragic Vision and the Christian Faith*, ed. N. A. Scott, Jr. New York: Association Press, 1957, pp. 281-305.

"The Function of Rhetorical Study at the Present Time." *ADE Bulletin*, no. 62 (Sept.-Nov. 1979), pp. 10-18.

"Geneva or Paris: The Recent Work of Georges Poulet." *University of Toronto Quarterly*, 39 (1969-70), 212-28.

"The Geneva School: The Criticism of Marcel Raymond, Albert Béguin, Georges Poulet, Jean Rousset, Jean-Pierre Richard, and Jean Starobinski." *Critical Quarterly*, 8 (1966), 305-21. Reprinted with annotated bibliography in *Modern French Criticism*, ed. John K. Simon (Chicago: Univ. of Chicago Press, 1972), pp. 277-310.

"Georges Poulet's 'Criticism of Identification.' " In *The Quest for Imagination*, ed. O. B. Hardison, Jr. Cleveland: Case-Western Reserve Univ. Press, 1971, pp. 191-224. Pp. 191-205 are revised from "The Literary Criticism of Georges Poulet," *infra*; pp. 205-20, from "Geneva or Paris," *supra*.

"A Guest in the House." *Poetics Today*, 2, no. 1b (1980-81), 189-91.

"History as Repetition in Thomas Hardy's Poetry: The Example of 'Wessex Heights.' " In *Victorian Poetry*, ed. M. Bradbury and D. Palmer. London: Edward Arnold, 1972, pp. 222-53. An expanded version of " 'Wessex Heights,' " *infra*.

" 'I'd have my Life unbe: La Ricerca dell'obblio nell'opera di Thomas Hardy." *Strumenti Critici*, 3 (1969), 263-85.

"The Interpretation of *Lord Jim.*" In *The Interpretation of Narrative*, ed. Morton W. Bloomfield. Cambridge, Mass.: Harvard Univ. Press, 1970, pp. 211-28.

"Introduction." *Bleak House*, ed. Norman Page. Harmondsworth: Penguin, 1971, pp. 11-34.

"Introduction." *Oliver Twist.* New York: Holt, Rinehart, and Winston, 1962, pp. v-xxiii.

"Introduction." *The Well-Beloved.* London: Macmillan, 1975, pp. 11-21.

"Introduction." *William Carlos Williams: A Collection of Critical Essays*, ed. J. Hillis Miller. Englewood Cliffs, N.J.: Prentice-Hall, 1966, pp. 1-14.

"Kenneth Burke." In *International Encyclopedia of the Social Sciences.* New York: Free Press, 1979, vol. 18, pp. 78-81.

"The Linguistic Moment in 'The Wreck of the Deutschland.' " In *The New Criticism and After*, ed. Thomas D. Young. Charlottesville: Univ. Press of Virginia, 1976, pp. 47-60.

"The Literary Criticism of Georges Poulet." *MLN*, 78 (1963), 471-88.

"Literature and Religion." In *Relations of Literary Study*, ed. James Thorpe. New York: Modern Language Association, 1967, pp. 111-26.

"Middlemarch, Chapter 85: Three Commentaries." *Nineteenth Century Fiction*, 35 (1980), 441-48.

"Myth as 'Hieroglyph' in Ruskin." *Studies in the Literary Imagination*, 8, no. 2 (1975), 15-18.

"Narrative and History." *ELH*, 41 (1974), 455-73.

"Narrative Middles: A Preliminary Outline." *Genre*, 11 (1978), 375-87.

"Nature and the Linguistic Moment." In *Nature and the Victorian Imagination*, ed. U. C. Knoepflmacher and G. B. Tennyson. Berkeley: Univ. of California Press, 1977, pp. 440-51.

"On Edge: The Crossways of Contemporary Criticism." *Bulletin of the American Academy of Arts and Sciences*, 32, no. 4 (1979), 13-32.

"Optic and Semiotic in *Middlemarch*." In *The Worlds of Victorian Fiction*, ed. Jerome H. Buckley. Cambridge, Mass.: Harvard Univ. Press, 1975, pp. 125-45.

" 'Orion' in 'The Wreck of the Deutschland.' " *MLN* 76 (1961), 509-14.

Poets of Reality: Six Twentieth-Century Writers. Cambridge, Mass.: Harvard Univ. Press, 1965.

"The Problematic Ending in Narrative." *Nineteenth-Century Fiction*, 33 (1978), 3-7.

"Recent Studies in the Nineteenth Century." *Studies in English Literature*, 9 (1969), 737-53; 10 (1970), 183-214.

"The Rewording Shell: Natural Image and Symbolic Emblem in Yeats's Early Poetry." In *Poetic Knowledge: Circumference and Center*, ed. Roland Hagenbuchle and Joseph T. Swann. Bonn: Bouvier, 1980, pp. 75-86.

"Some Implications of Form in Victorian Fiction." *Comparative Literature Studies*, 3 (1966), 109-18.

"The Sources of Dickens's Comic Art: From *American Notes* to *Martin Chuzzlewit*." *Nineteenth-Century Fiction*, 24 (1970), 467-76.

"Stevens' Rock and Criticism as Cure." *Georgia Review*, 30 (1976), 5-31; 330-48.

"The Still Heart: Poetic Form in Wordsworth." *New Literary History*, 2 (1971), 297-310.

"The Stone and the Shell: The Problem of Poetic Form in Wordsworth's Dream of the Arab." In *Mouvements premiers: études critiques offertes à Georges Poulet*. Paris: Corti, 1972, pp. 125-47.

"The Theme of the Disappearance of God in Victorian Poetry." *Victorian Studies*, 6 (1963), pp. 207-27.

"Theology and Logology in Victorian Literature." *Journal of the American Academy of Religion*, 47, no. 2, Supplement (1979), pp. 345-61.

"Theoretical and Atheoretical in Stevens." In *Wallace Stevens: A Celebration*, ed. Frank Doggett and Robert Buttel. Princeton: Princeton Univ. Press, 1980, pp. 274-85.

"Theory and Practice: Response to Vincent Leitch." *Critical Inquiry*, 6 (1980), 609-14.

"Thomas Hardy: A Sketch for a Portrait." In *De Ronsard à Breton: Hommages à Marcel Raymond*. Paris: Corti, 1967, pp. 195-206.

Thomas Hardy: Distance and Desire. Cambridge, Mass.: Harvard Univ. Press, 1970.

"Three Problems of Fictional Form: First-Person Narration in *David Copperfield* and *Huckleberry Finn*." In *Experience in the Novel*, ed. Roy Harvey Pearce. New York: Columbia Univ. Press, 1968, pp. 21-48.

"Tradition and Difference." *Diacritics*, 2, no. 4 (1972), 6-13. Review of Abrams, *Natural Supernaturalism*.

"Virginia Woolf's All Soul's Day: The Omniscient Narrator in *Mrs. Dalloway*." In *The Shaken Realist*, ed. Melvin J. Friedman and John B. Vickery. Baton Rouge: Louisiana State Univ. Press, 1970, pp. 100-27.

"Wallace Stevens' Poetry of Being." *ELH*, 31 (1964), 86-105.

"Walter Pater: A Partial Portrait." *Daedalus*, 105, no. 1 (1976), 97-113.

" 'Wessex Heights': The Persistence of the Past in Hardy's Poetry." *Critical Quarterly*, 10 (1968), 339-59.

"William Carlos Williams: The Doctor as Poet." *Plexus*, 3, no. 4 (1968), 19-20.

"Williams' *Spring and All* and the Progress of Poetry." *Daedalus*, 99, no. 2 (1970), 405-34.

"*Wuthering Heights* and the Ellipses of Interpretation." *Notre Dame English Journal*, 12 (1980), 85-100.

"The Year's Books: J. Hillis Miller on Literary Criticism." *New Republic*, 29 Nov. 1975, pp. 30-33.

Moynihan, Robert. "Interview with Geoffrey Hartman, Yale University, March 19, 1979." *Boundary 2*, 9, no. 1 (1980), 191-215.

Nemerov, Howard. "Figures of Thought." *Sewanee Review*, 83 (1975), 161-69. Review of Bloom, *The Anxiety of Influence*.

Norris, Christopher. "Deconstruction and the Limits of Sense." *Essays in Criticism*, 30 (1980), 281-92.

——. *Deconstruction, Theory and Practice*. London: Methuen, 1982.

——. "Derrida at Yale: The 'Deconstructive Moment' in Modernist Poetics." *Philosphy and Literature*, 4 (1980), 242-56.

——. "Poetics of Reconstruction." *British Journal of Aesthetics*, 20 (1980), 67-76. On Bloom.

Ozick, Cynthia. "Judaism and Harold Bloom." *Commentary*, 67 (Jan. 1979), 43-51.

Poirier, Richard. Review of Hartman, *The Fate of Reading. New York Times Book Review*, 20 Apr. 1975, pp. 21-26.

Riddel, Joseph N. "Juda Becomes New Haven." *Diacritics*, 10, no. 2 (1980), 17-34. On Bloom.

——. "A Miller's Tale." *Diacritics*, 5, no. 3 (1975), 56-65.

——. Review of Bloom, *Kabbalah and Criticism* and *Poetry and Repression. Georgia Review*, 30 (1976), 989-1006.

——. Review of Hartman, *Beyond Formalism. Comparative Literature*, 25 (1973), 178-80.

Rimmon-Kenan, Shlomith. "Deconstructive Reflections on Deconstruction: In Reply to Hillis Miller." *Poetics Today*, 2, no. 1b (1980-81), 185-88.

Rorty, Richard. "Nineteenth-Century Idealism and Twentieth-Century Textualism." *Monist*, 64 (1981), 155-74. Rpt., as is following entry, in *Some Consequences of Pragmatism*. Minneapolis: University of Minnesota Press, 1982.

——. "Philosophy as a Kind of Writing." *New Literary History*, 10 (1978), 141-60. On Derrida.

Rosenfeld, Alvin. " 'Armed for War': Notes on the Antithetical Criticism of Harold Bloom." *Southern Review*, 13 (1977), 554-66.

Sabin, Margery. Review of de Man, *Allegories of Reading. Comparative Literature*, 33 (1981), 69-73.

Said, Edward W. "A Configuration of Themes." *Nation*, 202 (1966), 659-61. Review of Miller, *Poets of Reality*.

———. "The Problem of Textuality: Two Exemplary Positions." *Critical Inquiry*, 4 (1978), 673-714.

——. "Reflections on Recent American 'Left' Literary Criticism." *Boundary 2*, 8, no. 1 (1979), 11-30.

——. Review of *A Map of Misreading. New York Times Book Review*, 13 Apr. 1975, pp. 23-25.

Sitter, John E. "About Ammons' *Sphere*." *Massachusetts Review*, 19 (1978), 201-12. On Bloom.

Sprinker, Michael. "Hermeneutic Hesitation: The Stuttering Text." *Boundary 2*, 9, no. 1 (1980), 217-32. Review of *Criticism in the Wilderness*.

The Structuralist Controversy: The Languages of Criticism and the Sciences of Man, ed. Richard Macksey and Eugenio Donato. Baltimore: Johns Hopkins Univ. Press, 1972. Slightly revised from the 1970 edition in which the above title and subtitle are reversed.

Ulmer, Gregory L. "Jacques Derrida and Paul de Man on-in Rousseau's Faults." *Eighteenth Century: Theory and Interpretation*, 20 (1979), 164-81.

Vendler, Helen. "Defensive Harmonies." *Times Literary Supplement*, 25 June 1976, pp. 775-76. Review of Bloom, *Poetry and Repression*.

——. Review of Bloom, *Yeats. Journal of English and Germanic Philology*, 70 (1971), 691-96.

Wieseltier, Leon. "Summoning Up the Kabbalah." *New York Review of Books*, 19 Feb. 1976, pp. 27-31. Review of Bloom, *Kabbalah and Criticism*.

Contributors

Jonathan Arac, who teaches at the University of Illinois, Chicago is the author of *Commissioned Spirits: The Shaping of Social Motion in Dickens, Carlyle, Melville, and Hawthorne*. His essays on recent criticism have appeared in *Diacritics, boundary 2*, and *Salmagundi*.

Paul Bové is author of *Destructive Poetics: Heidegger and Modern American Poetry*, which appeared in 1980. He is Associate Editor of *boundary 2* and teaches at the University of Pittsburgh.

Stanley Corngold, who teaches German and comparative literature at Princeton, has written on Kafka (*The Commentators' Despair*), Dilthey, Nietzsche, Freud, Thomas Mann, and Heidegger.

Rodolphe Gasché, author of *Die hybride Wissenschaft* and *System und Metaphorik in der Philosophie von George Bataille*, translator into German of Derrida's *L'Ecriture et la différence*, teaches comparative literature at the State University of New York, Buffalo. His essays have appeared in *MLN, Diacritics, Glyph* and *boundary 2*; he is currently finishing a book on deconstruction and reflexivity.

Wladyslaw Godzich is Director of the Comparative Literature Program at the University of Minnesota. He is co-author of *An Essay on Prosaics* (forthcoming) and serves on the editorial committee of *Glyph*.

Donald Marshall, who teaches at the University of Iowa, has contributed articles on criticism to *Philological Quarterly, boundary 2*, and *Diacritics*.

Wallace Martin teaches at the University of Toledo and is the author of *"The New Age" under Orage: Chapters in English Cultural History*. His articles on critical theory have appeared in *Comparative Literature, Critical Inquiry*, and *Diacritics*.

Daniel O'Hara is author of *Tragic Knowledge: Yeats's Autobiography and Hermeneutics*, which appeared in 1981. He teaches at Temple University and has contributed to *boundary 2*, the *Journal of Aesthetics and Art Criticism, Contemporary Literature*, and other journals. He is currently completing a study of the revisionary will in modern criticism.

Donald Pease, who teaches at Dartmouth College, has published articles on Hart Crane, Tennessee Williams, Stephen Crane, Blake, Milton, and Whitman, in connection with his continuing interest in the poetics of modernism.

Michael Sprinker, author of *A Counterpoint of Dissonance: The Aesthetics and Poetry of Gerard Manley Hopkins*, teaches at Oregon State University. His essays have appeared in the *Journal of the History of Ideas, boundary 2*, and *Diacritics*. He is currently co-editor of *The Minnesota Review*.

Index

Index